THE DEVELOPMENT OF ACCOUNTING IN AN INTERNATIONAL CONTEXT

This collection of commissioned papers from some of the world's most renowned scholars in accounting celebrates the academic achievements of Professor Bob Parker. Reflecting his multi-faceted contributions to the history of accountancy and to internatinal accounting, the volume studies the development of accounting in an international context.

The book has a foreword by Sir Bryan Carsberg and an introduction by the editors. Basil Yamey then analyses the interesting diversity of accounting in Europe from late medieval times to 1800. The nineteenth-century development of the profession in the UK and Australia is examined by Tom Lee and by Edwards, Carnegie and Cauberg. Lee Parker looks at the topical area of professional conduct. Richard Morris charts the influence of England on Australia in the development of one type of corporate legal form. Bell and Peasnell, and Tweedie and Whittington, analyse aspects of current value accounting. Steve Zeff adds to his work on political influence on standard setting by looking at a recent US example. Gray and Roberts seek to explain patterns of foreign listing on the London Stock Exchange. Finally, Segun Wallace studies the development of accounting research in the UK, with emphasis on the journal which Bob Parker edited for many years.

T. E. Cooke is Professor of Accounting at the University of Exeter.
C. W. Nobes is Coopers & Lybrand Professor of Accounting at the University of Reading.

ROUTLEDGE INTERNATIONAL STUDIES IN
BUSINESS HISTORY
Series editor: Geoffrey Jones

THE DEVELOPMENT OF ACCOUNTING IN AN INTERNATIONAL CONTEXT

A Festschrift in honour of R. H. Parker

Edited by
T. E. Cooke and C. W. Nobes

ROUTLEDGE

London and New York

First published 1997
by Routledge
11 New Fetter Lane, London EC4P 4EE

Simultaneously published in the USA and Canada
by Routledge
29 West 35th Street, New York, NY 10001

Typeset in Garamond by Mathematical Composition Setters, Salisbury, UK

Printed and bound in Great Britain by Mackays of Chatham PLC, Chatham, Kent

British Library Cataloguing in Publication Data
A catalogue record for this book is available from the British Library

Library of Congress Cataloging in Publication Data
The development of accounting in an international context:
  a Festschrift in honour of R.H. Parker/
  edited by T.E. Cooke and C.W. Nobes.
    p.   cm.
  Simultaneously published in the USA and Canada.
    1. Accounting--History.   2. International business enterprises-
-Accounting.   3. Parker, R. H. (Robert Henry)   4. Accountants-
-Biography.   5. Comparative accounting.   I. Parker, R. H. (Robert
Henry)   II. Cooke, Terence E., 1952- .   III. Nobes, Christopher.
HF5605.D477   1997
657'.09--dc21
                                                        96-37762
                                                        CIP

ISBN 0-415-15528-2

CONTENTS

CONTENTS

ILLUSTRATIONS

CONTRIBUTORS

Philip W. Bell is semi-retired Professor of Accounting at Boston University

Garry D. Carnegie is Professor of Accounting and Finance, Deakin University

Sir Bryan Carsberg is Secretary General of the International Accounting Standards Committee

Jules H. Cauberg is a member of the Professional Associations Division, Deakin University

Terry Cooke is Professor of Accounting at the University of Exeter

John Richard Edwards is Professor of Accounting at the Cardiff Business School

Sidney J. Gray is Professor of International Business at the University of Warwick

Tom Lee is Hugh Culverhouse Endowed Chair of Accountancy at the University of Alabama

Richard D. Morris is Senior Lecturer in Accounting at the University of New South Wales

Chris Nobes is Coopers & Lybrand Professor of Accounting at the University of Reading

Lee D. Parker is a Professor and Associate Dean (Research) in the School of Commerce at the University of Adelaide

Ken Peasnell is a Professor of Accounting at Lancaster University

Clare B. Roberts is Reader in International Accounting at the University of Exeter

Sir David Tweedie is Chairman of the UK's Accounting Standards Board

R. S. Olusegun Wallace is Research Professor of Accounting and Finance at the Middlesex University Business School

NOTES ON CONTRIBUTORS

Geoffrey Whittington is Price Waterhouse Professor of Financial Accounting at the University of Cambridge

Basil Yamey is Professor Emeritus of Economics at the London School of Economics

Stephen A. Zeff is Herbert S. Autrey Professor of Accounting at Rice University

FOREWORD
Sir Bryan Carsberg

It must have been in 1966, more than half my lifetime ago, when I first met Bob Parker. He had come to spend a year at the London School of Economics where I had begun my academic career two years earlier. I remember those times with great affection. We had a small but lively accounting group led by Will Baxter and Harold Edey and including Peter Bird, Michael Bromwich and John Flower as well as myself. We seemed to have more time for discussion and debate in those days, and we learned from each other in the process. Bob was a stimulating member of the group. His academic contributions ranged from the important general areas of valuation and income measurement, where the book of readings which he edited with Harcourt made such an important contribution, to esoterica such as whether a French writer had suffered the misfortune of having an accent left off one of his words in the printing and this had changed the impact and assessment of his work! He also had, I remember, on a lighter note, a nice line in parody of people who say – as we all do from time to time – something a little different from what they mean. A favourite example, at the time, was 'a much needed gap in the literature' rather than a gap much in need of filling.

The late 1960s, in the UK, was also a time for challenging the existing order of academic accounting and laying foundations for its growth, the potential for which was starting to be evident. There was, at that time, an enormous and regrettable gulf between accountants in practice and accountants in academe. Academe had little influence on practice. And there were differences of opinion about how to change that situation. Some newcomers to the scene, notably Professor Eddie Stamp who had just returned to the UK from working in Canada and New Zealand, favoured gingering things up through a revitalised Association of University Teachers of Accounting (as it was then called). I was reminded of the dramas of those times, and of the appalling lack of interest in education by many senior members of the profession, only recently, on reading a draft of a history of that part of AUTA's life, written by Bob Parker. Bob himself deserves great credit for the contribution he made to bringing people together and generating new arrangements which would provide an effective organisation for academic accountants.

Another of Bob's major contributions has been his work on international accounting. His text with Chris Nobes on the subject has been notably successful in a field where there have been few competitors and I have used it myself in teaching international accounting in postgraduate courses.

My own career touched Bob's again briefly when he was appointed to his chair at Exeter. The university had asked me to act as its external adviser in making the appointment. I well remember the pleasure of the university at Bob's candidacy for the position and the general feeling of the committee that he would be an excellent fit for the needs of Exeter. And so it proved to be. The potential of the university is very high because of its ability to attract well-qualified students, and Bob built up a strong department there, several of his young colleagues going on to achieve great things in other departments.

Chris Nobes says, later in this book, that Bob Parker might now be regarded as a 'grand old man' of academic accounting. This, I confess, came as a bit of a shock to me. Can Bob have aged while I was not looking? Undeniably, retirement looms. And what, I wonder, will he do with it? I understand that his interest in accounting history has spilled over into a pastime of researching family history. With characteristic resourcefulness, finding Parker to be a difficult name to research, because there are so many of them, he has concentrated on his mother's line with the much more helpful name of 'Bunkell'. As I know from my own experience, researching family history can occupy a great deal of time in a fascinating manner.

Perhaps, however, the link between accounting history and family history, the link between work and play, holds the key to the future for Bob in a deeper way. One of the features of academic life, I have often thought, is that in it, it is more difficult than in most activities to tell the difference between work and play. So perhaps, freed from the burdens of administration, which clearly is work, Bob will be busier than ever and yet not really knowing whether he is working or playing at the time. I rather hope so. But whatever the outcome, I wish him a long time at it and great pleasure from it.

Bryan Carsberg

1

INTRODUCTION

Terry Cooke and Chris Nobes

ABOUT THIS BOOK

This volume celebrates the life and works of Professor Robert Henry Parker. Bob's career in academic accounting has been largely spent in Australia, England and Scotland, and began when there were few professors of accounting in any of those countries. His influence has been widespread, notably on:

- his colleagues and students;
- scholarship in historical and international accounting, and
- academic journals and organisations.

An appreciation of his academic life forms part of this chapter. A bibliography of his works is printed as an appendix to this chapter.

The theme of this book is the historical development of accounting in an international context. The authors of the chapters are all well known as researchers into one or other aspect of this composite theme, and the papers also concern one or both of them. The other linking theme of the contributors to this volume is their previous collaboration with Bob Parker as research student, colleague, co-author or co-editor (or, in some cases, all four).

In this book, Basil Yamey combines history, development and international issues by looking at bookkeeping methods from 1300 to 1800 in several countries of Western Europe. Then Chapters 3 and 4 look at aspects of the nineteenth-century development of the accountancy professions in Scotland and Australia; this is classic Parker territory. Tom Lee analyses the influence of one man on the Edinburgh Society; and then Edwards, Carnegie and Cauberg look at the backgrounds of the founders of the Incorporated Institute in Victoria, leading them to question some earlier scholarship. Lee Parker brings us into the first half of the present century and looks at the development of ethical accounting issues in several English-speaking countries.

The next three papers concern technical issues. Richard Morris takes up another Parker theme: the international transfer of technology. He looks at the influence of British legal forms on the development of the 'no-liability'

1

company in Australia. A further matter for which Bob Parker is famous is the introduction to Parker and Harcourt (or, indeed, Parker, Harcourt and Whittington) on the subject of concepts of income and value. The papers here by Bell and Peasnell and Tweedie and Whittington (all well known for their writings in these areas) take up two issues related to this: deprival value depreciation and the international collapse of current cost as a practical accounting method.

Steve Zeff, who has been working closely with Bob Parker in recent years on the research side of the Institute of Chartered Accountants of Scotland, adds to the literature on the politicisation of standard setting, by looking at the recent US case of employee stock options. Gray and Roberts examine the facts about, and the motives for, the listing of foreign companies on the London Stock Exchange.

Segun Wallace looks at the development of accounting research in the UK, with particular reference to the journal that Bob Parker edited for many years.

The editors of this volume are most grateful for the efforts of the contributors in producing a worthy tribute to Bob. Because we concentrated on those colleagues with close working connections to him, there are many of Bob's academic friends who are not contributors here but who would have been eager to join us in celebrating his achievements. Fortunately, we have been able to include one such long-standing academic friend as the writer of the Foreword. Sir Bryan Carsberg has now happily returned to the world of this book's title: the development of accounting in an international context.

We are most grateful to the Institute of Chartered Accountants of Scotland for sponsoring this publication. The sponsors and the editors are joined by the contributors and those many other academic friends not represented here in acknowledging the great beneficial influence of Bob Parker on academic accounting in several countries over several decades. We wish him a long, happy and busy retirement.

A BIOGRAPHY[1]

Parker, Robert Henry (1932–   )

Bob (or R. H.) Parker was born and educated in Norfolk and, as a pastime, has traced his family's long roots there. Like many accounting academics of his generation, he studied economics at the University of London. After graduation he qualified (in 1958) as a chartered accountant in the City, and had published his first article even before that. Soon after, he went to Nigeria for a year or so, with a firm that later joined Peat Marwick, and then to Adelaide briefly (as lecturer) and Perth until 1966 (as senior lecturer). So began a distinguished academic career and a lifelong association with Australia. His earliest book (Bennett *et al.* 1964) was published there; the next (Parker and Harcourt 1969), with another Adelaide colleague, is a classic.

The return to Europe saw Parker at the LSE (as P. D. Leake Research Fellow); at Manchester Business School (as a Reader in Management Accounting!); at INSEAD (as Associate Professor of Finance!); at Dundee (including as Dean of the Law Faculty!); and finally (perhaps) at Exeter (as Professor of Accounting). Meanwhile, there have been frequent stays in or trips to Australasia, where he has been a visiting professor at the University of New South Wales, the University of Sydney, Edith Cowan University and the University of Newcastle.

Books and papers have continued to flood from Parker's pen, unstemmed by increasing rank, age or administrative pressures. His papers can be found in most of the world's leading accounting journals, including two even in the *Journal of Accounting Research* in the days when his topics would be considered for such a journal; Parker is keen on things classical, but prefers to keep Greek out of accounting papers. There are also many serious, clear articles in the professional press which are of great value to enquiring practitioners and students. Books, too, range from those relating to somewhat obscure, scholarly accounting history (e.g. Parker and Pryce-Jones 1974, or Kitchen and Parker 1980), to a major collection of his papers on history (Parker 1984), to a standard textbook (Nobes and Parker 1981), and 'popular' works (e.g. Parker 1972). Perhaps his most obvious specialisms have been nineteenth-century Anglo-Saxon accountancy and international aspects of consolidation, but no-one would usefully accuse Parker of having narrow interests, and new researchers in many fields often find an old Parker paper which addressed many of the problems years ago.

In many ways, Parker is one of the grand old men of academic account-ing in the close-knit enclave of the UK and Australasia. For some years now, a large proportion of senior accounting scholars have worked with him, written with him, been appointed to chairs by a committee containing him or advised by him, used him as a personal referee, or been examined for a PhD by him. He edited one of the UK's major academic journals (*Accounting and Business Research*) from 1975 to 1993; was an *éminence grise* in the resuscitation of what is now the British Accounting Association and founded the predecessor journal to the *British Accounting Review*; has been on several editorial boards; has sat on several research-oriented committees of professional accountancy bodies (and is now Professorial Fellow of the Scottish Institute); and is a great contributor to international conferences. However, can one be a 'Grand Old Man' when one shows disturbing signs of irreverence, lack of conservatism and general irrepres-sibility? These latter qualities have contributed to his success in launching, fostering or moulding the careers of many now successful academics, which will be perhaps his most influential achievement.

NOTES

1 This biography was written by Christopher Nobes. An edited version has appeared in Chatfield and Vangermeersch (1996).

REFERENCES

Bennett, J. W., Grant, J. McB. and Parker, R. H. (1964) *Topics in Business Finance and Accounting*, Melbourne: Cheshire.

Chatfield, M. and Vangermeersch, R. (1996) *The History of Accounting: An International Encyclopedia*, New York: Garland.

Kitchen, J. and Parker, R. H. (1980) *Accounting Thought and Education: Six English Pioneers*, London: Institute of Chartered Accountants in England and Wales.

Nobes, C. W. and Parker, R. H. (1981) *Comparative International Accounting*, Oxford: Philip Allan (and 1985, 1991 and 1995).

Parker, R. H. (1972) *Understanding Company Financial Statements*, Harmondsworth: Penguin (and 1982, 1988 and 1994).

—— (1984) *Papers on Accounting History*, New York: Garland.

Parker, R. H. and Harcourt, G. (1969) *Readings in the Concept and Measurement of Income*, Cambridge: Cambridge University Press (and, with G. Whittington, 1985).

Parker, R. H. and Pryce-Jones, J. (1974) *Accounting in Scotland: A Historical Bibliography*. Edinburgh: Institute of Chartered Accountants of Scotland (and 1976).

APPENDIX TO CHAPTER 1
Bibliography of R. H. Parker

BOOKS

1 (with J. W. Bennett and J. McB. Grant) *Topics in Business Finance and Accounting*, Melbourne: Cheshire, 1964.
2 (with G. C. Harcourt) *Readings in the Concept and Measurement of Income*, London: Cambridge University Press, 1969; 2nd edition with G. C. Harcourt and G. Whittington, published by Philip Allan, Oxford, 1986.
3 *Management Accounting: A Historical Perspective*, London: Macmillan, 1969.
4 *Understanding Company Financial Statements*, Harmondsworth: Penguin, 1972; 2nd edition 1982; 3rd edition 1988; 4th edition 1994.
5 (with Janet Pryce-Jones) *Accounting in Scotland: An Historical Bibliography*, Edinburgh: Institute of Chartered Accountants of Scotland, 1974; 2nd edition 1976; reprinted New York: Garland, 1984.
6 *Readings in Accounting and Business Research*, London: Institute of Chartered Accountants in England and Wales, 1978.
7 (with T. A. Lee) *The Evolution of Modern Financial Reporting*, London: Nelson, 1979; reprinted New York; Garland, 1984.
8 (with J. Kitchen) *Accounting Thought and Education: Six English Pioneers*, London: Institute of Chartered Accountants in England and Wales, 1980; reprinted New York: Garland, 1984).
9 *British Accountants: A Biographical Sourcebook*, New York: Arno Press, 1980.
10 *Bibliographies for Accounting Historians*, New York: Arno Press, 1980.
11 (with C. W. Nobes) *Comparative International Accounting*, Oxford: Philip Allan, 1981; 2nd edition 1985; 3rd edition London: Prentice Hall, 1991; 4th edition 1995.
12 (with R. Ma) *Consolidation Accounting in Australia*, Melbourne: Longman Cheshire, 1983.
13 *Papers on Accounting History*, New York: Garland 1984.
14 *Macmillan Dictionary of Accounting*, London: Macmillan, 1984; 2nd edition 1992.

15 *Accounting Standards and the Law: An Australian Experiment*, Sydney: University of Sydney Accounting Research Centre, 1986.

16 *The Development of the Accountancy Profession in Britain to the Early Twentieth Century*, Birmingham, AL: Academy of Accounting Historians, 1986.

17 (with C. W. Nobes) *Issues in Multinational Accounting*, Oxford: Philip Allan, 1988.

18 (with S. James) *A Dictionary of Business Quotations*, London: Routledge, 1990.

19 *Accounting in Australia. Historical Essays*, New York: Garland, 1990.

20 (with R. Ma and G. Whittred) *Consolidation Accounting*, Melbourne: Longman Cheshire, 1991.

21 (with S. James) *Collins Dictionary of Business Quotations*, Glasgow: HarperCollins, 1991.

22 (with T. E. Cooke) *Financial Reporting in the West Pacific Rim*, London: Routledge, 1994.

23 (ed., with B. S. Yamey) *Accounting History: Some British Contributions*, Oxford: Oxford University Press, 1994.

24 (with C. W. Nobes) *An International View of True and Fair Accounting*, London: Routledge, 1994.

25 (with A. Bishop and T. A. Lee) (eds) *Accounting History from the Renaissance to the Present*, New York: Garland, 1996.

26 (with S. A. Zeff) (eds) *Milestones in the British Accounting Literature*, New York: Garland, 1996.

27 (with C. W. Nobes and P. W. Wolnizer) *Readings in True and Fair*, New York: Garland, 1996).

28 (with Y. Lemarchand) *Accounting in France/La comptabilité en France: Historical Essays/Etudes historiques*, New York: Garland, 1996.

CHAPTERS IN BOOKS

1 'Accounting Practices – translation and consolidation', in M. Z. Brooke and H. L. Remmers (eds) *The Multinational Company in Europe*, London: Longman, 1972.

2 'Harmonisation of company financial reporting', in A. T. McLean (ed.) *Business and Accounting in Europe*, London: Saxon House, 1973; and in National Association of Accountants, *Management Accounting for Multinational Corporations*, vol. 1, New York: 1974.

3 'British accounting and the EEC', in McLean, op.cit.

4 (with G. C. Harcourt) 'An eclectic approach', in T. J. Fiflis and H. Kripke (eds) *Accounting for Business Lawyers – Teaching Materials*, St Paul, MN: West, 2nd edition 1977.

5 Accounting in Europe', in B. V. Carsberg and A. Hope (eds) *Current Issues in Accounting*, Oxford: Philip Allan, 1977; 2nd edition 1984.

6 (with C. W. Nobes) 'Chronology of the development of company financial reporting in Great Britain 1844–1977', in T. A. Lee and R. H. Parker (eds) *Evolution of Corporate Financial Reporting*, London: Nelson, 1979.

7 'History of accounting for decisions', in J. Arnold, B. Carsberg and R. Scapens (eds) *Topics in Management Accounting*, Oxford: Philip Allan, 1980.

8 'The want of uniformity in accounts: a nineteenth century debate', in D. M. Emanuel and I. C. Stewart (eds) *Essays in Honour of Trevor R. Johnston*, Auckland: University of Auckland, 1980.

9 'The study of accounting history', in A. Hopwood and M. Bromwich (eds) *Essays in British Accounting Research*, London: Pitman, 1981.

10 'Reckoning, merchants' accounts, book-keeping, accounting or accountancy? The evidence of the long titles of books on accounting in English, 1543–1914', in B. V. Carsberg and S. Dev (eds) *External Financial Reporting*, Hemel Hempstead: Prentice Hall International, 1984.

11 (with C. W. Nobes) 'The Fourth Directive and the United Kingdom'. in S. J. Gray and A. G. Coenenberg (eds) *EEC Accounting Harmonisation: Implementation and Impact of the Fourth Directive*, Amsterdam: North-Holland, 1984.

12 'Regulating British corporate financial reporting in the late 19th century', in J. St G. Kerr and R. C. Clift (eds) *Essays in Honour of Louis Goldberg*, Melbourne: Department of Accounting and Business Law, University of Melbourne, 1989.

13 'Importing and exporting accounting: the British experience', in A. G. Hopwood (ed.) *International Pressures for Accounting Change*, Hemel Hempstead: Prentice Hall, 1989.

14 'Accounting basics: language writing materials, numerals and calculation', in A. T. Craswell (ed.) *Collected Papers of the Fifth World Congress of Accounting Historians*, Sydney: University of Sydney Accounting and Finance Foundation, 1988 and in G. Macdonald and B. A. Rutherford (eds) *Accounts, Accounting and Accountability*, London: VNR International, 1989.

15 'Australian writings on accounting, 1871–1900', in R. H. Parker (ed.) *Accounting in Australia: Historical Essays*, New York: Garland, 1990.

16 'Misleading accounts? Pitfalls for historians', in O. F. Graves (ed.) *The Costing Heritage. Studies in Honor of S. Paul Garner*, Harrisonburg, VA: The Academy of Accounting Historians, 1991.

17 'Accounting regulation, the business corporation, taxation and professional accountancy in 19th century Europe: a comparative essay', pp. 41–79 of A. Tsuji (ed.) *Collected Papers of the Sixth World Congress of Accounting Historians*, vol. 1, Accounting History Association, Japan, 1992.

18 'Bowring and financial reform: government accountancy and decimalisation', pp. 71–85 of J. Youings (ed.) *Sir John Bowring 1792–1872. Aspects of his Life and Career*, Exeter: The Devonshire Association, 1993.
19 (with J. Tay) 'Measuring international harmonization and standardization', pp. 381–403 of S. J. Gray, A. G. Coenenberg and P. D. Gordon (eds) *International Group Accounting: Issues in European Harmonization*, London: Routledge, 2nd edition 1993.
20 (with J. Kitchen) 'Lawrence Robert Dicksee (1864–1932)', in J. R. Edwards (ed.) *Twentieth-Century Accounting Thinkers*, London: Routledge, 1994.
21 (with J. Kitchen) Frederick Rudolf Mackley de Paula (1882–1954)' in J. R. Edwards (ed.) *Twentieth-Century Accounting Thinkers*, London: Routledge, 1994.

REFEREED ARTICLES

1 'A note on the use of accounting statements by business historians', *Bulletin of the Business Archives Council of Australia* January 1961.
2 'Accounting history: a select bibliography', *Abacus* September 1965; revised version in M. Chatfield, *Contemporary Studies in the Evolution of Accounting Thought*, Belmont, CA: Dickensen, 1968.
3 'Lower of cost and market in Britain and the United States: an historical survey', *Abacus* December 1965; reprinted in B. S. Yamey, *The Historical Development of Accounting: A Selection of Papers*, New York: Arno Press, 1978.
4 'A note on Savary's "Le Parfait Négociant"', *Journal of Accounting Research* Autumn 1966.
5 'Discounted cash flow in historical perspective', *Journal of Accounting Research* Spring 1968.
6 'Principles and practice in translating foreign currencies – an essay in comparative accounting', *Abacus* December 1970.
7 'Some international aspects of accounting', *Journal of Business Finance* Winter 1971; revised version in S. J. Gray, *International Accounting and Transnational Decisions*, London: Butterworths, 1983.
8 'Hendriksen's 'Accounting Theory"', *Abacus* June 1972.
9 'Explaining national differences in consolidated accounts', *Accounting and Business Research* Summer 1977.
10 'Research needs in accounting history', *Accounting Historians Journal* Fall 1977.
11 'British men of account', *Abacus* June 1978 (*Men of Account*, Inaugural Lecture, University of Exeter, 1977); reprinted in T. A. Lee (ed.) *The Closure of the Accounting Profession*, New York: Garland, 1990, vol. 2, pp. 145–57.
12 'Memorial – Frank Sewell Bray, 1906–1979', *Accounting Review*, April

1980; reprinted in D. A. R. Forrester, *Frank Sewell Bray, Master Accountant 1906–1979*, Glasgow: Strathclyde Convergencies, 1982; and in Thomas A. Lee, *Transactions of the Chartered Accountants Societies of Edinburgh and Glasgow*, New York: Garland, 1984.

13 'The Third International Congress of Accounting Historians', *Journal of European Economic History* Fall 1981.

14 'Bookkeeping barter and current cash equivalents in early New South Wales', *Abacus* December 1982.

15 'John Manger Fells (1958–1925)' and 'Sir William Barclay Peat (1852–1936)', in *Dictionary of Business Biography*, vols 2 and 4, London: Butterworths, 1984, 1985.

16 (with G. Peirson and A. L. Ramsay) 'Australian accounting standards and the law', *Company and Securities Law Journal* November 1987.

17 'Select bibliography of works on the history of accounting 1981–1987', *Accounting Historians Journal* Fall 1988.

18 (with J. S. W. Tay) 'Measuring international harmonization and standardization', *Abacus* March 1990.

19 'Regulating British corporate financial reporting in the late nineteenth century', *Accounting, Business and Financial History* October 1990.

20 (with C. W. Nobes) '"True and Fair": A survey of UK financial directors', *Journal of Business Finance Accounting* April 1991.

21 (with C. W. Nobes) '"True and Fair': UK auditors' view', *Accounting and Business Research* Autumn 1991.

22 '"Capital", "Stock", "Assets', economists and accountants', *History of Economic Thought Newsletter* Autumn 1991.

23 'Misleading accounts? Pitfalls for historians', *Business History* October 1991.

24 (with J. S. W. Tay) 'Measuring international harmonization and standardization: a reply', *Abacus*, 28 (2): 217–20, September 1992.

25 'The scope of accounting history: a note', *Abacus* March 1993.

26 'Finding English words to talk about accounting concepts', *Accounting Auditing and Accountability Journal* 7 (2) 1994.

27 (with G. D. Carnegie) 'The first Australian book on accounting: James Dimelow's *Practical Book-Keeping Made Easy*, *Abacus* March 1994.

28 'Debating true and fair in Australia. An exercise in deharmonization', *Journal of International Accounting, Auditing and Taxation* July 1994.

29 'David Solomons and British accounting', *Accounting and Business Research* Autumn 1995.

30 (with T. E. Cooke), 'A reply to "Financial Reporting in the West Pacific Rim – An Extension and an Update"', *Research in Emerging Economies* vol. 3, 1995.

31 (with G. D. Carnegie) 'The transfer of accounting technology to the Southern Hemisphere: the case of William Butler Yaldwyn', *Accounting, Business and Financial History* March 1996.

32 'Harmonizing the notes in the UK and France. A case study in de jure harmonization', *European Accounting Review* 5(2), 1996.

OTHER ARTICLES

1 'Down with double entry', *Accountancy*, April 1957.
2 'The measurement of profit', *Accountant* October 1957.
3 'Some thoughts on balance sheets', *Accountants' Journal* 1957.
4 'Bookkeeping and the African slave trade', *Accountant's Magazine* February 1958.
5 'The first English double entry books of account', *International Accountants' Journal* March 1958.
6 'Company law in Nigeria', *Accountant* 6 December 1958.
7 'The Deed of Settlement of the South Australian Company', *Chartered Accountant in Australia* February 1961.
8 'The nature and purpose of accounting', *Accountant* 10 June 1961.
9 'Australia's oldest accountancy body – the Adelaide Society of Accountants', *Chartered Accountant in Australia* December 1961.
10 'Some aspects of company law amendment in the United Kingdom', *Australian Accountant* October 1961.
11 'Materials and labour variances in standard costing', *Accountant* 7 July 1962.
12 'Accountants, economists and stock valuation', *WA Management Quarterly* June 1962.
13 (with J. W. Bennett and J. McB. Grant) 'Financial mathematics and the accountant', *Australian Accountant* March 1964.
14 (with D. H. Briggs) 'Some comments on the new recommendations on accounting principles', *Chartered Accountant in Australia* June 1964.
15 'Depreciation, replacement and the measurement of business income', *Economic Activity in Western Australia* January 1965.
16 (with D. H. Briggs) 'Executorship accounts in Western Australia', *Chartered Accountant in Australia* 1965.
17 (with E. Stamp) 'Accounting for inflation', *Financial Times* January 1971.
18 'British accounting practice and the EEC', *Bankers' Magazine* June 1973.
19 'Inflation accounting in France', *Accountancy* July 1977.
20 'Questions and answers on the Fourth Directive', *Accountant's Magazine* September 1978; reprinted in J. W. H. Trueman, *Developing Accounting Principles in the European Economic Community*, University of New England, Australia, 1979.
21 (with C. W. Nobes) 'Landmarks in accounting history', *Accountancy* June 1979.
22 'Concepts of consolidation in the EEC', *Accountancy* February 1977;

reprinted in American Accounting Association, *Notable Contributions to the Periodical International Accounting Literature – 1875–78*; in F. D. S. Choi and G. G. Mueller, *Essentials of Multinational Accounting: An Anthology*, University Microfilms International, 1979; and in S. J. Gray, *International Accounting and Transnational Decisions*, London: Butterworths, 1983.

23 'Those first councillors ...', *Accountancy* May 1980.

24 'Accounting historians' guide to London', Supplement to *Accounting and Business Research*, Special Accounting History Issue, 1980.

25 'Chronological list of books and articles on Australian accounting history', *Accounting History Newsletter* no. 4, Summer 1981–2.

26 'Group accounts: amending the Seventh Directive', *Accountant's Magazine* February 1982.

27 'Company legislation and accounting standards in Australia', *Accountant's Magazine* February 1982.

28 'Why are Australian accounting standards different?', *Australian Accountant* August 1982.

29 'The Seventh Directive: some first impressions', *Accountant's Magazine* October 1983.

30 'The tercentenary of the first Scottish book on accounting', *Accountant's Magazine* November 1983.

31 'Founding fathers – Scots almost to a man', *Accountancy* September 1983.

32 'Burning down Parliament: a story of accounting change', *Accountancy* October 1984.

33 (with B. R. Pearson) 'Roger North, gentleman accountant and economist', *Fourth International Congress on the History of Accountancy. Congress Proceedings*, University of Pisa Faculty of Economics and Commerce, 1984.

34 'History of accounting', *Australian Accountant* January, March, April, May, June, July, August, September, October, November and December 1986.

35 'The first Scottish book on accounting: Robert Colinson's *Idea Rationaria* (1683)', *Accountant's Magazine*, 1974; reprinted in T. A. Lee (ed.) *A Scottish Contribution to Accounting History*, New York: Garland, 1986.

36 'Creative accounting medieval style', *Accountancy* October 1988.

37 'The first 5000', *Career Accountant* September 1989.

38 'How accountants invented counting and writing', *Accountant's Magazine* January 1990.

39 'Foreword', *Research in Third World Accounting* vol. 1, 1991.

40 'True and fair: an international perspective', *CA News* December 1994.

2

DIVERSITY IN MERCANTILE ACCOUNTING IN WESTERN EUROPE, 1300–1800

Basil Yamey

'Merchants do differ much in the manner of keeping their accompts'.[1] This was the opinion of Mr Wakefield, a seventeenth-century English merchant. Available evidence suggests that this statement applies to England, indeed to Western Europe, for the period 1300 to 1800 which is dealt with in broad-brush manner in this paper.

The major differentiations in accounting arrangements can be stated simply: (a) some merchants had no written accounting records at all; (b) many used what is called single-entry bookkeeping; (c) yet others used the double-entry bookkeeping system; and (d) within each of the last two categories there were many differentiating features in practice. In this paper I illustrate the diversity of arrangements, and suggest some explanation. For this latter purpose I draw attention to some instances of uniformity amidst the general diversity.

BOOKKEEPING WITHOUT WRITTEN RECORDS

Leon Battista Alberti, Renaissance architect, painter and writer, referred to a kinsman of his, experienced in commerce, who

> considered it essential for a merchant or anyone who does business with a large number of persons always to write everything down, to note all transactions, and to keep a record of every item brought in or taken out. As he watches over the enterprise, he should almost always have his pen in his hand.[2]

In a manuscript dated 1458, and first published much later, Benedetto Cortrugli, a merchant of Ragusa, explained that a merchant should not rely on his memory in matters concerning his business unless he had a memory like King Cyrus of Persia, who knew each soldier in his large army by name. He must keep accounting records: they 'not only preserve and keep in the memory [all] transactions, but they also are a means to avoid many litigations and disputes'.[3]

12

Yet there were merchants who did not keep written accounts at all. When Francesco Datini, the 'merchant of Prato', returned to his native town from Avignon towards the end of the fourteenth century, he complained that the Pratesi kept their books only in their heads, for four out of six of them had neither book nor ink-well, and those who had ink-well had no pen. He added, however, that for that reason they were able to recall things after thirty or forty years better than most men could do after a month.[4] If the inventories of deceased estates are to be believed, many merchants in Amiens at the beginning of the seventeenth century had no account books, but relied on documents of their debts assembled in files.[5] Samuel Mitz, a merchant of Cologne, explained in 1625 that he wrote entries in his account books only in connection with those transactions he made in partnership with others.[6] An Englishman, James Cope, who died in Smyrna in 1685, had no account books. His executor was 'forct to make up by his coppy booke of letters' when settling the estate.[7]

Some traders, especially those in a modest way of business, were able to dispense with account books and keep the information they needed by other visual means. Some of these means are mentioned in Daniel Defoe's observation that the compound distillers or rectifiers in London 'keep no books but their slate, and no pen and ink but their chalk and tallies'.[8] The making of marks on a convenient surface to record debts is illustrated in a story told by the Piovano Arlotto (1396–1484), who acquired a reputation as 'a ribald story-teller and home-spun moralist' in Tuscany:

> The story describes how the Piovano and the innkeeper at his favourite haunt, the Uccellatoio, kept their accounts, the Piovano recording each jug of wine he consumed with a charcoal mark on the wall. Asked by his friend Messer Falcone the reason for this practice, the Piovano told the tale of a simple innkeeper who kept an account by scratching lines on a door. When a dispute arose with a customer, and the *podestà* required him to produce evidence, the innkeeper went home and returned struggling under the weight of the door. The Piovano explained that for this reason he preferred to mark his debts on an immovable wall.[9]

However, many of those engaged in commercial activities would have had some form of written accounting records. The account books that have survived the hazards of neglect, fire, flood, recycling and deliberate destruction reveal a remarkably wide array of bookkeeping arrangements.[10]

SINGLE-ENTRY BOOKKEEPING

Fabio Besta, the distinguished Italian accounting theorist and historian, explained that the only defining characteristic of single-entry bookkeeping is a negative one: single entry is any bookkeeping that is not double entry. It therefore includes a variety of methods or arrangements that have no necessary uniformities, no *norme e aspetti constanti*.[11]

The variety of different arrangements that, for convenience, are grouped together under the umbrella title of single-entry bookkeeping is amply illustrated and discussed in Raymond de Roover's magisterial survey (1956) of business accounting records before 1500.[12] In this section I refer to some examples not in de Roover as well as others dated after 1500.

Personal accounts, i.e. accounts of the merchant's debtors and creditors, naturally are prominent in surviving single-entry records; and, as de Roover showed, several early account books have entries only for the creation of debts and their settlement (e.g. loans, and sales and purchases on credit terms).[13] But a merchant or his bookkeeper who was not using the double-entry system was free to open accounts for other subjects as well. Thus accounts for different lots or categories of merchandise were opened in many ledgers or in special account books, either systematically or sporadically. In some cases there is evidence of careful recording of quantities in such accounts, which could also disclose the profit or loss made on a particular category or lot of goods. The account book (1398–9) of Giovanni Canale of Pinerlo in Piedmont is an early example. In his *liber numeri* he opened a separate account for each lot of cloth, and recorded the lengths sold to each customer, with the amount of the transaction. When a lot was completely disposed of, the profit, *lucrum*, was inserted.[14] Another example is the 'book of the shop' (*lu libru di la putiga di mi matteu di avicu*) of 1432–4 of Matteo da Vico who had a shop in Palermo.[15]

There are also examples of single-entry ledgers that include, besides personal and merchandise accounts, accounts relating to expenses. An interesting illustration is provided by the fragments of a ledger (with entries from 1364 to 1383) attributed to the important Schürstab family of Nuremberg.[16] The accounts, in paragraph form (and not in the familiar bilateral account form), include accounts for persons, merchandise and expenses. The pages with personal accounts are divided in two by vertical lines, with different accounts in the two halves. Accounts are separated from each other by horizontal lines. Settlement of a personal account is indicated by several oblique cancellation strokes, and the addition of the words *Ab, Ab, Ab* or *pez[alt]*.

Two English ledgers, with bilateral accounts, also include a variety of classes of accounts. The ledger (1558–65) of John Isham, a mercer and merchant adventurer, has accounts for persons, goods, voyages and a house. The profits (losses) on the various goods and voyage accounts are rarely shown as entries.[17] The ledger (1538–50) of John Smythe, a merchant of Bristol, has a greater range of accounts. There are several goods accounts as well as many personal accounts, including one for an employee in Spain (with entries in Spanish currency). There is an account, really a list, of 'dessperid dettes' brought forward from a previous ledger. There is also a profit and loss account (Gaynes for my owne acownt), but no capital account.[18]

Moreover, if the merchant wanted to know how big his capital was at a particular date, or by how much it had increased or decreased since an earlier reckoning, he could take an inventory of his assets and liabilities. Early examples include the annual inventories of the Pisan merchant Biagio Delle Brache from 1326 to 1347, the subject of a scholarly study by Tito Antoni;[19] the occasional inventories of Andrea Banchi, a leading fifteenth-century Florentine silk merchant and manufacturer;[20] the occasional inventories of the Fugger of Augsburg, the earliest surviving example being that of 1527 (its lost predecessor having been made sixteen years earlier in 1511);[21] the annual compilations (1616–64) made by Sir Thomas Cullum, draper and Restoration baronet;[22] and the frequent inventories entered by Sir William Turner, a prosperous merchant, in his so-called 'book of sales' or in his 'stock book' (second half of seventeenth century).[23] One of Turner's inventories dated 16 December 1664 has this title:

> This is the estate God Almighty has blest me with, I beseech him bless me with a heart that will be truly thankfull for it, and enable me to use it to his glory.

Another inventory of his, dated 10 December 1674, shows a total of £36,746.12.00 – an increase of more than £10,000 in ten years. The 1674 inventory contains six entries for assets ('Mony abroad upon severall securities at interest ...', 'My houses ...'; 'My Plate ... including other houshold stuf woorth ...'; 'My Cloath and bayes being measured amounts to ...'; 'My Cash amounts to ...'; and 'My Booke debts being cast up ...'), and one liability ('I owe to Christ. Conyers at 5^L p.C').

De Roover regarded single-entry bookkeeping as imperfect. Nevertheless, he emphasised (in an earlier article) that 'medieval merchants were able to adapt this imperfect (*imparfait*) instrument to meet the requirements of their businesses and attain their objectives ... they found solutions which astonish us by their flexibility and their extraordinary variety'.[24] The same verdict can be applied also to the single-entry accounting arrangements fashioned by the successors of those medieval merchants.

DIVERSITY IN DOUBLE-ENTRY BOOKKEEPING

In his *Summa de arithmetica* of 1494 Luca Pacioli wrote that he was expounding 'the Venetian method (*el modo de vinegia*) which certainly among the others is much recommended and which can be used as a guide to all others'. Although it is not altogether clear what Pacioli meant by his words *el modo de vinegia*, he was most likely referring to differences in the practice of double-entry bookkeeping in different Italian commercial centres.[25]

There certainly were such differences, so much so that it led de Roover to conclude that double-entry bookkeeping must have emerged independently and almost concurrently in several centres in Italy.[26] Differences concerned nomenclature, the arrangement of account books (e.g. the ledger in Tuscany was often divided into two books, one for personal accounts and the other for goods accounts), the form of journal entries and of ledger entries, and the treatment of the effects of foreign exchange fluctuations in the accounts for a merchant's foreign correspondents.[27]

The double-entry system nevertheless imposed definite constraints on its practitioners. For every debit entry there had to be a credit entry. Moreover, although historians are not unanimous as to what they consider to be the other indispensable features of double entry, there is general agreement that it is necessary for there to be other categories of accounts in addition to personal accounts, i.e. accounts for other assets, incomes, expenses and capital.

These constraints, however, left considerable freedom to the merchant or bookkeeper who decided to use the double-entry system. Several of these differences I have discussed and illustrated elsewhere in the context of practice in Italy in the fifteenth and sixteenth centuries and in England in the seventeenth and eighteenth centuries.[28] There are differences, for example, in procedures for the opening and closing of a ledger, the regularity or otherwise of the compilation of a balance account in the ledger (or separately outside it), and the extent to which use was made of the check on arithmetical accuracy that is incorporated in the double-entry system (the art 'carries its own proof').[29]

For present purposes it is more useful to survey briefly differences in what we now refer to as the valuation of assets (taking receivables and fixed assets as examples) and the assignment of expenditures and receipts to accounting periods. These practices naturally affect the amount of profit or loss shown in the profit and loss account in the ledger, and also the balance on the capital account.

Amounts owed by debtors (receivables) were usually a major part of a merchant's business assets. They were subject to loss of value for a variety of reasons, including the debtor's disappearance, bankruptcy, obduracy or contentiousness. The merchant could treat a bad or doubtful debt in various ways. He could write a bad debt off to the profit and loss account, thereby eliminating it as an 'asset'; or he could simply ignore the recognised dubiousness of a receivable and keep the debt at its face value in the ledger and in its balance account (*bilancio*); or he could accumulate it with other bad and doubtful debts in a collective 'asset' account for 'desperate debtors' (*debitori di poco speranza*, as the account is called in the 1560 balance account of an Affaitadi company);[30] or he could establish a reserve account (today known as a provision account) to reflect, as an offsetting credit balance in the ledger, the loss from receivables that were likely to be partly or wholly uncollectible. The last-named treatment was rarely used. There are some early Italian examples.[31] Two late eighteenth-century examples are in the accounts of James Finlay and Company of Glasgow ('Fund for bad debts') and of the Manufacture de Papier Peints of Rixheim (near Mulhouse). An entry in the latter firm's journal, dated 1798, indicates a credit to a reserve account, the balance on which was 15 per cent of the *dettes actives*.[32]

A similar variety of 'valuation' methods is also evident in respect of fixed assets such as office furniture, business implements and utensils, ships and buildings. Expenditure on furniture and implements might be written off to the profit and loss account, the capital expenditure not being capitalised in an asset account. (According to the idiosyncratic view of the late Federigo Melis, the use of this treatment should disqualify a ledger from being considered a proper double-entry ledger.)[33] Another method was to take the arithmetical balance – the difference between the totals of the debit entries and the credit entries on the asset account – as the asset's closing 'value'. This meant that the asset was shown as yielding neither a profit nor a loss.[34] Another method was to maintain the acquisition cost of the asset as its closing balance. Yet another method was to revalue the asset, whether upwards or downwards, according to market conditions at the time of drawing up the balance account.

In a few ledgers there are examples of the modern treatment for depreciation: regularly part of the acquisition cost of the asset would be written off to the profit and loss account on a systematic basis (e.g. *x* per cent a year). An interesting example is that of the London merchants, Herries & Company.[35] A memorandum (1766) concerning the conduct of its counting house includes the following instruction:

> Trade Necessaries: To this Account we place the Cost of all Uttensils as Weights & Measures & c. for our Warehouse or Cellars as well as all Desks, Book Cases ... placing yearly Ten per Cent of their amount to Profit & Loss for Wear & Tear.

Another example is provided by a Marseille partnership agreement of 1776 that stipulated that 10 per cent be deducted to reflect the depreciation (*dépérissement*) of the firm's furniture.[36]

Different methods for dealing with fixed assets can be found in the same ledger, or even in the same account over time. It is not at all clear why a merchant or his bookkeeper sometimes applied one treatment and at other times another, or applied one treatment in one asset account and a different treatment in another.

Expenditure on a fixed asset such as a ship or furniture and fittings is an example of an outlay whose benefits to the firm are likely to straddle several accounting periods. As noted above, many merchants used accounting treatments that did not seek to assign portions of the expenditure to the profit and loss account of each of the periods in which the asset was used. Similarly, merchants in our period generally were not fussy about apportioning payments of rent or salaries to the two or more accounting periods affected. Again, the receipt of a lump sum as a fee for taking on an apprentice was usually credited in total to the profit and loss account in the year of its receipt and not spread over the years in which the apprentice was being trained. There is little evidence, in short, of the meticulous accrual accounting that is standard today.

Several things follow. First, the amount of profit or loss and the capital account balance shown in the ledger could differ greatly according to the 'valuation' treatments adopted. Broadly, one can endorse Professor Lemarchand's remark made in connection with the inclusion of bad and doubtful debtors among the asset balances, but extend it more widely to mercantile bookkeeping in our period: *La comptabilité a une fonction descriptive, avant d'être un instrument de calcul ou de mesure.*[37] Second, special calculations outside the account books (calculations that were *extra-comptable* or *ausserbuchmässig*) were necessary if and when the proprietor(s) of a business required realistic profit or capital figures. Thus when a partnership or company was being dissolved or terminated, or for any other reason the owner wanted to have a reliable indication of profits or of capital employed, he would compile a special inventory. On those occasions the users of the double-entry system had recourse to the same device of inventorisation as was used by many merchants who practised single-entry bookkeeping.[38] Third, because of the kinds of differences considered above, it is doubtful how accurate it is to suggest that double entry by the eighteenth century had become, in Charles Carrière's words, *une sorte de langage international, un moyen de l'unité du grand commerce.*[39] If double entry had become an international language, it was one which had several versions. (The differences, incidentally, were not national.) Moreover, if double entry had the advantage of being recognised as an international language of commerce, and if its use in that role had been significant, one would expect the system to have been used more widely in, say, the eighteenth century than it appears to have been, though, admittedly, there is little reliable evidence of the extent of its use in various countries or centres in particular periods.

Finally, it is clear that the double-entry system, whatever its virtues, did not correspond to any 'needed kind of measurement in that it was objective and measured something existing independently of the observer'[40] – as objective, say, as the measurement of time by means of a mechanical clock. The balance of profit (or loss) shown in a double-entry profit and loss account was not and could not be an objective datum. On the other hand, entries in a personal account for the origination or the settlement of a debt were objective whether that account was in a single-entry or in a double-entry ledger.

OFFICIAL REGULATION OF BOOKKEEPING

In the five centuries compressed within the limits of this paper there were virtually no external pressures on the merchant as to how he should keep and organise his account books or how he should calculate his profits or losses. His freedom to choose the scope and arrangement of his bookkeeping was unconfined. There were no mandatory rules or even guidelines.

There were a few isolated attempts at legislation. Thus in 1491 Ferdinand and Isabella promulgated a law that required merchants in Castile to keep accounts – an obligation designed to make it more difficult for them to evade the *alcabala*, a sales tax. But the law did not stipulate which books had to be kept, or in what manner. Further measures were introduced in 1549, designed on this occasion largely to curb the illegal outflow of coins and precious metals. The law decreed that each business had to have a journal (*manual*) and a ledger (*libro de caja*),[41] kept on the debit and credit system (*debe y ha de haber*). According to Dr Hernandez Esteve, these terms suggest the double-entry system. It seems, however, that greater emphasis was placed on the crucial role of keeping a chronological journal in bound-book form, a loose-leaf account book (*pliego horadado*) having been much used previously. It is not clear to what extent and for how long the legislation was effectively implemented.[42]

The best-known attempt at legislating for business accounts was the French Ordonnance de Commerce of 1673, associated with the names of Colbert and Savary, the latter a merchant who made his money in the textile business. This wide-ranging edict covered many subjects including accounting, and its enactment reflected public concern over the frequency of bankruptcies. Merchants, both wholesalers and retailers, had to keep a book which would cover all their trading (*négoce*), bills of exchange, debts payable and receivable, and household expenses. Every two years a merchant had to compile an inventory of all his movable and immovable assets and his debts receivable and payable. However, the accounting provisions of the code, which did not prescribe double-entry bookkeeping, were not enforced rigorously at any time, and they became a dead letter.[43]

Throughout Western Europe, entries in merchants' account books could be accepted, in certain circumstances, as evidence in courts of law. The degree of credence given to such evidence varied from place to place, and was subject to change over time. Generalisation is difficult. At first, it seems, account books may have had little value in law courts as evidence of debts receivable. A law enacted in Castile by Alfonso X in 1265 declared that an entry in an account book did not provide acceptable proof of a debt: it could be erroneous, incomplete or malicious.[44] A merchant sometimes insisted that his debtors made the relevant entries in his ledger, or at least signed them. The account book (1414–26) of Martin Bursa, a merchant from Bruges who traded in Valencia, includes entries with signed acknowledgements of debt in several languages – Valencian, Castilian, French, Latin and Arabic.[45] Nevertheless, it seems that courts were apt to give credence to a merchant's account books, having regard to the reputation or standing of the merchant, the condition of his account books, and the orderliness and clarity of his account books and the entries in them. It helped if the entries were written by the merchant himself or by an accredited employee. The 1520 laws of the city of Freiburg provided that a merchant's books could carry weight in a court of law if they were securely bound in stout covers, were written up by the merchant himself or his nominated employee, and did not have erasures and crossing out of entries.[46] The 1612 statutes of Avignon prescribed that a merchant's books would have probative value for three years provided that the entries in them were in the merchant's hand or that of his *agent fidelle et légitime*.[47] The available evidence suggests that the courts did not give any special weight to account books kept by double entry.

CAUSES OF DIVERSITY

The 1828 partnership agreement of a firm of *charrons carrossiers* in Grenoble included a statement to the effect that the partners themselves would do the bookkeeping in the way that seemed best to them and according to their custom, and that they would keep their accounts in such a manner that they did not need the help of anyone else. They noted also, in effect, that their bookkeeping requirements were simple: they bought and sold mainly for cash, and paid their workers regularly at short intervals. As Lemarchand has observed, the same attitude was displayed by many small-scale businesses, whether single proprietorships or partnerships, in the period before 1800. Indeed, it was characteristic of some of the most important merchants as well. Thus Jean Pellet (1694–1772), one of the more considerable wholesalers of Bordeaux of his time, was satisfied with fairly basic accounting arrangements.[48]

Pellet did his own bookkeeping. Some other prominent merchants also were their own bookkeepers, or at least made entries in their main books. Examples across the centuries include Pacino di Tommaso Peruzzi, the last head of the Peruzzi fourteenth-century international business; Sir Dudley North (1641–91), Turkey merchant and later active in public life in England; and Sir Charles Peers, an important merchant with business in Spain, Lord Mayor of London (1715–16) and a director of the Bank of England.[49]

Such merchants naturally adapted their bookkeeping arrangements to suit their particular business needs as they saw them. The organisation of their account books and their bookkeeping practices would also be influenced by considerations such as their knowledge and understanding of bookkeeping methods, the 'love' (or lack of it) they bore to 'this science',[50] their aptitude for this part of commercial life, and the competing demands on their time. Some merchants, moreover, were more anxious than others to keep secret the details of their business affairs, and therefore were less inclined to employ bookkeepers, except perhaps to keep subsidiary account books that revealed little about the owner's wealth.

But even when merchants did not act as their own bookkeepers, and instead employed full-time or part-time bookkeepers, they were likely to determine their bookkeeping arrangements as they thought fit in accordance with their own perceptions of their requirements. If the merchant did not understand the double-entry system, he might not have that system used in his business even if his bookkeeper was skilled in it. When Matthäus Schwartz returned from his *Wanderjahre* in Italy, having acquired in Venice a mastery of the double-entry system, and began to work as bookkeeper for the Fugger in 1516, he soon realised that he might as well have remained in Augsburg.[51] As Malachy Postlethwayt wrote in 1751, unless the merchant was capable of keeping his own books by double entry, he would not know whether his bookkeeper was keeping the books properly, or be able by inspection of his ledger to be 'duly acquainted with the state of his own affairs'.[52] And although knowledge of the double-entry system was widely diffused by the eighteenth century, it seems that there were merchants who ran large businesses but did not understand double-entry bookkeeping. According to Matthieu de la Porte, an *écrivain juré* and author of an eighteenth-century best-seller on accounting, writing at the beginning of the eighteenth century, *Il y a néanmoins des Négocians que font des affaires assez considérables, qui se contentent de tenir leurs Livres à Parties simple, parce qu'ils ne sçavent pas les Parties doubles.*[53] Paul Jakob Marperger (1656–1730) included several books on accounting among the ninety-four books he is said to have had published. In one of them he wrote that many merchants preferred single-entry bookkeeping, which they could manage 'without outside assistance'. He commented that single entry was perfectly suitable, being 'simpler and more natural' than the Italian double-entry system.[54] It is interesting that the French Code de Commerce of 1673 required that merchants' apprentices had to know single-entry as well as double-entry bookkeeping.

The personal influence of the merchant on his accounting practices can be illustrated by three admittedly idiosyncratic examples. Giovanni Borromeo, a Florentine with a business in Milan and interests abroad, showed credit balances on some merchandise accounts in his ledger (1428) and carried them to the credit side (i.e. liabilities side) of his balance account – as Zerbi expressed it, a 'kind of fictitious liability' – a procedure that makes no sense.[55] A Venetian, Leonardo Donà, in 1611 credited his capital account with the amount of 2,664 ducats. At 6 ducats a month over his long business career, it represented money which he 'could easily have spent' on his desires, and his sacrifice in 'abstaining from all kinds of personal pleasures'.[56] Sir John Banks, a wealthy seventeenth-century merchant, financier and landowner, incurred a sizeable loss on the sale of his remaining holding of East India Company stock. He could not face up to the fact that he had made a mistake. So he debited the loss, incongruously, to his Doubtfull Debts account in the ledger he wrote up himself.[57]

In any event, even well-informed bookkeepers would not have had the same ideas as to how to keep a set of books by single entry or by double entry. There were no uniform standards or professional norms. Moreover, to judge from the contents of the numerous books on accounting that were available from Pacioli onwards, it is unlikely that all teachers had the same views on the organisation of account books within a double-entry framework, or had reasonably similar views as to the treatment, for example, of assets account balances on the closing of the ledger. In fact, few of the treatises dealt seriously with the latter subject; this is true of the best-selling eighteenth-century texts such as de la Porte's *Science des négocians* and John Mair's *Bookkeeping methodiz'd*. Moreover, it seems that many merchants and bookkeepers acquired their knowledge of bookkeeping as apprentices or employees of established merchants – a process that would have tended to perpetuate diversity rather than reduce it. The fact that young men frequently had training periods abroad, rather than only or mainly in their native city or country, would have worked against uniformity in bookkeeping practice even in particular commercial centres or regions.

Some ledgers were models of punctuality of entries, good order and arrangement, and clarity. Others fell into muddle and disorder for a variety of reasons such as pressure of other work, shortage of staff, or incompetence. According to the Dutch historian, Buist, some Dutch merchants were several years in arrears with their books, and did not know what their profits had been five years earlier.[58] Justo Forchaudt, the representative in Cadiz of a Flemish partnership (towards the end of the seventeenth century) had fallen so far behind in his bookkeeping that he could not furnish customers with the abstracts of their ledger accounts they requested. Another Flemish merchant in the same city, Juan Fernicourt, had made no entries in his ledger between 1668 and 1672.[59] William (later Sir William) Hedges was head of the premier English trading house (*ragione*) in Constantinople in the second half of the seventeenth century, and later became governor of Bengal. The accounts of his firm were so 'intricated' that its credit was endangered, and there were no 'plain means to charge the debtors or good grounds to recover at law'.[60] In all, the quality of bookkeeping performance among merchants differed widely – yet another aspect of diversity.

SOME EXAMPLES OF UNIFORMITY

In the preceding sections I have been illustrating and emphasising diversity in mercantile accounting in our period. The sources of this diversity can be further elucidated by examining briefly some particular elements of uniformity that were to be found in the midst of the general lack of it.

By the end of the sixteenth century the Venetian form of ledger appears to have become widely used by merchants and other business firms throughout Italy as well as further afield. The ledger *alla veneziana* or *a sezione contrapposte* (with debits and credits respectively on facing pages in the ledger) had replaced the use of other forms of ledger, such as the ledger *a sezione sovrapposte* (with the debit and credit sections placed one above the other on the same page) that had been commonly used in Tuscany, or the bilateral ledger (with debits and credits on the same page) that had been customary in Genoa and Milan.[61] The success of the Venetian ledger can be ascribed to its greater convenience and clarity, which evidently outweighed its tendency to use ledger space prodigally. Convenience and clarity were general business desiderata in the counting house; and ledger space could be economised through the use of bookkeeping devices such as compound journal and ledger entries which came to be widely used. In contrast, the distinctive style of the early Venetian journal entry was not widely adopted outside Venice, and eventually fell into disuse even in that city.[62] Apart from a certain elegance, it offered no practical advantages over other forms.

Another example relates to certain partnerships (*compagnie*) in late fourteenth- and fifteenth-century Tuscany. Their double-entry ledgers reveal a certain uniformity of practice, including the recording of loss of value in fixed asset accounts, and the careful pro-rating of expenditures (e.g. on salaries) at ledger-balancing dates. It seems that this large measure of uniformity was the result of common features of those partnerships. The partnerships were for specified periods of a few years; at the termination of one partnership it was replaced by another, possibly with some change in the composition of the partnership (including the entry of a new partner, the exit of an old partner, or a change in partners' profit shares); the new partnership would use the same merchant's mark as its predecessor; and there was no interruption in the entity's commercial activities. Third parties might not even know that there had been a change in ownership. But the change in ownership on the occasion of what has been called a *liquidazione fittizia* called for a realistic assessment of asset values and obligations. These realistic values and the recognition of the effects of unexpired receipts or payments were reflected in entries in the ledgers of the continuing business. Practices appropriate for the liquidation of a partnership seem to have been used also at ledger-closings during the life of a partnership: this was not dictated by the same need, but presumably reflected the routine application of the same procedures. The large measure of uniformity may have been further promoted by the location of the particular partnerships in the same relatively small region. It is probable that they drew on a commonly trained pool of bookkeeping talent.[63]

Finally, the diversity of mercantile accounting in the first centuries of our chosen period can be contrasted with the uniformity of a certain category of non-mercantile accounts in England. Uniformity is a feature of manorial accounting in the hundred years from around the middle of the thirteenth century. In spite of the 'rapid proliferation' of these accounts across the country, this uniformity was striking, as P. D. A. Harvey has shown:[64]

> Yet everywhere – whether the estate was large or small, whether it was lay or ecclesiastical, whether its centre was at one end of the country or the other – these accounts closely follow a single pattern, both in external form and in the methods of accountancy.

The uniformity reflected primarily the presence of common management problems and common accounting requirements, which imposed a common purpose on the accounting process: the minimisation of fraud, and the determination of the indebtedness between steward and owner at regular intervals. The circulation of didactic treatises and the teaching of business methods to clerks at Oxford may also have promoted uniformity.[65]

Manorial accounting related predominantly to agricultural activities, but it was not the nature of the activities that itself promoted uniformity. The surviving account books of ordinary farmers in the earlier part of our period show considerable diversity. Unlike in the case of manorial farming, there were no overriding objectives strong enough to mould and standardise the bookkeeping arrangements of farmers running their own farming businesses and keeping their own books.[66]

CONCLUDING NOTE

In closing the present account, diversity in mercantile accounting has to be emphasised once more. In the absence of strong internal or external pressures to induce uniformity, a sort of *laissez-faire* prevailed as regards the bookkeeping and accounts of commercial firms. The only bookkeeping imperative that was common to the great majority of commercial (and also industrial) enterprises sprang from the business need to keep records of debts receivable and debts payable, including records of dealings between principals and agents and among partners in a partnership. This need was not enough to impose a standard pattern on accounting arrangements or to require the adoption of, for example, the same accounting treatment of bad and doubtful debts or of fixed assets.

NOTES

1 R. Grassby, *The English Gentleman in Trade: The Life and Works of Sir Dudley North 1641–1691*, Oxford, 1994.

2 L. B. Alberti, *The Family in Renaissance Florence* (translation by R. N. Watkins of *I Libri della Famiglia*), Columbia, SC, 1969, p. 197.

3 B. Cotrugli, *Il Libro dell' Arte di Mercatura* (ed. U. Tucci), Venice, 1990, p. 171.

4 F. Melis, *Aspetti della Vita Economica Medievale* (Studi nell' Archivio Datini di Prato), Siena, 1962, p. 344, n. 3.

5 P. Deyon, *Amiens Capitale Provinciale: Etude sur la Societé Urbaine au 17e Siècle*, Paris and The Hague, 1967, p. 99.

6 G. S. Gramulla, *Handelsbeziehungen Kölner Kaufleute zwischen 1500 und 1600*, Vienna, 1972, p. 398.

7 Grassby, *The English Gentleman*, op. cit., p. 40.

8 Quoted in M. D. George, *London Life in the Eighteenth Century*, 1925 (p. 43 in Penguin edition, 1992).

Defoe also explained how a certain tradesman who could not write was able to keep track of his debtors with 'many ingenious knacks of his own'. Defoe often told this dealer, who became mayor of the considerable city where he had his business, that with 'half of the study and application' that those 'knacks' involved 'he might have learned to write, and keep books too'. D. Defoe, *The Complete English Tradesman*, ch. 20. This book was first published in 1726.

9 F. W. Kent and A. Lillie, 'The Piovano Arlotto: new documents', in P. Denley and C. Elam (eds), *Florence and Italy: Renaissance Studies in Honour of Nicolai Rubinstein*, London, 1988, pp. 331–2. A *pievano* – from which *piovano* is derived – is a parish priest.

10 Some account books met their fate in odd ways. A converted Jew lived in Venice with his Christian wife. She informed the Inquisition that her husband every evening beat her over the head with the only book in the house, a ledger. She burned it. B. Pullan, *The Jews of Europe and the Inquisition of Venice, 1550–1670*, Oxford, 1983, p. 106.

On the other hand, Balthasar de Groote, an important merchant in Antwerp, was able to save his current ledger and journal when an explosion in 1646 of some stored gunpowder caused deaths, damage and fire. Several account books were lost. The surviving account books have been used effectively in R. Baetens, *De Nazomer van Antwerps Welvaart: De Diaspora en het Handelshuis De Groote tijdens de Eerste Helft der 17 de Eeuw*, Antwerp, 1976, vol. 2, p. 32.

11 F. Besta, *La Ragioneria*, Milan, 1920, vol. 2, pp. 435–6.

The view has been expressed that all other 'methods' of keeping accounts, i.e. single-entry bookkeeping in any form, could be subsumed under double-entry bookkeeping. Thus Roger North wrote: 'I need only say, that the Method comprehends all other Methods, which particular Persons have occasionally Instituted, for their own private Concerns; and that all those Methods, whatsoever they are, were, or can be invented, for the use of any Accompts, are Parts of, and as it were taken out of the *Dr.* and *Cr* ...'. North used the term 'Debtor and Creditor' for the double-entry method. (A Person of Honour (R. North), *The Gentleman Accomptant*..., London, 1714.) Two years later Thomas Watts quoted North at length, and commented: 'From all which 'tis abundantly evident, how ridiculous that common Error, which many are apt to fall into, that BOOK-KEEPING is so different among Merchants and Men of Business, that hardly two make use of the same Method ...'. Watts dismissed single entry as 'no Method'. Thomas Watts, *An Essay on the Proper Method for Forming the Man of Business*, London, 1716, p. 24.

12 R. de Roover, 'The development of accounting prior to Luca Pacioli according to the account-books of medieval merchants', in A. C. Littleton and B. S. Yamey (eds) *Studies in the History of Accounting*, London, 1956, pp. 114–74; reprinted in R. de Roover, *Business, Banking, and Economic Thought in Late Medieval and Early Modern Europe*, Chicago, 1974.

13 Further examples, before and after 1500, are discussed or reproduced in the following publications: M. Schwab, *Livre de Comptes de Mardoché Joseph (Manuscrit Hébréo-Provencal)*, Paris, 1913; W. von Stromer, 'Das Schriftwesen der Nürnberger Wirtschaft vom 14. bis zum 16. Jahrundert', in *Beiträge zur Wirtschaftsgeschichte Nürnbergs*, vol. II, 1967; A. Represa (ed.) *Libro Mayor del 'Banquiero de Corte' de los Reyes Catolicos, Ochoa Perez de Salinas (1498–1500)*, Bilbao, 1980; O. Pickl, *Das älteste Geschäftsbuch Österreichs*, Graz, 1966; E. Andersen, *Malmøkobmanden Ditlev Enbeck og hans Regnskabsbog*, Copenhagen, 1954; F. Treml, *Das Handelsbuch des Judenburger Kaufmannes Clemens Körbler, 1526–1548*, Graz, 1960; A. Louant, *Arnould Lison. Orfevre Montois (+1638)*, Brussels, 1960.

14 I. Naso, *Una Bottega di Panni alle Fine del Trecento: Giovanni Canale di Pinerlo e il suo Libro dei Conti*, Genoa, 1985.

15 C. Trasselli, 'Il mercato dei panni a Palermo nella prima metà del XV secolo: La bottega di Matteo da Vico', *Economia e Storia* 4: 286–333, 1957.

16 Von Stromer, 'Das Schriftwesen', op. cit., pp. 776–80.

The Schürstab ledger fragments are one example of the preservation of an old account book by means of its recycled use: the surviving forty-eight pages had been used as part of the cover of a register of the Nuremberg city court. Another example is the ledger of a carpet business. The pages of this large book had been torn out one by one, and used as protective covers for other documents. The bulk of the pages have been recovered; all consist of personal accounts. E. Duverger, *Jan, Jacques en Frans de Moor, Tapijtwevers en Tapijthandelaars te Oudenaarde, Antwerp en Gent (1560 tot ca. 1680)*, Ghent, 1960.

17 G. D. Ramsay, *John Isham, Mercer and Merchant Adventurer: Two Account Books of a London Merchant in the Reign of Elizabeth I*, Northampton, 1962.

18 J. Vanes, *The Ledger of John Smythe, 1538–1550*, London, 1974.

19 T. Antoni, *Il Libro dei Bilanci di una Azienda Mercantile del Trecento*, Pisa, 1967.

20 F. Edler de Roover, 'Andrea Banchi, Florentine silk manufacturer and merchant in the fifteenth century', in *Studies in Medieval and Renaissance History*, vol. 3, 1966.

21 J. Strieder, *Die Inventur der Firma Fugger aus dem Jahre 1527*, Tübingen, 1905.

22 B. S. Yamey, 'Some topics in the history of financial accounting in England, 1500–1900', in W. T. Baxter and S. Davidson (eds) *Studies in Accounting Theory*, London, 1962, pp. 21–4.

23 Guildhall Library (London), MSS 5105, 5109A.

24 R. de Roover, 'Le formation et l'expansion de la comptabilité à partie double', *Annales d'Histoire Économique et Sociale*, nos 44–45: 193, 1937.

25 For discussion of this question, see B. S. Yamey, 'Notes on Pacioli's first chapter', *Accounting, Business & Financial History*, 4: 56–60, 1994.

26 R. de Roover, 'New perspectives on the history of acounting', *Accounting Review*, 30: 405, 413, 1955.

27 On the last mentioned, see R. de Roover, 'Early accounting problems of foreign exchange', *Accounting Review*, 19, 1944.

28 B. S. Yamey, 'Some seventeenth and eighteenth century double-entry ledgers', *Accounting Review*, 34, 1959; reprinted in B. S. Yamey, *Essays on the History of Accounting*, New York, 1978; and 'Balancing and closing the ledger: Italian practice, 1300–1600', in R. H. Parker and B. S. Yamey (eds), *Accounting History: Some British Contributions*, Oxford, 1994.

Major aspects of accounting in France are discussed in the first part of Y. Lemarchand, *Du Dépérissement à l'Amortissement*, Nantes, 1993.

29 'This Way of accounting... carries with it its own proof: And here lies the supreme Excellency and Usefulness of this mystery...'. S. Monteage, *Debtor and Creditor made easie...*, London, 1675, preface.

30 An interesting variant is exemplified in the bookkeeping records (1774–82) of the Krügerey Compagnie of Viborg. There was a ledger account for bad and doubtful debts (*Böse & Zweifelhafte Schulden Conto*). Its balance was closed by transfer to the profit and loss account (*Generale Avantz Conto*). A Grandell, *Äldre Redovisningsformer i Finland*, Helsingfors (Helsinki), 1944, pp. 85–6. The Italian word *conto* was often used in North European ledgers.

31 See Yamey, 'Balancing and closing the ledger', op. cit., p. 264.

32 The Finlay records are in the library of Glasgow University, UGD 91. Information kindly provided by Professor I. Watanabe. For the French example, see Lemarchand, *Du Dépérissement*, op. cit., p. 237. The company soon changed its procedure. Instead of crediting a *compte de reserve*, an account with the title *débiteurs de nulle valeur* was credited. The net amount of the debtors was shown in the balance account, with the *débiteurs de nulle valeur* shown in the margin.

33 On this question, see Yamey, 'Notes on Pacioli's first chapter', op. cit., pp. 62–4.

34 Lemarchand (*Du Dépérissement*, op. cit., p. 259) has suggested that the arithmetical balance method of 'valuation' may be interpreted as representing the reimbursement by the asset itself of its initial cost. He links this with the theory of the 'personification' of accounts. This interpretation may be correct, at least for some users of the method.

For relevant material culled from accounting texts of the eighteenth century and early decades of the nineteenth century, see my 'Cost, market or something else: asset valuation in some early treatises', in B. Carsberg and S. Dev (eds) *External Financial Reporting: Essays in Honour of Harold Edey*, London, 1984, pp. 177–9.

It seems to me more likely that the arithmetical balance method was an expedient used to save effort: the need to make entries (in the journal and the ledger) for any profit or loss was avoided.

35 J. M. Price, 'Directions for the conduct of a merchant's counting house, 1766', in R. P. T. Davenport-Hines and J. Liebenau (eds), *Business in the Age of Reason*, London, 1987, p. 144.

36 C. Carrière, *Négociants Marseillais au XVIIIe Siècle*, Marseille, 1973, p. 722.

37 Lemarchand, *Du Dépérissement*, op. cit., p. 236.

38 An excellent example is presented and discussed by Lemarchand, concerning the Compagnie Royale d'Afrique. A letter written by the directors, dated 1760, explained why it was necessary to have two documents. The ordinary balance account (*bilan ou bordereau des effets*) does not inform one of the real state of affairs of the company; it only proves the correctness of the entries in the ledger, of which it is no more than an extract. To remedy this lack of illumination (*défaut de clarté*), the balance account had for several years been supplemented by a general inventory, which was a more realistic account of the state of affairs. This procedure was subsequently changed, without changing the intention. Instead of a supplementary *inventaire général*, a *dépouillement du bilan* was compiled to accompany the *bilan*. Lemarchand reproduces the company's *bilan* (in the form of an opening balance account) as at the end of 1776, and the *dépouillement* that sets out the corrections

necessary to calculate the *fonds réel*. Deductions are made for bad and doubtful debts, and also for certain fixed assets (such as furniture) and a large loan to the King of France. The net reductions reduce the total debit balances from some L.5,237,000 in the *bilan* to L.4,565,000 (if the loan to the King is included) and to L.3,411,000 (if it is excluded). The adjustments in the *dépouillement* were not carried through in the ledger. (Lemarchand, ibid., pp. 248–52.

The English East India Company also conducted such exercises from time to time. Thus a 'committee of [7] proprietors' reported in December 1780 on their investigations. Their adjustments reduced the 'balance in favour of the Company' (as shown in the ledger) from some £5.9 million to an amount between £3.1 and £3.8 million, according to the severity of the adjustments. *Report of the Committee of Proprietors of East-India Stock...*, London, 1780.

39 Carrière, *Négociants Marseillais*, op. cit., vol. 2, p. 763. Carrière links the statement quoted with his view that *les extraits de comptes courants* were identical in form throughout Europe. However, *comptes courants*, being personal accounts, were not peculiar to the double-entry system.

40 F. L. Nussbaum, *The Triumph of Science and Reason, 1660–1685*, New York and Evanston, 1962, p. 16.

41 Although the word *caja* or *caxa* means 'cash', the *libro de caja* was a term used for the ledger. This usage is explained in the first chapter of B. de Solorzano, *Libro de Caxa y Manuel de Cuentas de Mercaderes...*, Madrid, 1590. The author explains that the ledger is commonly called the *libro de caxa* because it contains the cash account which is the most important account.

42 E. Hernandez Esteve, 'Castilian laws of the Later Middle Ages and beginning of the Renaissance relating to merchants' accounting and account books', paper presented at *Journées internationales d'histoire du droit*, Valladolid, June 1981.

43 On the code, see Lemarchand, *Du Dépérissement*, op. cit., pp. 113–23.

44 Hernandez Esteve, 'Castilian laws', op. cit.

45 H. Lapeyre, 'Les marchands étrangers dans le royaume de Valence aux XVe et XVIe siècles', in H. Kellenbenz (ed.), *Fremde Kaufleute auf der Iberischen Halbinsel*, Cologne and Vienna, 1970, p. 103.

For another example, see P. Wolff, *Commerce et Marchands de Toulouse (vers 1350–vers 1450)*, Paris, 1954, p. 521.

46 B. Penndorf, *Geschichte der Buchhaltung in Deutschland*, Leipzig, 1913, p. 168.

47 Lemarchand, *Du Dépérissement*, op. cit., p. 115.

48 Ibid., p. 125.

49 E. S. Hunt, *The Medieval Super-companies: A Study of the Peruzzi Company of Florence*, Cambridge, 1994, p. 212; Grassby, *The English Gentleman*, op. cit., p. 75; B. S. Yamey, 'A seventeenth century double-entry journal', *Accountancy*, November 1960 (reprinted in Yamey, *Essays*, op. cit.).

50 The words quoted are in R. Dafforne, *The Merchants Mirrour*, London, 1635, Epistle Dedicatory.

51 A. Weitnauer, *Venezianischer Handel der Fugger*, Munich and Leipzig, 1931, p. 184.

52 M. Postlethwayt, *The Merchant's Public Counting-House: or, New Mercantile Institution*, London, 1751, p. 24.

53 M. de la Porte, *La Science des Négocians et Teneurs de Livres*, Paris, 1704, p. 4.

54 P. J. Marperger, *Nuetzliche Fragen*, p. 264, as quoted in J. Kulischer, *Allgemeine Wirtschaftsgeschichte*, Berlin, 1929, vol. 2, p. 299.

55 T. Zerbi, *Le Origini della Partita Doppia*, Milan, 1952, p. 333.

56 J. C. Davis, *A Venetian Family and its Fortune*, Philadelphia, 1975, p. 42.

57 Yamey, 'Some seventeenth and eighteenth century ledgers', op. cit., p. 545.
58 M. G. Buist, comment, in M. Aymard (ed.), *Dutch Capitalism and World Capitalism*, Cambridge, 1982, p. 279.
59 J. Everaert, *De Internationale en Koloniale Handel der Vlaamse Firma's te Cadiz, 1600–1700*, Bruges, 1973, pp. 69–70.

On the other hand, the Bordeaux merchant, Abraham Gradis, recorded in 1741 that he was anxious to ensure that his books were never in arrears. P. Butel, *Les Négociants Bordelais: L'Europe et Les Isles au XVIIIe Siècle.* Paris, 1974, p. 171.
60 Grassby, *The English Gentleman*, op. cit., p. 35.
61 John Dodson, writing in 1750, noted that the debit and credit entries in an account should be separated, 'otherwise the Design of the Account will not be answered'. He continued: 'The manner of separating such Transactions being a matter perfectly indifferent, various Methods have been used for that Purpose; but the most common way is to make the Account consist of two opposite Pages, and to enter those Transactions whereby *B* becomes Debtor, on the Left Hand Page, hence called the Debtor Side of the Account; and those whereby he is credited, on the Right Hand Page, called therefore the Creditor Side'. J. Dodson, *The Accountant*, London, 1750, p. ii.

The convention of having debit entries on the left-hand side of a ledger account seems to have been followed throughout Europe. Exceptions, which are rare, include the account book (1369) of Guillaume Ruyelle, a Bruges money-changer, and the ledger of Tönnis Smidt, a sixteenth-century merchant of Reval. R. de Roover, *Le Livre de Comptes de Guillaume Ruyelle, Changeur à Bruges (1369)*, Bruges, 1934, p. 21; G. Mickwitz, *Aus Revaler Handelsbüchern*, Helsingfors, 1938, p. 202.
62 The body of a 'Venetian' journal entry had six elements in the following order: (a) the word *Per*; (b) the title of the account to be debited; (c) two short sloping lines; (d) the word *A*; (e) the title of the account to be credited; and (f) the description of the transaction. See Yamey, 'Notes on Pacioli's first chapter', op. cit., pp. 56–8.
63 On the last point, see Melis, *Aspetti della Vita Medievale*, op. cit., pp. 343–4.
64 P. D. A. Harvey, 'Manorial accounts', in Parker and Yamey (eds), op. cit., p. 100.
65 D. Oschinsky, *Walter of Henley and other Treatises on Estate Managenent and Accounting*, Oxford, 1971, p. 148.

Christopher Woolgar draws attention to the absence of uniformity in medieval *household* accounts, and provides ample illustration from the accounts of aristocratic households, ecclesiastical households and knightly families. He ascribes the diversity to the lack of didactic literature for the medieval household, and to lack of specialisation of clerks responsible for the accounts. C. M. Woolgar, *Household Accounts from Medieval England*, London, 1992, part 1, p. 48.
66 The following are studies of the account books of four farmers of the sixteenth and seventeenth centuries: N. W. Alcock, *Warwickshire Grazier and London Skinner: The Account Book of Peter Temple and Thomas Heritage*, London, 1981; B. H. Slicher van Bath, 'Een Fries Landbouwbedrijf in de Tweede Helft van de Zestiende Eeuw', in *Agronomisch-Historische Bijdrage*, vol. 4, 1958; G. E. Fussel (ed.) *Robert Loder's Farm Accounts, 1610–1620*, London, 1936; D. Woodward (ed.) *The Farming and Memorandum Books of Henry Best of Elmswell, 1642*, London, 1984.

3

THE INFLUENCE OF THE INDIVIDUAL IN THE PROFESSIONALISATION OF ACCOUNTANCY

The case of Richard Brown and The Society of Accountants in Edinburgh, 1892 – 6

Tom Lee

INTRODUCTION

The purpose of this paper is to demonstrate the validity of the profession-alisation proposition that, within the context of an institutional strategy to control markets for professional services by means of various functionalist activities, the role of an individual within the institutional elite is crucial to the strategy's success. The proposition was first enunciated explicitly in the accountancy literature by Lee (1996a) when introducing historical biographies of three early Scottish professional accountants. It is an extension of two well-accepted theories of professionalisation. The first is the conventional functionalist approach to professional behaviour which characterises the latter in terms of various social attributes of a professional (e.g. Carr-Saunders and Wilson 1933). The second theory is an extension of the earlier one, and suggests that professional behaviour has a principal economic objective to control service markets (e.g. Larson 1977). The Lee (1996a) theory extends the social and economic arguments by suggesting that neither works effectively without the intervention of key individuals within the ruling institutional elite of a profession.

Little research has been published on the role of the individual in the development of the accountancy profession. Most of what exists in this area can be labelled as biography. For example, Kitchen and Parker (1981) reviewed the achievements of six English accountants, and Zeff (1987) reported on fourteen American accountants who had 'made a difference' in the development of the US accountancy profession. Neither study, however, was set within a specific theoretical context, and neither examined beyond the broad influences each of the individuals had in their specific

30

areas of expertise. The current study attempts to address these issues by, first, specifying a theory relating to the professionalisation of accountancy and, second, providing detailed evidence of the influence of an individual on the professionalisation process.

The individual used in this study is Richard Brown, who was Secretary and Treasurer of The Society of Accountants in Edinburgh (SAE) between 1892 and 1916. His biography has been recently published (Lee 1996b), and the current study extends the general information about Brown into the specific area of the institutional process of professionalisation. The focus of the study is a series of events which took place between 1892 and 1896 (particularly between 1895 and 1896). These events were concerned with attempts by Scottish chartered accountants to create a professional service monopoly by means of the chartered designation 'CA', and involved a UK-wide strategy involving Scottish, English and Irish chartered accountants. As the chief executive of an established and respected professional accountancy body for twenty-four years, Brown was in a unique position to exercise direct influence over events and strategies such as these in the early history of professional accountancy.

Data for this study have been derived mainly from the early records of the SAE, particularly its Council Minute Books (designated 'CMB' here) and Letter Books (designated 'LB') kept by The Institute of Chartered Accountants of Scotland (ICAS).[1] Other data have come from published research on the SAE and other similar bodies (e.g. Kedslie 1990; Macdonald 1985; Walker 1991). Each of these publications examines different aspects of the various challenges, defences and strategies concerning Scottish chartered accountancy in the late nineteenth and early twentieth centuries. None, however, reports research on the influence of individuals in these events. The current study redresses this imbalance and, by doing so, hopefully creates better insight into the professionalisation process of yesterday and today.

RICHARD BROWN AND THE SAE

It would be inappropriate to study the actions of Richard Brown within the context of the SAE without briefly presenting some relevant biographical detail. Much of what follows is taken from a detailed biography of Brown (Lee 1996b).

Richard Brown had a remarkable life. He was born in 1856, the fourth and youngest son of a tenant sheep farmer located on the outskirts of Edinburgh. He also had two sisters. Brown was educated in the local parish school from 1860 until 1870. He then worked as a clerk for two years prior to entering an apprenticeship with Kenneth Mackenzie, an Edinburgh chartered accountant. Mackenzie was one of the original planners of the SAE and a founding member in 1853 (Lee 1996c). He was the SAE

Treasurer from 1853 to 1863, and on its Council from 1863 to 1873. Thus, when Brown signed his contract of indenture with Mackenzie in 1872, he was relating himself to a well-established and respected member of the SAE. Mackenzie was the son of the landowner for whom Brown's father was a tenant farmer. His partner, John Turnbull Smith, was also connected to Brown. Smith's father was Brown's schoolmaster.

Brown served his five-year apprenticeship uneventfully, and was satisfactorily discharged from it in 1877. He passed the final examinations of the SAE in first place in 1878, and was admitted to membership in 1879. He continued to work for Mackenzie and Smith for six years until the dissolution of that partnership in 1885 when Smith was appointed Manager of the Life Association of Scotland. Smith's audit clients were transferred to Brown, and he practised as a sole practitioner until 1893 when he admitted two partners (one probably related to a brewing client, and the other a nephew of Kenneth Mackenzie). This was the year immediately following Brown's appointment as Secretary and Treasurer of the SAE.

Brown's humble origins did not prevent him from progressing rapidly in a profession which was founded on elitism and closely connected to landowners and lawyers (Lee 1996c). Much of his early success was obviously due to his good fortune in being connected to the Mackenzie and Smith families. Later success was due to a combination of intellectual ability, hard work and the earlier connections (particularly as these related to his accountancy practice and involvement in the SAE). The SAE was founded in 1853 and obtained its royal charter in 1854 (thus providing the designation of chartered accountant or CA). The Secretaryship of the SAE was its senior executive position and, *inter alia*, meant its holder was continuously working with a changing Presidency and Council. This mix of continuity for the Secretary and change for the office-bearers provided an ideal opportunity for the chief executive to shape events in the early history of the SAE.

Brown joined the Council of the SAE in 1891 aged 35 years and, in 1892, was elected to its Secretaryship. He held this office until 1916 when he was elected SAE President. He died in that office in 1918. During his tenure of the Secretary's office, Brown was responsible for a number of different and related tasks, all of which significantly influenced the organisation and determined its nature to the present day. There were 265 members and 93 apprentices when Brown became SAE Secretary in 1892. When he demitted office in 1916, the respective figures were 584 and 117. During that period, Brown acted as Secretary and Treasurer, worked with sixty-five Council members, and served eight Presidents. The position of Secretary and Treasurer entailed serving Council and other SAE meetings; maintaining financial, membership and indenture records; dealing with SAE investment of funds; purchasing and refurbishing the SAE headquarters in Edinburgh; establishing and maintaining the SAE library; the entire education and examination system (including SAE classes for apprentices and the secretaryship of the General Examining Board from 1893);[2] editing *The Accountant's Magazine* from 1897 onwards;[3] establishing educational links with the University of Edinburgh (eventually leading to the founding of a chair of accountancy in 1919, one year after his death); administering SAE responses to various pieces of Scottish and UK legislation affecting accountants (e.g. in bankruptcy); the effects of the First World War and the emergence of women accountants as a result; and the complex events to which the current study relates (involving competitive pressures and responses, protection of the CA designation, and attempts at registering professional accountants).

Thus, as well as managing a successful accountancy practice, Brown had what must have amounted to a full-time job as SAE Secretary. For his services, he was paid an annual fee of £100 from 1892 (increasing to £200 in 1909) and various *ad hoc* fees for specific services (e.g. with respect to various legal actions to protect the CA designation). Brown was also heavily involved in Church of Scotland affairs, and in various non-accounting bodies. He travelled extensively throughout the world, and wrote several contributions to the literature (of which his history of accounting and accountants is the best known; Brown 1905). Brown was very much a Victorian 'man of affairs', and a good example of the emerging professional middle class of that period in Scotland.

THE SAE AND COMPETITION

The SAE was well established by the time Richard Brown became its Secretary in 1892. It was the first professional accountancy body founded in Scotland[4] (and, indeed, the world) and, like most pioneering organisations, was advantaged and disadvantaged by that position. In particular, the SAE quickly found that obtaining a royal charter in 1854 was insufficient to create the work monopoly which was undoubtedly a major factor in the desire for its formation (Kedslie 1990; Walker 1995). The SAE was an elitist organisation (Lee 1996c). It was formed by a small group of Edinburgh accountants in mid-century, and its initial membership was very deliberately chosen to mimic other well-established professional bodies. It therefore excluded accountants as well as including them. In addition, the Glasgow (IAAG) and Aberdeen (SAA) bodies were a constant source of irritation to it (Shackleton and Milner 1996). This irritation appears to have arisen partly as a result of a long-standing rivalry between Edinburgh and other Scottish cities such as Glasgow, and partly because the IAAG (particularly) and SAA adopted different and apparently lower standards of membership than the SAE. Thus, the formation and development of the SAE not only created an 'external' schism between SAE members and other

Scottish accountants, it also produced an 'internal' rivalry between competing Scottish bodies of chartered accountants. These divisions characterised a long-standing series of challenges to the superiority of Scottish chartered accountants, and the responses by the three chartered bodies. The responses were particularly difficult to sustain because of the 'internalised' disputations that persisted. This was the world of professional accountancy which Richard Brown entered in 1892. Events prior to this date described in this section are examined in greater detail by Kedslie (1990) and Walker (1991).

The first challenge to the privileged position of Scottish chartered accountants came in 1884 when a small body of accountants based in Glasgow petitioned Queen Victoria for a royal charter. The petitioning body was the Scottish Institute of Accountants (SIA) founded in 1880. The essence of its petition was a desire to permit SIA members to use the designation CA, thus appearing to be designated in the same way as chartered accountants. The three Scottish chartered bodies (led by the SAE) briefed the Lord Advocate on the matter, and the petition was rejected by the Privy Council without a hearing (following receipt of a report from the Lord Advocate). The main feature of this incident was the close co-operation between the senior law officer in Scotland and the SAE Council. Following rejection of the petition, the SIA attempted in 1886 to get the three chartered bodies to come to unify with it as one profession in Scotland with a national charter. This approach was firmly and immediately rejected by the chartered bodies.

The next SIA challenge to the Scottish chartered bodies came in 1889 with a further petition for a royal charter. The petition was supported by several thousand individual signatures of influential Scots. Opposition was organised by each of the three bodies with some attempt to ensure consistency and compatibility. For example, the SAE Secretary, James Howden, was instructed by his Council to ask the SAE law agent to draft a counter-petition (CMB, 2/2, 69) based on arguments concerning the educational superiority of chartered accountants and the inferiority of SIA members (most of whom were not employed in accountancy). The correspondence of the SAE Secretary in 1890 reveals that the Dean of the Faculty of Advocates and two colleagues were appointed to represent the SAE (LB, 78); a conference of the Councils of the SAE, IAAG and SAA was held to organise the opposition to the petition (LB, 79); Scots MPs were asked not to support the petition (LB, 90); and the petition was refused in July 1890 (LB, 92). The management of the opposition on this occasion was clearly in the hands of the individual Councils, although there were signs of an emerging unification on such matters with leadership from the SAE.

Several other events should be mentioned prior to the appointment of Richard Brown as SAE Secretary. They reveal that not all competitive events were regarded as important by the Scottish chartered bodies. For example, in 1890 and 1891, The Institute of Chartered Accountants in England and Wales (ICAEW) promoted the Chartered Accountants Bill which attempted to restrict the use of the CA designation to UK chartered accountants (with the caveat that the description should include the holder's professional body if he did not practise in the country of that body). The Bill failed to progress in Parliament, and there was no mention of it in the SAE Council Minute Books or Secretary's Letter Books.

In 1891, the SIA attempted to incorporate under the Companies Act 1867. The SAE Council suitably adjusted its previous counter-petition to the 1889 SIA petition, and submitted it to the Board of Trade (CMB, 2/2, 112–13). Incorporation did not take place. Also in 1891, a second Scottish rival to the chartered bodies (the Corporation of Accountants Limited (CAL), an offshoot of the SIA) attempted to incorporate as a body of corporate accountants with the explicit intention of using the designation CA. On this occasion, the three Scottish chartered bodies took joint court action to prevent such use in 1892. They were successful under appeal in 1893, and effectively obtained legal protection for the CA designation in Scotland from that time onwards.

The ICAEW made another attempt in 1892 to create a UK-wide monopoly of the CA designation. It promoted a further Chartered Accountants Bill which was defeated largely through the opposition of a rival English body, the Society of Accountants and Auditors Incorporated (SAAI). There is no mention of this Bill in the SAE Council Minute Books and Letter Books, indicative that the 1892 CAL court action was regarded by at least the SAE Council as sufficient to provide the monopoly use of the CA designation.

Finally, in 1892, the CAL made the first attempt in the UK to register or license accountants. Its Public Accountants Bill related only to accountants in Scotland. It failed in Parliament and, as with other similar legislation, did not prove to be sufficiently significant to warrant discussion by the SAE Council. This was not the case with later legislation dealt with by Richard Brown when he succeeded James Howden as SAE Secretary in 1892.

RICHARD BROWN, COMPETITION AND REGISTRATION

The first legislation dealing with the registration of accountants, and which Richard Brown was required to monitor, was the SAAI's Public Account-ants Bill (No. 1) in 1893 and 1894. This proposed statute suggested registration of members of five UK chartered bodies (including those in Scotland), the SAAI and the SIA. SAE Council minutes reveal that Brown was informed of this Bill early in 1893, and that Council decided at that point that legislation of this type was not required for its members (CMB,

2/2, 172–3). However, despite this decision, Brown wrote to the SAAI on 21 April 1893 suggesting amendments to the Bill, and informing it that the Bill would be supported in Parliament by Sir Charles Pearson MP (the SAE's Parliamentary adviser). It is unclear why there was this contradiction with respect to the actions of Council and Brown – particularly whether or not Brown was acting on the instructions of his Council. In the event, it mattered little as the Bill was defeated in Parliament.

The Council of the SAE took greater interest in a competing Bill on registration in 1893 and 1894. This was the Public Accountants Bill (No. 2), sponsored by the ICAEW, and covering the registration of ICAEW and SAAI members only. Thus, unlike the SAAI Bill, Scottish chartered accountants were excluded, and the issue arose of what would happen to Scottish chartered accountants working in England and Wales. Not surprisingly, the SAE Council Minute and Letter Books indicate the issue was taken seriously. On 6 February 1893, Brown wrote to his ICAEW counterpart to arrange a meeting to discuss the Bill (LB, 60). On his return by 11 February, he wrote in very general terms to the IAAG Secretary, Alexander Sloan, informing him of how the ICAEW and SAAI Bills were progressing through Parliament (LB, 64). He wrote more revealingly on 14 February to Walter Reid, the SAA Secretary, saying the SAAI Bill was 'harmless' whereas the ICAEW Bill was not (LB, 66).

On 17 March, Brown sent a copy of the ICAEW Bill to Sloan to allow the IAAG Council to discuss it (LB, 100).[5] The day before, he had written to his President, James Howden, expressing his major concern that all English accountants would be designated as CAs by the ICAEW Bill (LB, 102). The SAE Council met on 24 March to discuss the Bill (CMB, 2/2, 174–81). It disapproved of its exclusion of Scottish chartered accountants from practising as CAs in England. Brown was asked to instruct the SAE law agents to draft an amending clause to prevent such exclusion, and proceeded to London to discuss this and further amendments with Scottish MPs. Sir Charles Pearson MP opposed the Bill's reading, and it (and the SAAI Bill) were withdrawn.

Events of 1893 therefore witnessed significant changes in the approach of the Scottish chartered bodies to the issue of protecting the CA designation and to the registration of accountants. First, the SAAI approach to registration embraced all major UK accountancy bodies (including the SIA), and was presumably regarded as non-threatening by Richard Brown and his colleagues because of the inclusion of the SIA. The latter body had persistently been denied professional respectability by the Privy Council, the Board of Trade, and the Scottish courts. The ICAEW Bill, on the other hand, not only permitted SAAI members to be chartered, but also had the effect of preventing Scottish chartered accountants from practising as CAs in England. As a number of such individuals had been working in England for a number of years, their interests required protection – hence the SAE intervention in the Bill's progress. The second change was the active involvement of Richard Brown in the legislative process. He appears to have become by 1893 the principal actor for the Scottish bodies in terms of gathering and disseminating information and activating policy. The third change was the realisation that there was a need to co-ordinate effectively responses to any challenges to Scottish chartered accountancy. On 18 November 1893, Richard Brown wrote to the Secretary of the ICAEW requesting him to send any future registration Bills to a special Joint Committee of the three Scottish chartered bodies. Thus, for the first time, these bodies formally acknowledged the potential consequences of registration as driven by the English bodies, and the need to act efficiently and effectively in response.

The Scottish chartered bodies did not have to wait long for the next round of proposed legislation. In 1894, the SAAI introduced a Public Accountants Bill similar to that defeated in 1893. The SAE Council noted it, instructed its law agents to continuously monitor such legislation, and decided to take no action (CMB, 2/2, 187–8). The Bill failed in October 1894. Richard Brown wrote to the ICAEW Secretary in January 1894 stating an SAE Council view that such legislation was not needed in Scotland but that the SAE should be informed of any proposed statutes (LB, 267). The scene was therefore set for the greatest and most complex challenge to the Scottish chartered bodies – the third petition of the SIA for a royal charter in 1895 and 1896. It was within the events surrounding this petition that Richard Brown can be seen to have had a major role.

THE SIA PETITION OF 1895

The 1895–6 petition of the SIA expressly asked that it be called the Scottish Provincial Institute of Accountants, and that its members be designated as CPIAs. Developments in the presentation of the petition extended over at least two years. Richard Brown was informed in 1893 of the SIA's intention to petition (its third). On 21 March 1893, he passed this news to his President (James Howden) and to the Secretaries of the IAAG (Alexander Sloan) and SAA (Walter Reid) (LB, 103). What the SIA had done was send a 'Memorial of Intent' to the Scottish Office prior to petitioning, and Brown was instructed by his Council on 24 March to write to the Secretary of State for Scotland asking for a hearing on the matter (CMB, 2/2, 175). Brown, however, had already done so on 22 March (pointing out previous failed SIA petitions) (LB, 105), and had written on the same day to Sloan asking him to write in similar terms to the Secretary of State, and to come with him to London to lobby Scottish MPs on the matter (LB, 107). Following his Council's meeting on 24 March, Brown wrote to Reid with the request to write to the Secretary of State but without the London invitation (LB, 108). He and Sloan also met with the ICAEW

President in London, and reported this to Reid (LB, 110). Thus, competition and registration events appear to have been driven from Brown's SAE office, with subsequent ratification from the SAE Council and physical presence from the IAAG but not the SAA Secretary.

Nothing relevant appears to have occurred between early 1893 and late 1894. Then, on 10 November 1894, Brown informed Sloan of the emergence of the SIA petition, and asked whether it should be taken directly to the three chartered Councils or the Joint Committee formed in November 1893 as a result of the ICAEW and SAAI registration Bills of that year (LB, 384). Taking the matter to the Joint Committee appears to have been agreed by Brown and Sloan, and Reid was informed of this by Brown on 14 November (LB, 390). The SAE Council on 19 November received a letter from the SIA in which it informed the SAE of its intention to petition for a royal charter, and hoping that the three Scottish chartered bodies would join with it in a scheme to regulate Scottish accountants (CMB, 2/2, 198–214 and 222–31).[6] The SAE set up a subcommittee (including Brown) to organise opposition to the petition and to promote the idea of national registration.

A letter from Brown to Reid on 20 November outlines this tactic – that is, to oppose the proposed royal charter, and go for a Bill of registration similar to those which regulated legal and medical practitioners (LB, 399). A letter on the same day to Sloan informed him of the SAE subcommittee and the strategy which the SAA had agreed with Brown (LB, 401). The SIA was informed by Brown on 4 December of the opposition to its petition and the consensus regarding a Scottish registration scheme (LB, 410). A letter to Brown from the SIA on 24 December agreed to the registration idea (LB, 425). The SAE Council was informed by Brown on 4 January 1895 that the SIA would set its petition aside if legislation to register was introduced. Brown was instructed by his Council to proceed to draft such legislation. This was the Accountants (Scotland) Bill which was intended to restrict the use of the term 'accountant' in Scotland to those practitioners registered there.

Brown instructed the SAE law agent on 7 January 1895 to draft the Bill (LB, 434), and wrote to Sir Charles Pearson MP on 2 February inviting him to see the Bill through Parliament (LB, 463). Thus, as a result of the threat of a third SIA petition, the SAE generally, and its Secretary particularly, had taken charge of the issue by using the registration Bill tactic. The degree to which Brown felt he was in charge is evidenced by his letter to the SAA Secretary, Walter Reid, on 2 February 1895, in which he chastised Reid for mentioning the proposed Scottish Bill in the SAA annual report (LB, 466). Further amendments to the draft Bill were notified to the IAAG Secretary, Alexander Sloan, on 4 February (LB, 467) and, at the request of former SAE President, George Auldjo Jamieson, Brown informed the ICAEW President of the Bill (LB, 470). On 9 February,

Brown acknowledged receipt from the ICAEW President of its Chartered Accountants Bill to register English, Welsh and Irish chartered accountants (LB, 476). The Scottish chartered bodies were therefore faced with three simultaneous issues: the proposed SIA petition dependent on Scottish registration legislation, draft Scottish registration legislation, and ICAEW-inspired non-Scottish chartered registration legislation. Richard Brown's hands were filling fast.

Brown wrote to Reid, the SAA Secretary, on 13 February 1895 regarding the ICAEW Bill (LB, 482). He stated that the IAAG Council wished to register all Scottish accountants who had been in practice for at least two years. In particular, he articulated the SAE objection to the ICAEW Bill (i.e. that only English CAs could be designated as CAs in England). He ended by warning Reid not to talk about these matters outside of the Joint Committee. On 19 February, Brown wrote to Reid, Sloan, the SAE President (James Haldane) and Sir Charles Pearson MP, enclosing his memorandum on the ICAEW Bill to the Joint Committee (LB, 487–90). He had received the Bill from Pearson. It was receiving its second reading in Parliament. Pearson was also notified by Brown that the drafting of the Scottish registration Bill was being held up by the IAAG Council (LB, 489). The letter to Haldane indicates that Brown rather than the SAE Council was the initiator of opposition to the ICAEW Bill (LB, 490).

A further letter from Brown to Pearson on 23 February gives the reason for objecting to the ICAEW Bill (i.e. the exclusion of Scottish chartered accountants from practising as CAs in England) (LB, 494). Brown stated that he had written on 23 February (LB, 496) to the ICAEW asking for removal of the exclusion in return for SAE support for the Bill. The IAAG and SAA were making similar overtures through their representative MPs. Brown then returned to the issue of the SIA. On 2 March 1895, he sent the SIA's lawyer a copy of the draft Accountants (Scotland) Bill (LB, 504). The SIA reply was communicated to the SAE Council by Brown on 28 March. The SIA wished to have the right to be designated as CAs, and rejected the proposed Bill. A letter was sent by Brown in response to the SIA indicating that the Scottish chartered bodies could not agree to a registration Bill which deprived them of their distinctive CA designation. The letter to the SIA had been drafted by the SAE law agent, and approved by the SAE President, James Haldane, and by Brown (LB, 528).

Brown's orchestration of opposition to the SIA petition can be evidenced in a series of letters from him in May 1895. He wrote to his President, James Haldane, on 1 May stating a need to fight the SIA, and to call a meeting of the SAE Council as soon as possible (LB, 534). Also on 1 May, he wrote to both his IAAG and SAA counterparts saying that, in the absence of Council meetings, there was an immediate need to send a circular letter to all Scottish MPs asking them not to sign the SIA petition (LB, 538–9). The SAE Council agreed to this idea on 9 May, and to revisiting the idea of a UK registration Bill. Writing to MPs appears to have been successful as it was reported to the SAE Council that names had been removed from the petition (CMB, 2/2, 227). Brown was empowered to travel to London with his President to lobby MPs (CMB, 2/2, 229), and also met Sir Charles Pearson MP in London with the objective of introducing a UK-wide Bill to Parliament (LB, 547 and 549). He was accompanied by the IAAG Secretary, Alexander Sloan.

The most immediate task for Brown at this time was organising a coherent and relevant case against the SIA petition. He did so in a number of ways. For example, on 4 June 1895, he wrote to SAE members in Dundee and Inverness asking them to research and inform him about the nature of the work they typically undertook in these locations (LB, 565). He wrote to Walter Reid, the SAA Secretary, on 5 June requesting that Reid inform Lord Provosts and Town Councils in the Aberdeen area of SAA opposition to the SIA petition (LB, 573). On 12 June, Brown wrote directly to the Lord Provost of Perth asking for his support against the petition. His main arguments were that the petition was delaying the Accountants (Scotland) Bill which would permit registration of eminent Perth accountants who were not chartered accountants, the SIA did not represent the 'provinces', and the petition created confusion regarding use of the CA designation (LB, 581). Sloan and Reid were requested on 12 June to provide data on SIA members rejected for membership by the IAAG and SAA (LB, 583). Sloan was asked on 21 June to provide information on auditors appointed by Sheriffs under the Burgh Police Act 1892 (LB, 589). And Sloan and Reid were invited on 24 June to give Brown information on the business of SIA members in Glasgow and Aberdeen (LB, 591). Thus, Brown took responsibility for gathering a considerable amount of information to support a counter-petition to the SIA. On 28 June 1895 he informed the SAE President that the counter-petition had gone to the Privy Council on 22 June (LB, 605). This is somewhat surprising, given the data searches initiated by Brown subsequent to the delivery of the counter-petition. At the very least, it provides reason for speculating that the policy to involve the Secretaries of the IAAG and SAA was less than whole hearted. Alternatively, the information gathered would be of use at a later date if further challenges to the Scottish chartered bodies emerged.

It was reported at an SAE Council meeting on 29 July 1895 that James Haldane and Richard Brown had been to London to lobby MPs as part of the opposition to the SIA petition. In addition, Brown continued to rally support from non-accounting constituents (e.g. parish councils) (LB, 625). He also returned to the issue of registration legislation when he wrote to the Secretary of State for Scotland on 12 August 1895 asking that the Secretary and the Lord Advocate meet with him and the Presidents of the SAE and IAAG concerning such a matter (LB, 645). As no meeting took place, this tactic seems to have failed. However, Brown continued to orchestrate opposition to the SIA petition. Reid of the SAA was asked to write 'one or two' letters to Scottish MPs suggesting they were supporting the SIA petition on inadequate information (LB, 651). Sloan of the IAAG was asked by Brown to change the wording of the IAAG annual report regarding the SIA petition (presumably it was too conciliatory) (LB, 730).

The registration issue continued to develop. By 25 January 1896, Brown was able to report to Sloan that he, the SAE President, and the SAE law agent had met with the Lord Advocate, and that the latter person's advice was that registration legislation should not be seen as an argument against granting a royal charter to the SIA (LB, 738). In other words, whereas Brown and the other opponents to the SIA petition had attempted to use registration legislation as a ploy to defeat the petition, the senior law officer in Scotland was recommending that the two issues should be kept separate. On 29 January, Brown recommended to the SAE law agent further changes to the proposed Accountants (Scotland) Bill prior to a meeting of the Joint Committee (presumably in line with the Lord Advocate's advice) (LB, 740). Brown asked J A Campbell MP (now the SAE Parliamentary adviser) to ballot for the Bill on 5 February (LB, 758). Campbell agreed on 7 February, and Brown travelled to London to discuss tactics with him (LB, 761).

The Accountants (Scotland) Bill was intended to restrict the use of the term 'accountant' in Scotland to those individuals who were registered to practise as such. The register was to be similar to those maintained for legal and medical practitioners. The term 'chartered' was to be used only by members of the SAE, IAAG and SAA. There was to be a Registrar and Council appointed by the Lord President of the Court of Session. The Council's responsibility was to determine rules for educating, examining and training accountants for registration. Brown drafted a letter to go to members of the SAE, IAAG and SAA (enclosing a copy of the Bill) (LB, 781 and 782). However, a letter to Sloan on 28 February 1895 indicates that the IAAG Council was not happy with this procedure, wishing instead to examine the detail of the Bill before it went to members (LB, 783). Brown's advice was not to do this, particularly as the Bill was on its way to the Secretary of State for Scotland and Scottish MPs. This event further suggests that, despite a Joint Committee, co-operation between the three Scottish chartered bodies was not fully effective, and that Brown was a primary influence in events.

On 2 March 1895, Brown informed Sloan that the Privy Council wanted to know if the chartered bodies wished to appear before it in relation to the SIA petition (LB, 787). Brown stated the need to do so, and to prepare the appropriate case and immediately introduce the Accountants (Scotland) Bill. At the same time (5 March), Brown asked Reid, the SAA Secretary, to do nothing in London regarding the Bill or to let the ICAEW or SAAI know of its existence until he sent them copies (LB, 794). This suggests that Brown did not fully trust Reid's ability to remain a member of a team or to retain confidentiality. It also suggests that the English bodies were not being kept informed by Brown of Scottish registration developments in the same manner as he had requested the ICAEW to keep the Scottish bodies informed of English registration plans.

On 6 March 1896, the final version of the Accountants (Scotland) Bill went to J. A. Campbell MP, other supporting MPs, Sloan and Reid (LB, 797). The accompanying letters from Brown to the MPs stated the urgency of the Bill's introduction, and the need for their presence in Parliament when it was. On 12 March, Sloan was informed by Brown that there would be no meeting of members regarding the Bill, and he was sending it to the ICAEW and SAAI, *The Scotsman* and *The Glasgow Herald* (both with a small article), and all non-CA accountants in Scotland (LB, 811). He wrote to the ICAEW, ICAI (Institute of Chartered Accountants in Ireland) and SAAI on the same day, adding that, if similar legislation were introduced by them, the Scottish bodies would seek reciprocal arrangements for the various registers (LB, 814). The SAAI reintroduced its Public Accountants Bill in 1896 (including the three Scottish chartered bodies and the SIA). There was no mention of this legislation in the SAE Council minutes. The ICAEW also introduced its Accountants (No. 2) Bill in 1896. Like the SAAI Bill, it included all chartered bodies in the UK, the SAAI and SIA, and, for one year only, any other accountant approved by a General Council of Accountants. Three competing Bills therefore emerged in Parliament during 1896.

Meantime, the Scottish Bill was pursued by Brown. On 14 March 1895, he wrote to Reid of the SAA asking him to send the Bill to the *Aberdeen Press and Journal* (LB, 824). The Bill was also sent by Brown to *The Accountant* on 17 March, emphasising the desire of the Scottish bodies for reciprocation should the English Bills succeed (LB, 829). On 19 March, Brown reported to Sloan and Reid that the article he had sent to *The Glasgow Herald* was published, but that *The Scotsman* one was not (it was published several days later) (LB, 836). Brown also continued to seek more evidence of the frailties of SIA members (presumably for the Privy Council hearing). He sought from Sloan and Reid data on SIA members who had failed chartered accountancy examinations (LB, 836).

The strain of these events on Richard Brown must have been considerable. He was essentially running the show on his own, with occasional help from his IAAG and SAA counterparts. How much he was affected is clear in certain exchanges he had in the spring of 1896. For example, on 24 March, he wrote to the ICAEW Secretary (and J. A. Campbell MP) complaining about inaccuracies in *The Accountant* regarding the Scottish position over possible reciprocation on registration (LB, 861). He sent his *Scotsman* article to all Scottish CAs, and various letters to Scottish CAs in England reassuring them that, with reciprocation, they would be able to continue to practise in England. Brown was at his most testy in a letter to Reid on 21 April prior to the hearing with the Privy Council (which Reid would not attend) (LB, 899). He wrote that he would not be able to give Reid a copy of the minutes of the meeting, although he might have a spare copy of the Scottish bodies' case. By 22 April, he was complaining to Campbell about Parliamentary changes to the Bill which were destroying its intention and aiding the SIA and CAL (LB, 894). On 23 April, he bluntly refused the SIA's law agent access to SAE membership records (LB, 896).

The registration events affected organisations other than the professional accountancy bodies. Brown had to write to the Commercial Bank of Scotland to reassure its management that the Accountants (Scotland) Bill was not intended to prevent bank accountants being described as such (LB, 916). The more weighty problems affecting Brown, however, were those associated with the tactics of getting the proposed legislation through Parliament. For example, he wrote on 19 May 1896 to the Bill's sponsor, J. A. Campbell MP, informing him that the ICAEW was blocking all attempts to present registration Bills to a Select Committee of Parliament, and that he should present the Accountants (Scotland) Bill in the 'normal way' (LB, 919).

By this time, the SIA petition had been rejected for the third time by the Privy Council (CMB, 2/2, 248–9). Brown had attended the meeting at the beginning of May. The cost to the SAE of responding to the petition was £506 (CMB, 2/2, 254). Brown wrote a second letter to Campbell on 19 May seeking an amendment to the Accountants (Scotland) Bill which would permit cross-frontier reciprocation (this had been agreed with the ICAEW and SAAI and, in his opinion, would likely be agreed by the SIA because of its petition failure) (LB, 921). Brown's testiness was further demonstrated on 19 May when he wrote to, first, the Editor of *The Accountant* bluntly complaining of its misleading editorial on the failed SIA petition (LB, 923) and, second, the Secretary of the ICAEW (which he stated subsidised *The Accountant*) repudiating the article (LB, 936). The curious aspect of these letters is that Brown was authorised to write them on behalf of his Council at its meeting of 28 May – five days later (CMB, 2/2, 250). It is apparent that he was acting independently of his Council and seeking a retrospective approval of his actions. Whether SAE Council members were aware of this behaviour is unclear.

The Accountants (Scotland) Bill was sent in May 1896 to all SAE members for comment (CMB, 2/2, 247–8). However, it failed at its second reading in the same month (CMB, 2/2, 248). Despite this, Brown sent a further letter to J. A. Campbell MP on 8 June 1896 (LB, 944). In it, he stated that the Bill had received support from the Edinburgh Chamber of Commerce (by public report) and the Solicitors to the Supreme Court in Edinburgh and Aberdeen (by petition). As a result of the Bill's failure,

Brown's communications with the IAAG and SAA on the issue ceased for several months. Then Brown was authorised by his Council on 6 November 1896 to reintroduce the Bill. Alexander Sloan, Secretary of the IAAG, was informed of this intention on 10 November 1896 (LB, 52). Walter Reid, Secretary of the SAA, was not. Neither of these individuals had been written to by Brown on the issue of a Scottish Bill since mid-March 1896. This is not to say that there had been no other communications or meetings, merely that there is no record of them taking place.

The failure of the Accountants (Scotland) Bill meant that accounts required settling. Brown submitted his (undisclosed) fee note to the SAE law agent on 8 June 1896 (LB, 945). Several months later, on 16 December 1896, he asked the SAE law agent to submit his account for the Bill (LB, 102) and, on 24 December, wrote to Reid (for the SAA share of £9. 9s. 9d.) (LB, 111), and to Sloan for the (unstated) IAAG share. However, the Accountants (Scotland) Bill was not completely dead. On 29 December, Brown wrote to Reid asking for SAA permission for J. A. Campbell MP to ballot to reintroduce it to Parliament (LB, 116). A similar letter on 31 December was sent to Sloan regarding IAAG permission, with the following addendum which reflected that the action was regarded by Brown as political rather than practical:

> In reference to your letter of yesterday relating to the Accountants Scotland Bill. You may have an opportunity before Tuesday of pointing out to any members of your Council, that the use made of the Bill in the hearing before the Privy Council seems to us to impose a moral obligation to re-introduce the Bill in the forthcoming session of Parliament. It is not the least likely that our doing so will have any practical result, but as a matter of common honesty, we think we are bound to put it forward. In a matter of Policy also, unless we keep ourselves to the front regards legislation, there is a risk of Bills being passed at the instance of other bodies, which would be inimical to our interests, and in any event it is particularly desirable that our position should be made manifest. Yours very truly, Richard Brown.

EVENTS AFTER 1896

The proposed legislation was introduced as the Scottish Chartered Accountants Bill in March 1987 (CMB, 2/2, 264). It desired registration only for Scottish chartered accountants. Also in 1897, the ICAEW reintroduced its 1896 Accountants (No. 2) Bill, having failed to get its members to agree to a Chartered Accountants Bill which would have absorbed SAAI and ICAEW members into one body. On 18 January 1898, it was reported by Brown to the SAE Council that both the Scottish and English Bills had failed (CMB, 2/2, 281). The Scottish chartered accountants had one further attempt at registration in 1898, but this was blocked in Parliament on behalf of the ICAEW (CMB, 2/2, 286).

The registration issue persisted for some time into the twentieth century, and continued to involve Richard Brown as SAE Secretary. Although all proposed legislation failed in Parliament, its introduction meant a rapid and meaningful response from the Scottish chartered bodies generally and Brown particularly. The Scottish strategy was that Scottish chartered accountancy required separate registration as proposed in the Accountants (Scotland) Bill. For example, when the SAAI introduced a Bill in 1899, the Joint Committee responded with this argument (CMB, 2/2, 305–6). An ICAEW Bill was introduced and failed in 1905 with little comment from the Scottish chartered bodies (CMB, 2/3, 32 and 34). In 1909, a further ICAEW attempt at registration was made despite a lack of enthusiasm from the Board of Trade (CMB, 2/3, 104). In this case, the legislation was intended to include only England and Wales. Despite Scottish pressure to have UK-wide registration, the ICAEW would not amend it to include Scotland (CMB, 2/3, 111–12 and 114). The Bill failed, but the ICAEW introduced a further Bill in 1910, this time including Scotland (CMB, 2/ 3, 126). The Bill failed at the committee stage (CMB, 2/3, 144). It was followed by a further Bill by the SAAI which failed in 1912, and an ICAEW Bill in 1913 which was never introduced to Parliament. This was the last registration issue with which Richard Brown dealt during his secretaryship.

CONCLUSIONS

The early histories of the UK professional accountancy bodies include extensive discussions of the significant issues of competition between and registration of professional accountants (e.g. Kedslie 1990; Macdonald 1985; Walker 1991 in relation to the Scottish chartered bodies). At the heart of these rivalries and disputes lay the right to the CA designation as a signal of professional respectability and status, and as a means of securing an economic monopoly over certain accountancy services. The issue was therefore a complex mix of social and economic factors. Previous research has not investigated the impact of individuals in these matters, particularly from the point of view of determining whether or not policy and action was influenced by either individuals (such as Richard Brown of the SAE) or groups (such as the SAE Council). Indeed, previous research implies that policy and action were group-induced matters.

This study argues to the contrary – that is, that the early professionalis-ation process in the UK was shaped in large part by the actions of a few key individuals. One of these men was Richard Brown of the SAE. Because of his position as chief executive of the SAE over a twenty-four year period in the early history of the UK accountancy bodies, Brown was able to shape events well beyond his proportional presence on the Council of one of five chartered bodies in the UK. Indeed, as evidence from the SAE Letter Books reveals, he influenced policy and practice in a number of important ways.

First, Brown became SAE Secretary during a period when Scottish chartered accountants were continuously challenged over their privileged economic and social position. The challenges were persistent and increasingly well managed. They needed to be responded to in an equally effective way. The SAE Council generally, and Brown particularly, appear to have taken the lead on these matters. The competition and registration events of the 1890s suggest that the IAAG and SAA were only supporting actors in the events. Often, the SAA did not appear to be involved at all.

Second, Brown took a lead role in these matters at a time when rivalries between the Scottish chartered bodies were as persistent as those with which the latter were attempting to cope vis-à-vis the SIA, ICAEW and SAAI. This is not to suggest that the Scottish chartered rivalries were as deep seated as the others. Despite the rivalries, Brown managed to fashion a unified Scottish approach to the royal charter petitions of the SIA, and the English-only registration attempts of the ICAEW. This was particularly the case in 1895 and 1896 when he had to deal with petitions and registration Bills at the same time. His major tactic appears to have been one of formulating policy and intended action (whether this was with the SAE Council is unclear at times), and then communicating these matters to the IAAG and SAA (and his President).

Third, Brown engineered events in such a way that he involved everyone who had to be involved without surrendering his position of leadership. In particular, despite the existence of a Joint Committee and three separate Councils, the responses to the charter petitions and registration Bills were skilfully orchestrated to allow others to participate without necessarily having significant involvement. For example, the IAAG and SAA Secretaries, Sloan and Reid, appear to have been reduced to gatherers of data and receivers of information on several occasions. Brown's correspondence to his counterparts in the IAAG and SAA suggest that the Joint Committee was not the primary source of policy and action with respect to petition and Bill responses. At times, Brown felt comfortable enough to put his counterparts in their place when he felt they were likely to stray from his designated strategy.

Fourth, despite his actions to include and exclude, Brown successfully managed the responses to the petitions and Bills without destroying other efforts at unifying the Scottish chartered accountancy profession, and relationships with the English and Irish bodies. For example, in Scotland several unification events took place during Brown's tenure as Secretary. The General Examining Board was formed in 1893 with Brown as its Secretary (CMB, 2/2, 152). A Joint Committee was constituted in 1894, also with Brown as Secretary. It met frequently without a constitution until its constituted formation in 1915 as the Joint Committee of Scottish Councils (CMB, 2/3, 244). *The Accountant's Magazine* was launched in 1897 largely as a result of Brown's efforts, and with him as its founding Editor (CMB, 2/2, 256). A Joint Committee of the Councils of the Chartered Bodies of Accountants in the United Kingdom operated from 1902 onwards (CMB, 2/3, 342–3).

It would be wrong to suggest that Richard Brown ran a completely 'one-man' show during his SAE Secretaryship. He obviously had to involve SAE, IAAG and SAA Council members and his Secretarial colleagues in Glasgow and Aberdeen. Also, there are no surviving records of the actions of the Joint Committee formed by the three Scottish chartered Councils. However, the correspondence of Brown with respect to the competition and registration events examined in this study overwhelmingly suggest that he was 'in charge'. Thus, when examining the early development of the Scottish professional bodies, it is important to look for the influence of individuals such as Brown on events as well as the events themselves. Such a lesson should be extended to research of other bodies and their policies and actions. To do otherwise is to cause their histories to be incomplete.

NOTES

1. Permission by ICAS to access these sources is gratefully acknowledged.
2. The General Examining Board managed the complete examination system for the three chartered bodies in Scotland. It meant that, in one respect at least, Scottish chartered accountancy was a national system (Lee 1996b).
3. *The Accountant's Magazine* was also a national effort to which each of the three Scottish chartered bodies contributed intellectually and financially. It appeared as a response to anti-Scottish accountancy sentiment expressed in the English-based *The Accountant* (Lee 1996b).
4. The other bodies were The Institute of Accountants and Actuaries in Glasgow (IAAG) founded in 1855, and the Society of Accountants in Aberdeen (SAA) founded in 1867.
5. There is no evidence in the SAE records that the SAA was given the same opportunity.
6. The SAE Council's deliberations of the petition are captured in the Council Minute Book page references indicated. Individual events and comments are not separately referenced.

REFERENCES

Brown, R. (1905) *A History of Accounting and Accountants*, Edinburgh: Jack.
Carr-Saunders, A. and Wilson, P. A. (1933) *The Professions*, Oxford: Clarendon Press.
Kedslie, M. J. M. (1990) *Firm Foundations: The Development of Professional Accounting in Scotland 1850–1900*, Hull: Hull University Press.
Kitchen, J. and Parker, R. H. (1981) *Accounting Thought and Education: Six English Pioneers*, London: Institute of Chartered Accountants in England and Wales.

Larson, M. S. (1977) *The Rise of Professionalism: A Sociological Analysis*, Berkely, CA: University of California Press.

Lee, T. A. (1996a) 'Sociology of accountancy profession', in T. A. Lee (ed.) *Shaping the Accountancy Profession: The Story of Three Scottish Pioneers*, New York: Garland, pp. ix–xv.

——(1996b) 'Richard Brown, chartered accountant and Christian gentleman', in T. A. Lee (ed.) *Shaping the Accountancy Profession: The Story of Three Scottish Pioneers*, New York: Garland, pp. 153–221.

——(1996c) 'Identifying the founding fathers of public accountancy: the formation of The Society of Accountants in Edinburgh', *Accounting, Business & Financial History* 6(3): December.

Macdonald, K. M. (1985) 'Social closure and occupational registration', *Sociology* November: 541–56.

Shackleton, J. K. and Milner, M. (1996) 'Alexander Sloan: a Glasgow chartered accountant', in T. A. Lee (ed.) *Shaping the Accountancy Profession: The Story of Three Scottish Pioneers*, New York: Garland, pp. 81–151.

Walker, S. P. (1991) 'The defence of professional monopoly: Scottish chartered accountants and "Satellites in the accountancy firmament" 1854–1914', *Accounting, Organisations and Society* 16(3): 257–83.

——(1995) 'The genesis of professional organisation in Scotland: a contextual analysis', *Accounting, Organisations and Society* 20(4): 285–310.

Zeff, S. A. (1987) 'Leaders of the accounting profession: 14 who made a difference', *Journal of Accountancy* May: 46–71.

4

THE INCORPORATED INSTITUTE OF ACCOUNTANTS, VICTORIA (1886)

A study of founders' backgrounds

*John Richard Edwards, Garry D. Carnegie and Jules H. Cauberg**

INTRODUCTION

New South Wales, subsequently Australia, became a British settlement in 1788. Hence, accounting development in Australia at least during the colonial period to 1900 was influenced by Britain as the dominant cultural and business conveyor.[1] Previous studies have recognised the role of imperial Britain in the development of professional accounting in the Empire and Commonwealth (Johnson and Caygill 1971), in exporting accounting techniques, institutions and concepts (Parker 1989), and in the transfer of accounting technology to the southern hemisphere (Carnegie and Parker 1996).

Along with Canada, New Zealand and South Africa, Australia adopted the British model of professional accounting. The characteristics of this model included regionalism and duplication. By 1904, there was a separate accounting body in each Australian state while, in some states, duplication of bodies occurred. For instance, Victoria had four local professional accounting bodies in operation by 1900 (Parker 1989: 14–15; Carnegie 1993b). Johnson and Caygill (1971: 157) claimed that 'generally speaking, local associations were originally established by migrants from Britain, many of them members of the British accounting bodies'. The first known professional accounting body established in Australia was the Adelaide Society of Accountants, formed in South Australia in 1885 (Parker 1961). The earliest known professional accounting body established in Victoria was the Institute of Accountants in Victoria, formed in Melbourne on 12 April 1886 with forty-five foundation members, all of whom were men.[2] It was incorporated with the name the Incorporated Institute of Accountants, Victoria (IIAV) under the *Companies Statute* 1864 on 1 March 1887 as a company limited by guarantee (Macdonald 1936: 11). The IIAV soon

49

established itself as the premier accounting body in Victoria and by 1904 was attempting to obtain a royal charter (Carnegie 1993b; Chua and Poullaos 1993; Poullaos 1994). According to Chua and Poullaos (1996: 18), 'it potentially offered entree to the City's [Melbourne's] commercial classes at a time when urban capital was achieving economic and political dominance (Davison, 1978; Connell & Irving, 1992)'.

Through their professionalisation project, the IIAV's founders were able to close off entry to those individuals deemed unsuitable or unworthy of professional recognition in accounting. Their collective efforts may be seen as successful given that the IIAV is the earliest antecedent body of the Melbourne-based Australian Society of Certified Practising Accountants, which is the largest professional body in any field in Australia (Kenley 1963; Parker 1986; Carnegie and Goldberg 1996).[3] Prior to this study, little was known of the social and occupational backgrounds of the IIAV's founders (Chua and Poullaos 1996: 18) including the extent to which British migrants comprised the body's foundation membership and the contributions of British-qualified accountants to its establishment.

This study is intended to elucidate the interests which converged to form the IIAV and thus to shed light on the contingent nature of the structure of professional accounting in Australia at that time and since. It is the first prosopographical study of Australian-based pioneer accountants, although such studies have been conducted for Canadian (Richardson 1989) and Scottish accountants (Walker 1988; Kedslie 1990a, 1990b).

We examine attempts at professional formation by accountants in Victoria during 1885–6 and provide an overview of economic development and professionalisation in Victoria to the late 1880s. There follows an examination of the geographical origins, occupations on arrival, and social and religious origins of the IIAV's founders.

PROFESSIONAL FORMATION IN VICTORIA

Examination of the advent of professional accounting bodies in Victoria requires an understanding of the strategies adopted by the major British accounting bodies around this time. The three Scottish chartered accounting bodies – the Society of Accountants of Edinburgh (1853), the Institute of Accountants and Actuaries in Glasgow (1853), and the Society of Accountants in Aberdeen (1866) – allowed training in England and Wales in addition to Scotland (Parker 1989; 16). Formed in 1880 by means of the integration of five accounting bodies established in the 1870s, the Institute of Chartered Accountants in England and Wales (ICAEW) required English chartered accountants to be trained only in England and Wales (Howitt 1966: 22; Johnson and Caygill 1971: 157; Parker 1989: 16). Founded in 1885, the Society of Accountants and Auditors (Incorporated) (SAA) sought a wider sphere of influence given that its prospects at home were negated somewhat through the closure already achieved on the formation of chartered accounting bodies.[4] Garrett (1961: 14), the Society's historian, explained that 'at an early stage the Society [SAA] claimed for itself a "British Empire" policy'. To this end, it embarked on a course of establishing branches throughout the Empire to expand its membership and influence. According to Johnson and Caygill (1971: 157):

A major difference between the Society and Institute was between a body catering solely for public accountants, and one viewing industrial and commercial accountants as a potential source of recruits – an important factor, considering the frequent impossibility in pioneer communities for more than a minority of accountants to make a living purely from public practice.

In Australia, the SAA sought to establish a branch at Melbourne in December 1885. Charles Alfred Cooper, in the capacity as 'Commissioner for Australia', convened a meeting 'of the members of the profession' to consider 'the desirability of establishing a branch of the English society in Victoria' (Cooper 1886).[5] At the meeting held on 3 December 1885, a committee comprising Messrs Bolger, Crellin, Holmes, Lyell, Saunders, Tuckett and Tyler was appointed 'to consider Mr Cooper's proposals, and to bring up a Report to a Meeting to be called by them at as early a date as possible' (Crellin 1886a; see also *The Age* 4 December 1885: 5). At a subsequent meeting held on 4 February 1886 which was not attended by Cooper, it was agreed to establish a local society of accountants.[6] Cooper, who was in Sydney when the 4 February meeting was held, was clearly dissatisfied with these developments. In his letter to the editor of the *Argus* published on 10 March 1886, Cooper signalled his intention to proceed with the establishment of a Victorian branch of the SAA and stated:

It is for them [readers of the *Argus*] to judge whether a certificate of competency, granted by the English Society, having the special licence of the Board of Trade, will not have more weight in the commercial world than a certificate granted by such a society as the one now being formed on a purely local basis, and of narrow views.

(Cooper 1886)

In his response to Cooper published in the *Argus* on 16 March, William Crellin placed on public record the committee's resolution to establish a local body in quoting from clause 4 of its report:

After hearing Mr. Cooper's explanations, your committee is unable at present to see any advantage to be gained by forming a branch society, and recommends that the question of the relationship of a local society with this [i.e., Mr Cooper's] or any other society in Great

Britain, whether by affiliation or by correspondence only, be left to the council of the Victorian society, if one be formed.

(Crellin 1886b)

Crellin (1886b) also elucidated the cultural values underpinning this recommendation in stating:

surely those who have spent the best years of their life in the colony may be pardoned if they feel somewhat indisposed to sanction the idea that no good thing can be done here unless it bears the seal of a body of gentlemen sitting in London who are unknown to us, and to whom we are mostly unknown.

The founders' decision may also have been influenced by the ICAEW's condescending attitude to the SAA in the latter's early days (Stacey 1954: 28). For example, a leading article in *The Accountant* reported:

From references to various published directories and other sources, and an inspection of this society's list we find represented amongst its members a formidable array of clerks of all kinds, rent collectors, corn merchants, shopkeepers, valuers, collectors of taxes, bailiffs, secretaries of various concerns, civil engineers, school board clerks, overseers, timber agents, tobacconists, hairdressers, pawnbrokers, and manure merchants.

(*The Accountant* 1886: 160)

A little later in the year, *The Accountant* sought fit to print a letter from a newly qualified accountant which described the SAA's members as 'Jacks of all trades and masters of none' (Lucey 1886: 242). An awareness of such attitudes may have existed in Victoria and, if so, possibly contributed to a reluctance to join a branch of the SAA.

Although Cooper was most probably disappointed to learn of the advent of the new association on 12 April 1886, his actions nonetheless triggered the formation of this local accounting body. According to Crellin (1886b), 'all are agreed in admitting that by his [Cooper's] well-timed movement he has given an impetus to a project which has often been mooted, and has often been allowed to drop'. Cooper proceeded to establish the first branch of the SAA in 1886.[7] According to Garrett (1961: 14), Cooper 'endeavoured, but without success, to make the Society the nucleus of the then unformed profession in Australia'.

Nevertheless, the organised accounting profession developed along British lines as explained by Thomas Brentnall, a founder of the IIAV and a founding father of the Australian accounting profession, who wrote in his memoirs:

We knew the position attained by the Institute of Chartered Accountants in England and Wales, which had been incorporated by Royal

Charter in 1880, by the Society of Accountants and Auditors in 1885, as well as the three Scottish Institutes which had come into existence some years previously. With these examples before us, we had no difficulty in arriving at the conclusion that our object could best be attained by following in their footsteps.

(Brentnall 1938: 64)

Those who met on 12 April 1886 considered 'the propriety of establishing an association of those having kindred interests in their common calling and a desire to place their profession on a higher plane than it had previously occupied in public esteem' (Brentnall 1938: 64; Kenley 1963: 25).[8] In addition, it may have been perceived that British capitalists would have gained confidence from the adoption of this model for professional accounting in Australia.

Initially, this association was promoted as a body for 'those who were holding themselves out as public practitioners' (Brentnall 1938: 64). The *Argus* report of the foundation meeting referred to the list of members of the new body and claimed it included 'the names of nearly every public accountant in Melbourne' (17 April 1886).[9] According to Macdonald (1936: 9), the 'original intention [of its founders] was to admit to active membership only practising public accountants and their clerks, but ultimately, it was decided to admit persons having experience of accountancy in mercantile and government offices'. Membership diversification was actively encouraged from an early time and President Crellin, at the IIAV's first annual general meeting, expressed the hope that members:

> of the profession whether in public or private practice, connected with Government departments, banks, insurance and other incorporated companies, or in mercantile houses, will join [the IIAV] during the coming year and thereby add to its influence, and assist in promoting its object.

(IIAV, *Annual Report*, 1887)

Clearly, this membership strategy would not have placed the IIAV at a competitive disadvantage in the inevitable competition for members with the local branch of the SAA.

ECONOMIC DEVELOPMENT AND PROFESSIONALISATION IN COLONIAL VICTORIA

Settled by Europeans in the mid-1830s when known as the Port Phillip District of the Colony of New South Wales, Victoria became a separate British colony in August 1850. As detailed by Dunstan (1984: 15):

> Our stock images [of Victoria] are the land-rush years of the late 1830s and 1840s, the gold-rush years of the 1850s and the suburban

land-boom years of the 1880s, followed by the almost Biblical retribution of the Depression of the 1890s.

This cumulative image tends to mask the rapid transformation which took place in the pre-Federation period, a product of which was the development of 'Marvellous Melbourne',[10] nor does it adequately elucidate the advent of cultural values which underpinned 'the triumph of urban capital', a product of which was the establishment of a 'fully fledged market system' (Connell and Irving, 1992: 83).

The Victorian pastoral industry developed rapidly from the mid-1830s when settlers moved livestock onto productive grazing lands in the Port Phillip District. Based on the numbers of sheep depastured, the Port Phillip District provided around 60 per cent of the colony's wool clip by 1848–9 (Roberts 1935: 448). The discovery of gold in Victoria in 1851 led to a substantial increase in the population of the new colony and to changes in prevailing cultural values. The population of the colony rose from 77,345 in 1851 to 540,322 ten years later (Kiddle 1961: 203). Although essentially a commercial settlement from the mid-1830s, the gold rushes of the 1850s confirmed Melbourne's 'commercial destiny' (Davison 1978: 10). Importantly, ambitious gold-seekers delivered an abundance of energy, skills and enterprise which, combined with British capital, underpinned the rapid transformation of the new colony.

Macintyre (1991: 88) used the term 'settler capitalism' to depict the development of the colony in the first two decades of squatting occupation.[11] As explained by Macintyre (1991: 89) 'the productivity of settler capitalism concentrated wealth in the hands of a minority and restricted opportunities for the bulk of the population'. Connected with the arrival of large numbers of new settlers there emerged a culture of 'colonial liberalism' from the mid-1850s which embodied the rejection of the values underpinning settler capitalism (McNaughtan 1955: 98–144; Dunstan 1984: 15–16 and 55–6; Macintyre 1991: 88–9). According to Macintyre (1991: 5), the liberals 'sought to establish a sphere of freedom in which all citizens could meet each other, safe from interference and liberated from the hierarchical bonds of traditional society'. Working against the hegemony of the pastoralists (Carnegie 1993a: pp. 211–13), the liberals gained political influence and liberalism provided 'much of the framework and language of politics' (Dunstan 1984: 15). According to Dunstan (1984: 15), 'the colonists of the gold generation came to maturity at a time when the values of economic individualism that play so great a part in nineteenth century liberalism were in the ascendant'. The struggle between conservative pastoral capital and liberal urban capital resulted in the mercantile bourgeoisie comprising urban merchants, manufacturers and financiers gaining the ascendancy (Serle 1971: ch. 3; Sherington 1990: 69; Connell and Irving 1992: ch. 3).

Melbourne's first International Exhibition held in 1880 marked the dawn of a remarkable decade of economic expansion during which time the city's population nearly doubled (Davison 1978: introduction and ch. 1; Marshall 1982: 20). Fuelled by a plentiful supply of British capital, the expanding *laissez-faire* economy saw speculation rewarded. The land boom which had begun in the 1860s reached frenzied heights in the 1880s (Cannon 1967: ch. 2; Boehm 1971: 142–61). The mining and property booms resulted in a rapid expansion in the number of companies, the development of local capital markets, and the establishment of stock markets in Melbourne and Sydney. The company became the 'organising base for the mercantile bourgeoisie' (Connell and Irving 1992: 97).

In the 1880s, accounting associations and many other professional, trade and interest organisations were established 'to mobilize their members' collective strength in the intense competition of the metropolitan market-place' (Davison 1978: 10). Davison (1978) pointed to a demographic factor in the advent of professional associations. He referred to the generation born in the 1830s, many of whom had arrived in Victoria in the 1850s, as having developed Melbourne into a major commercial centre and, in middle age, were keen to ensure that their sons were provided with opportunities appropriate to their desired status in society. Commerce and the professions were seen to be suitable for this purpose. Davison (1978) thus argued that the professionalisation which occurred in Melbourne around this time was a distinctively middle-class movement. Poullaos (1994: 83) appeared to agree with this view in stating that 'those who wanted to make Melbourne's accountants into professional men did not find themselves on differing sides of the divide between labor and capital'.[12] Alternatively, Gollan (1960: 100) believed 'the professional classes [in Australia] differed perhaps from similar classes in older countries in that they included more who had seized the opportunities offered by colonial society to raise their social status above that of their parents'. This study presents an opportunity to examine these seemingly divergent views in the context of the professionalisation of accounting.

Britain provided both the precedents and models for professionalisation. Cooper's initiative for formation of the IIAV itself was symptomatic of an emerging British tradition of forming professional accounting bodies. Pointing to bodies of lawyers, doctors, architects, pharmacists, dentists, engineers and accountants, an observer commented in 1888 that 'every profession nowadays has its association' (cited in Leavitt and Lilburn 1888: 43). Although professionals in colonial Melbourne surrounded themselves with the paraphernalia of gentility then observable among professional groups in Britain, they 'practised a thorough-going commercialism' (Davison 1978: 112).

By 1891, 63 per cent of the inhabitants of Australia were Australian born (*Victorian Year-Book*, 1907–8: 178). Around this time, 'Australian nationalism' reflected the cultural values of constantly increasing numbers of inhabitants who, far distant from Britain, could see themselves as 'independent Australian Britons' (Hancock 1961: ch. 3).[13] According to Hancock (1961: 50), Australian inhabitants 'believed each word essential and exact, but laid most stress upon the last'. This national culture appears to be a key factor in explaining the willingness of colonial accountants to adopt the British model of the accounting profession but to form a local, independent body in Victoria rather than to come under the control of a British body. Further elucidation of this apparent influence is another potential benefit of this study.

Findings of this study

The findings of our investigations of geographical origins, occupations on arrival, and social and religious origins of the IIAV founders are presented in what follows.

Geographical origins

Particulars of the country of origin of forty-four of the forty-five founders of the IIAV are given in Table 4.1.[14] We were unable to establish whether Edward Nathan Brown was an immigrant or an indigenous founder. An overwhelming majority (forty, i.e. 88.9 per cent) of the founders were immigrants from the UK, while only four had been born in Australia (8.9 per cent).[15] Among the immigrants, thirty (70 per cent of total) were from England, seven from Scotland (17.5 per cent) and only three from Ireland (7.5 per cent). All of these immigrants came as free settlers. There is the possibility of a disproportionate number of immigrants among the IIAV's founders, but we were unable to test the validity of this proposition owing to the absence of appropriate demographic data.

Table 4.1 also shows the age on arrival of thirty seven of the forty known immigrants. Ten of these were under 21 years of age on arrival while six of these were less than 14 years old. The eldest immigrant was Lowry at 43. The average age of these thirty-seven immigrant founders on arrival was determined to be 23 years. These relatively youthful individuals or their parents were undoubtedly keen to realise the opportunities which presented themselves in the land of their adoption.

Table 4.2 presents a timeframe summary of the dates of arrival of these thirty-seven immigrant founders. As the table shows, just three of the founders had arrived in the Port Phillip District by 1850, but a majority of nineteen arrived in the newly constituted colony of Victoria during the 1850s. The other fifteen arrived in Victoria at a steady rate during the remaining period to 1883 when the last immigrant founder (James Edwin Moir) arrived. The first immigrant founder was William Henry Tuckett

Table 4.1 Geographical origins

	Country of origin	Year of arrival	Age on arrival	Age on formation of IIAV (1886)
Bickerton, James Knight	England, south*	1858	24	52
Blackwell, Richard Thomas	England, south	1853	21	54
Bolger, Frank Leear	England, south	—	—	—
Brentnall, Thomas	England, other	1878	31	39
Brown, Edward Nathan	—	—	—	—
Burns, Andrew	Scotland	1853	22	55
Cleveland, Arthur William	England, south	1871	25	40
Cole, James Henry	England, other	1862	22	46
Connell, John Minton	Ireland	1877	39	48
Crellin, William	England, south	1852	31	65
Dagnell, John Pickering	England	—	—	—
Danby, Henry William	England, south	1853	21	54
Davey, Thomas James	England, south	1857	12	41
Ellis, Christopher W.	England, south	1852	20	54
Ferdinando, Benjamin James	England, south	1880	25	31
Flack, Joseph Henry	England, south	1874	25	37
Foden, Isaac Clement	England, other	1863	29	52
Gilmour, Andrew	Scotland	1871	30	45
Hastings, Edward Percival	England, south	1873	23	36
Holmes, Charles Morrell	England, south	1860	13	39
Horrell, Robert Frederick	Australia	n/a	n/a	31
Howden, John McAlister	Scotland	1858	4	32
Hunt, Ebenezer	England, other	1852	20	54
Langton, Edward	England, south	1852	24	58
Lowry, Henry Wallace	Ireland	1852	43	77
Lucas, Charles James	England, south	1842	13	57
Lyell, Andrew	Scotland	1853	16	49
Macdonald, Alexander Cameron	Australia	n/a	n/a	58
Macdonald, John	Scotland	1855	35	66
Marquand, George	England, south	1864	22	44
McCaskie, Robert	Scotland	1853	26	59
McQuie, James Blackmore	England, other	1854	23	55
Moir, James Edwin	England, other	1883	29	32
Paterson, Laurance	Scotland	1875	19	30
Rainey, Phineas	Ireland	1867	32	51
Richardson, Charles John	England, south	1849	4	41
Rucker, William Sigismund	Australia	n/a	n/a	34
Saunders, Arthur Francis W.	England, south	—	—	—
Selby, George William	Australia	n/a	n/a	28
Smith, Benjamin Doughty	England, other	1857	21	50
Sprigg, William Gardiner	England, south	1854	22	54
Thompson, Walter	England, other	1853	4	37
Tuckett, William Henry	England, south	1841	24	69
Tulloch, Thomas Yelf	England, south	1868	37	55
Tyler, John Chatfield	England, south	1852	22	56

Source: Shipping records and death certificates

* Ipswich is the furthest north location of the founders who originated from England, south.

Table 4.2 Time of arrival in the Port
Phillip District/Victoria

Period	Number of immigrants
1840–4	2
1845–9	1
1850–4	14
1855–9	5
1860–4	4
1865–9	2
1870–4	4
1875–9	3
1880–4	2
	37
Unknown	3
	40

who arrived on the 'Ward Chipman' in 1841 (Sutherland Smith 1992). Most of the immigrant founders had been in their 'new country' for sufficiently lengthy periods to be holding values as 'independent Australian Britons' on the formation of the IIAV in 1886. At this time, the thirty-seven immigrant founders had been engaged with their new land for an average period of twenty-six years since their first arrival. Thus the average age of the immigrant founders on the body's formation was 49 years. Five of the seven immigrant founders who were members of the committee appointed to consider Cooper's proposals, and whose times of arrival are known, resided in Australia for an average period of thirty-four years to 1886. The average age of the thirty-seven immigrant founders whose times of arrival are known and the four locally born founders was 48 years at this time. The immigrant founders' ages on arrival and the period they generally spent in the colony preceding the formation of the IIAV provide elucidation of the impact of 'Australian nationalism' on the body's formation as reflected in Crellin's (1886b) explanation for rejecting Cooper's proposal to establish a local branch of the SAA.[16]

Occupations on arrival

Surviving shipping records of Victoria were examined to ascertain, as far as possible, the occupations of the immigrants of working age at the time of their arrival in Australia. In addition, surviving Melbourne and other directories, ICAEW membership lists and Australian and British marriage certificates were examined to identify the occupations of immigrant founders in the periods of up to three years before and after their arrival in Australia. This criterion was adopted to deduce the occupations around arrival time in the absence of official shipping records. In total, shipping records were located for twenty one of the thirty-four immigrant founders who were at least 14 years of age on arrival. Of these, occupations were recorded in twelve cases as summarised in Table 4.3.[17] Occupational particulars were obtained for a further eight immigrant founders in the surviving directories, ICAEW membership lists, and in the marriage certificates examined. The occupations deduced for these eight founders are also summarised in Table 4.3. This table indicates that four (20 per cent) of these twenty founders were accountants at or around their arrival time in Australia.

Of the forty-five founders, only two, Joseph Henry Flack and James Edwin Moir, were members of a British professional accounting body at the time of the IIAV's formation (Parker and Carnegie 1996). Flack was an associate member of the ICAEW in 1886, having joined that body as a founder in 1880. Moir joined the ICAEW in 1883, the year of his arrival in Australia. Hence, although the evidence supports the claim of Johnson and Caygill (1971: 157) that British migrants were generally responsible for establishing local professional accounting bodies, this study provides evidence which suggests that their assertion that many such migrants were British-qualified accountants is inaccurate. It is of course the case that a number of the founders emigrated from the UK subsequent to the formation of professional bodies in Scotland (commencing 1853) and

Table 4.3 Occupations on arrival

	Shipping	Other records	Total
Accountant		4	4
Builder		1	1
Butcher	1		1
Clerk	2		2
Draper	2		2
Gentleman	2		2
Labourer	2		2
Merchant	2	1	3
Sailor	1		1
Storekeeper		1	1
Warehouseman		1	1
	12	8	20

Sources: Shipping records, Sands and McDougall directories, ICAEW membership lists, and marriage certificates

England (commencing 1870). Therefore, the potential existed for local bodies to be established by British-qualified accountants. However, as discussed above, most of the immigrant founders with a known occupation on arrival came without an accounting background.

Social and religious origins

The occupations of the founders' fathers and fathers-in-law are presented in Table 4.4. Based on the details provided mainly in marriage certificates, we obtained information on the occupations of forty fathers and also thirty-three fathers of the founders' wives as at the respective dates of marriage of the founders. We were unable to trace occupational information for five fathers and eight fathers-in-law. In addition, four of the founders were unmarried and so remain absent from the second category. Limited evidence was identified of founders following in their fathers' footsteps and none of having adopted a wife's father's occupation. The fathers of Richard Thomas Blackwell, Frank Leear Bolger, James Henry Cole, Charles James Lucas and William Sigismund Rucker were each accountants.[18] Four of the founders' fathers and eight of their wives' fathers are listed as 'gentlemen' or of 'independent means'. The significance of the former caption, at least, is not clearly evident. It conveys the impression of the individual either having retired or having been sufficiently wealthy to negate the need for gainful employment. However, in our investigations examples were found of the use of the 'gentlemen' caption in certain cases where the individual was most probably gainfully employed. These limitations aside, it is evident that the vast majority of the fathers and fathers-in-law were in merchandising, trade, manufacturing, or a profession, demonstrating that the IIAV's founders were predominantly from what would today be described as middle-class origins. Indeed, one of the most striking features of Table 4.4 is the total absence of any reference to the labouring class. This study therefore provides strong support for Davison's (1978) rather than Gollan's (1960) thesis.

The founders, so far as we know, were all protestants. We have identified seventeen members of the established church and a similar number of non-conformists: five Independents; four Baptists; four Presbyterians; three Congregationalists; and one Methodist. Mindful of potential classification inconsistencies with official data, we have contrasted this distribution with that relating to residents of Victoria at the time the IIAV was established. Table 4.5 provides evidence which shows, in particular, a higher representation of the established church in our sample, while we find no Roman Catholics among the IIAV's founders despite the fact that these accounted for 24 per cent of the inhabitants of the colony. Around this time, the Irish were predominantly both working class and Roman Catholic (Madgwick 1937: 234–6; Kiddle 1961: 204; Clark 1987: ch. 5, esp. 86–7; de Serville 1991:

Table 4.4 Occupations of founders' fathers and fathers-in-law

	Father's occupation	Father-in-law's occupation
Bickerton, James Knight	Hat manufacturer	Hat manufacturer
Blackwell, Richard Thomas	Accountant[a]	Merchant
Bolger, Frank Leear	Accountant[b]	Gentleman
Brentnall, Thomas	Merchant[c]	Gentleman
Brown, Edward Nathan		
Burns, Andrew	Landing surveyor	Gentleman
Cleveland, Arthur William	Merchant	Sheep farmer and merchant[d]
Cole, James Henry	Accountant	Farmer
Connell, John Minton	Artist	n/a
Crellin, William	Merchant tailor	Merchant
Dagnell, John Pickering		
Danby, Henry William	Lace merchant	Brewer
Davey, Thomas James	Saddler	
Ellis, Christopher W.	Wine merchant	Independent means
Ferdinando, Benjamin James	Printer[e]	
Flack, Joseph Henry	Gentleman	Gentleman
Foden, Isaac Clement	Gentleman	Builder
Gilmour, Andrew	Wine merchant	Merchant
Hastings, Edward Percival	Wine merchant	Gentleman
Holmes, Charles Morrell	Leather merchant	Carriage builder
Horrell, Robert Frederick	Gentleman	Stock and station agent
Howden, John McAlister	Bootmaker and dealer	Merchant[h]
Hunt, Ebenezer	Farmer	Gentleman
Langton, Edward	Butcher	Chemist
Lowry, Henry Wallace		n/a
Lucas, Charles James	Accountant	Solicitor
Lyell, Andrew	Manufacturer	Surveyor
Macdonald, Alexander Cameron	Grazier	
Macdonald, John		
Marquand, George	Draper	Linen manufacturer
McCaskie, Robert	Hat manufacturer[f]	n/a
McQuie, James Blackmore	Merchant	Merchant
Moir, James Edwin	Silk manufacturer	Cotton spinner
Paterson, Laurance	Provisions merchant[b]	n/a
Rainey, Phineas	Ironmonger	Gentleman
Richardson, Charles John	Chemist and druggist[g]	Butcher
Rucker, William Sigismund	Accountant[i]	Surgeon
Saunders, Arthur Francis W.	Merchant	Grocer
Selby, George William	Land agent	Civil servant
Smith, Benjamin Doughty	Merchant	Merchant
Sprigg, William Gardiner	Baptist minister	Clergyman
Thompson, Walter	Bookseller	
Tuckett, William Henry		
Tulloch, Thomas Yelf	Wine merchant	Brewer
Tyler, John Chatfield	Gentleman	Merchant

Source: Marriage certificates except as indicated below:
[a] Actuary on son's death certificate; goldsmith on son's baptismal records.
[b] Information taken from birth certificate.
[c] Grocer on son's birth certificate and Civil Servant on son's death certificate.
[d] Second wife's father – occupation of first wife's father unknown.
[e] Weaver on son's birth certificate.
[f] Information taken from death certificate.
[g] Town clerk (Geelong) on son's death certificate.
[h] Shoemaker on son's birth certificate.
[i] Merchant on son's birth certificate.

Table 4.5 Religious backgrounds

	Founders (no.)	Founders (% of 'known')	Victorian male estimated (% of total)
Church of England (13), Church of Scotland (1), Church of England and Ireland (3)	17	49	36
Presbyterian	4	12	15
Independent denomination of Christians/Congregationalist	8	24	2
Baptist	4	12	2
Methodist	1	3	13
Other Protestant			3
Roman Catholics			24
Buddhist, Confucians, Jews, etc.			5
Known	34		
Unknown	11		
	45	100	100

Sources: Birth, marriage and death certificates; Brentnall (1938: 12); Victorian Year-Book (1886–7: 47)

212–13). As pointed out earlier, they were not well represented among the IIAV's founders. This evidence of religious preference does not necessitate a reassessment of the IIAV professionalisation project as a predominantly middle-class movement.

CONCLUSION

This study has shown that all the IIAV's founders were male, most of whom migrated from the UK as free settlers but few of whom identified themselves with an occupation in accounting on their arrival in Australia. Whilst the findings of this study support Johnson and Caygill's (1971) claim that local professional bodies were originally established by British immigrants, their assertion that many of these immigrants were British-qualified accountants on the formation of local bodies has been demonstrated to be inaccurate in the case of the advent of the IIAV. We have also shown that the immigrant founders had generally resided in Victoria for a considerable number of years at the time of the IIAV's formation. As firmly entrenched residents, the founders appeared to hold values as 'independent Australian Britons' as reflected in their preference to form a local, independent accounting body rather than to join a body under British control in adopting the British model of the accounting profession. Hence, this study provides further evidence of the impact of 'Australian nationalism' on the formation of the IIAV as evidenced in Crellin's public explanation for the rejection of Cooper's proposal to form a local branch of the SAA. We also acknowledge the possibility that the ICAEW's negative attitude towards the SAA influenced the decisions of Flack and Moir, both members of the ICAEW, and possibly others, to help found a local body rather than join a branch of the SAA.

Although in terms of representation the immigrants had an overwhelming influence on the IIAV's formation, it is evident that most of these immigrants of working age on arrival in Australia moved in the direction of an accounting career in the years following their arrival to 1886. Hence, the choice of a career in accounting appears to have been generally influenced by the availability of accounting opportunities as the economy expanded rather than any widely held desire to transfer the 'profession' of accounting to a new country. This finding suggests that caution should be exercised in assessing the contributions of pioneering members of colonial accounting bodies to the cross-national transfer of accounting technology. Further research in progress is examining when the IIAV's founders began their careers in accounting and what factors influenced this choice and their participation in the advent of an organised accounting profession in Victoria. Our exploration of the social and religious origins of the founders provided evidence of the IIAV professionalisation project as a predominantly middle-class movement, thus supporting Davison's rather than Gollan's thesis.

Prosopographical studies of the founders of other Australian professional accounting bodies would further elucidate the interests which converged to form such bodies. Further research of this genre would be expected to improve our understanding of the interests associated with the professionalisation project in the colonial era, and thus shed further light on the contingent nature of the structure of professional accounting in Australia since that period. Similar research conducted in other countries would assist in developing a 'comparative international accounting history' literature as advocated by Carnegie and Napier (1996).

NOTES

* The authors are grateful for the financial support provided for this project by the Scottish Committee on Accounting History of the Institute of Chartered Accountants of Scotland, the Australian Society of Certified Practising Accountants, and the Faculty of Business and Law, Deakin University. We thank Robert H. Parker, Christopher Poullaos and those who attended a session at the Seventh World Congress of Accounting Historians, Kingston, Ontario for their helpful comments on earlier drafts of this paper. We also thank Jill Bright and staff of the Australian Society of Certified Practising Accountants library for their assistance.

1 Federation of the six colonies within Australia into the Commonwealth of Australia occurred on 1 January 1901. On Federation, the colonies became states (Turner 1973: 327–56, first published in 1904).

2 A newspaper report referred to 'the 44 gentlemen' who had agreed to be foundation members of the body (*Argus* 17 April 1886). Our enquiries revealed that Crellin reported to the meeting of the Invitations Committee held on 5 April 1886 that 'he had received acceptances to the invitations [58 in all] sent out from 43 gentlemen' (Preliminary Minute Book, ASCPA Library, Series Number CIAO02). This list includes Edward Cox who did not proceed to membership, but not John Pickering Dagnell and Robert McCaskie who were admitted after the official date of formation (see minutes of meeting held on 13 April 1886). There is no evidence to suggest that any of those invited to join the IIAV were women.

3 The name of the IIAV was changed to the Incorporated Institute of Accountants, Commonwealth of Australia, in July 1918, and was changed again in October 1921 to the Commonwealth Institute of Accountants (CIA) (Macdonald 1936: 45–6). Incorporated on 13 October 1952, the Australian Society of Accountants (ASA) became the product of an amalgamation of the CIA and the Federal Institute of Accountants (*c.* 1894) (Kenley 1963: 1). The name of the ASA was changed to the Australian Society of Certified Practising Accountants in 1990 (Carnegie and Goldberg 1996).

4 Initially named the Society of Accountants, the body soon became the SAA and in 1908 was renamed the Society of Incorporated Accountants and Auditors. In 1954, the body became the Society of Incorporated Accountants (Garrett 1961: 1–2).

5 Born in London on 13 June 1852 to George Cooper, colonial agent, and Eliza Louise Cooper, née Standeven, Charles Alfred Cooper arrived in Melbourne in 1885 (Smith 1903: 398). He was an 'original' member of the SAA (Garrett 1961: 142) and was secretary of its Victorian Division at his death in Melbourne on 30 June 1917 (*Argus* 2 July 1917).

6 William Crellin was Convenor and was voted to chair the meeting held on 4 February 1886.

7 Overseas branches were also established in South Africa, Canada, India and Central Africa (Parker 1989: 16–17).

8 William Crellin was elected the inaugural President of the IIAV, a position he occupied for six years. Messrs Edward Langton and Andrew Lyell became the body's initial Vice-Presidents. Mr J. Chatfield Tyler was appointed the inaugural Honorary Treasurer, while Messrs Joseph Flack and Andrew Gilmour were made joint Honorary Secretaries.

9 As the 1886 Sands and McDougall *Melbourne Directory* contains the names of 116 'accountants', it may have rather been that the IIAV's foundation membership included *most* of the *leading* public accountants in Melbourne.

10 The celebrated English journalist, George Augustus Sala, christened the colony's capital 'Marvellous Melbourne' (*Argus* 15 August 1885).

11 Denoon (1983) interpreted 'settler capitalism' as the mode of production adopted in settler societies in the southern hemisphere during the nineteenth century and to 1914.

12 Chua and Poullaos (1996: 18) also pointed out that the IIAV's annual reports and coverage of its meetings in the *Australasian Insurance and Banking Record* and the *Journal of Commerce* gave strong indications of which side of the labour–capital divide the IIAV's leaders and members promoted.

13 Hancock (1961) was first published in 1930. See also Meudell (1882).

14 The birth, marriage and death certificates were obtained from the following sources: Registry of Births, Deaths and Marriages, Melbourne, Victoria; Registry of Births, Deaths and Marriages, Sydney, New South Wales; Office of the Register General, New Zealand; Office of Population Censuses and Surveys, General Register Office, Southport, England; General Register Office for Scotland.

15 Of the indigenous founders, Robert Frederick Horrell, William Sigismund Rucker and George William Selby were born in Melbourne in 1855, 1852 and 1858 respectively, while Alexander Cameron Macdonald was born in 1828 at Campbelltown, New South Wales.

16 Being 33 years of age in April 1886, Cooper was younger than nearly all the founders as evidenced in Table 4.1.

17 Although Flack's occupation is recorded as 'Grocer' in the Victorian shipping records, we have concluded that this entry appears to have been made in error. On his marriage in 1871 in the UK, Flack's occupation was recorded as accountant. He was also recorded as an accountant in the 1878 Sands and McDougall *Melbourne Directory*. Further, Jones (1995: 98) stated Flack 'emigrated to Australia to set up in practice'. William Henry Tuckett, according to the official shipping records, was a third mate (sailor) on arriving in Australia, and we have used this source for the purpose of Table 4.3. Sutherland Smith (1992: 57), however, believed that Tuckett arrived as a 'saloon passenger'.

18 We do not know whether the parents of any of the first four also emigrated to Australia; certainly none of them was found to be listed in the trade and professional directories we are able to consult commencing in 1857. Rucker's father, William Frederick Augustus, came to Melbourne from Hanover in 1837, and opened a branch of the Derwent Bank Company, Hobart, on 8 February 1838 (*Australasian* 11 March 1882: 308; Smith 1903: 398; Brownhill 1955: 12).

REFERENCES

Boehm, E. A. (1971) *Prosperity and Depression in Australia 1887–1897*, London: Oxford University Press.

Brentnall, T. (1938) *My Memories*, Melbourne: Robertson & Mullens.

Brownhill, W. R. (1955) *The History of Geelong and Corio Bay*, Melbourne: Wilke.

Cannon, M. (1967) *The Land Boomers*, Melbourne University Press.

Carnegie, G. D. (1993a) 'Pastoral accounting in pre-Federation Victoria: a case study on the Jamieson family', *Accounting and Business Research* 23 (91): 204–18.

—— (1993b) 'The Australian Institute of Incorporated Accountants (1892–1938), *Accounting, Business and Financial History* 3 (1): 61–80.

Carnegie, G. D. and Goldberg, L. (1996), 'Accounting', *The Australian Encyclopedia* 6th edition, Terrey Hills, NSW: Australian Geographic.

Carnegie, G. D. and Napier, C. J. (1996) 'Critical and interpretive histories: insights into accounting's present and future through its past', *Accounting, Auditing and Accountability*, 9 (3): 7–39.

Carnegie, G. D. and Parker, R. H. (1996) 'The transfer of accounting technology to the southern hemisphere: the case of William Butler Yaldwyn', *Accounting, Business and Financial History* 6 (1): 23–49.

Chua, W. F. and Poullaos, C. (1993) 'Rethinking the profession-state dynamic: the case of the Victorian charter attempt, 1885–1906', *Accounting, Organizations and Society* 18 (7/8): 691–728.

—— (1996) 'Colonialism, closure and distance: an episode from Australian accounting history', unpublished working paper.

Clark, M. (1987) *A Short History of Australia*, 3rd revised edition, New York: NAL Penguin.

Connell, R. W. and Irving, T. H. (1992) *Class Structure in Australian History*, 2nd edition, Melbourne: Longman Cheshire.

Cooper, C. A. (1886) 'The society of accountants', *Argus* 10 March: letter to the editor.

Crellin, W. (1886a) 'Proposal to form a society of accountants in Victoria', 28 January (original printed copy held at ASCPA archives, Melbourne).

—— (1886b), 'The society of accountants', *Argus* 16 March: letter to the editor.

Davison, G. (1978) *The Rise and Fall of Marvellous Melbourne*, Melbourne University Press.

Denoon, D. (1983) *Settler Capitalism: The Dynamics of Dependent Development in the Southern Hemisphere*, New York: Oxford University Press.

de Serville, P. (1991) *Pounds and Pedigrees: The Upper Class in Victoria 1850–80*, South Melbourne: Oxford University Press.

Dunstan, D. (1984) *Governing the Metropolis – Politics, Technology and Social Change in a Victorian City: Melbourne 1850–1891*, Melbourne University Press.

Garrett, A. A. (1961) *History of The Society of Incorporated Accountants 1885–1957*, Oxford: Oxford University Press.

Gollan, R. (1960) *Radical and Working Class Politics: A Study of Eastern Australia, 1850–1910*, Melbourne University Press.

Hancock, W. K. (1961) *Australia*, Brisbane: Jacaranda Press (first published in 1930 by Benn, London).

Howitt, H. G. (1966) *The History of The Institute of Chartered Accountants in England & Wales 1880–1965 and of its Founder Accountancy Bodies 1870–1880*, London: Heinemann.

IIAV Archives: Library of the Australian Society of Certified Practising Accountants, Melbourne.

Johnson, T. J. and Caygill, M. (1971) 'The development of accountancy links in the Commonwealth, *Accounting and Business Research* 1 (spring): 155–73.

Jones, E. (1995) *True and Fair: A History of Price Waterhouse*, London: Hamish Hamilton.

Kedslie, M. J. M. (1990a) *Firm Foundations: The Development of Professional Accounting in Scotland 1850–1900*, Hull University Press.

—— (1990b) 'Mutual self interest – a unifying force: the dominance of social closure over social background in the early professional accounting bodies', *Accounting Historians Journal* 17 (2): 1–19.

Kenley, W. J. (1963) *History of the Australian Society of Accountants and its Antecedent Bodies*, Melbourne: Australian Society of Accountants.

Kiddle, M. L. (1961) *Men of Yesterday: A Social History of the Western District of Victoria, 1834–1890*, Melbourne University Press.

Leading article (1886) ' "Incorporated" accountants', *Accountant* 20 March: 159–60.

Leavitt, T. W. H. and Lilburn, W. D. (eds) (1888) *The Jubilee History of Victoria and Melbourne*, vol. 1, Melbourne: Duffus Bros.

Lucey, F. S. (1886) 'The society of accountants', *Accountant* 24 April: 242.

Macdonald, O. R. (1936) 'Historical survey 1887–1936, in *The Commonwealth Accountants' Year Book 1936*, Melbourne: Commonwealth Institute of Accountants.

Macintyre, S. (1991) *A Colonial Liberalism: The Lost World of Three Victorian Visionaries*, Melbourne: Oxford University Press.

Madgwick, R. B. (1937) *Immigration into Eastern Australia 1788–1851*, London: Longmans, Green.

Marshall, N. J. (1982) *Accounting for a Century: A History of the Antecedent Firms of Touche Ross & Co., Australia 1882–1982*, Australia: Touche Ross.

McNaughtan, I. D. (1955) 'Colonial liberalism, 1851–92', in G. Greenwood (ed.) *Australia: A Social and Political History*, Sydney: Angus & Robertson.

Meudell, G. D. (1882), 'Australia for the Australians', *Melbourne Review*, 7: 316–24.

Parker, R. H. (1961) 'Australia's first accountancy body – the Adelaide Society of Accountants', *Chartered Accountant in Australia* 32 (6): 337–40.

—— (1986) 'Accounting in Australia', *Australian Accountant* 57 (10): 85–6.

—— (1989) 'Importing and exporting accounting: the British experience', in A. G. Hopwood (ed.) *International Pressures for Accounting Change*, Hemel Hempstead: Prentice Hall International.

Parker, R. H. and Carnegie, G. D. (1996), 'Professional segmentation: the case of co-membership of Australian and British accountancy bodies to 1914', paper presented at the Seventh World Congress of Accounting Historians, Kingston.

Poullaos, C. (1994) *Making the Australian Chartered Accountant*, New York and London: Garland.

Richardson, A. J. (1989) 'Canada's accounting elite: 1880–1930', *Accounting Historians Journal* 16 (1): 1–21.

Roberts, S. H. (1935) *The Squatting Age in Australia*, Melbourne University Press.

Serle, G. (1971) *The Rush to be Rich: A History of the Colony of Victoria, 1883–1889*, Melbourne University Press.

Sherington, G. (1990) *Australia's Immigrants 1788–1988*, 2nd edition, Sydney: Allen & Unwin.

Smith, J. (ed.) (1903) *The Cyclopaedia of Victoria: An Historical and Commercial Review, Descriptive and Biographical Facts, Figures and Illustrations, an Epitome of Progress*, vol. 1, Melbourne: The Cyclopaedia Company.

Stacey, N. A. H. (1954) *English Accountancy. A Study in Social and Economic History 1800–1954*, London: Gee.

Sutherland Smith, G. (1992) 'The firm of W. H. Tuckett and Sons', *Accounting History* 4 (2): 57–8.

Turner, H. G. (1973) *A History of the Colony of Victoria from its Discovery to its Absorption into the Commonwealth of Australia*, vol. 2, A.D. 1854–1900, Melbourne: Heritage Publications (first published in 1904 by Longmans, Green, London).

Walker, S. P. (1988) *The Society of Accountants in Edinburgh 1854–1914*, New York and London: Garland.

5

PRACTITIONER PERSPECTIVES ON PERSONAL CONDUCT

Images from the world of business, 1900 – 55

Lee D. Parker

INTRODUCTION

Researchers into the history of the formulation of ethical codes and disciplinary procedures have generally considered the accounting profession to have been a leader in developing formalised codes of ethical conduct and in maintaining supportive investigation and disciplinary systems (Millerson 1964; Wilensky 1964). Against this history of careful attention to ethical conduct stands the association of the accounting profession with many major corporate frauds and crashes that occurred in countries such as the UK and Australia in the 1980s (Parker 1996). Even the accounting profession itself saw its reputation as having been somewhat diminished because its members had acted as accountants, auditors or directors of companies that experienced difficulties and induced public criticism during that period.

The relationship between professional views on ethical conduct and the attitudes and pressures experienced by corporate managers is of course too large an issue and too significant in its import to be simply addressed in one paper. What is offered here is but a selection of images from the practical business literature of the first half of the twentieth century. The intention is to provide a sampling of the veritable smorgasbord of business manuals, instruction volumes, stories, anecdotes and personal philosophies that were very much in vogue during that period. They offer a radically different focus and mode of expression from the formal pronouncements on proper conduct that have been traditionally offered by professional accounting bodies. As such, they suggest new perspectives, new questions and new issues for further research into future means of enhancing the accounting profession's effective contribution to the ethical conduct of business.

This paper therefore offers a brief set of contrasting perspectives on the role of accountants and their conventional predispositions in the first half of this century. It then moves on to outline a variety of approaches recommended by writers to those who sought to prosper in business. The reflections of a number of writers on the responsibilities of managers, particularly to their employees, are also then reviewed as examples of attitudes to management practice within the firm. Finally, a number of management concepts put forward by various writers are briefly discussed. They represent various approaches to business conduct, which were recommended or cautioned against by writers. While their style of expression and formulation of argument might mark these as curiosities today, their underlying messages still have currency of debate in the present international business world.

RESEARCH METHOD EMPLOYED

This study is based on Carnegie and Napier's (1996) advocacy of the broadening of the archive in accounting research. Recognising the increasing investigation of accounting as a social practice, they argue that accounting historians should adopt a broader notion of what constitutes the 'archive'. This allows historians to tap into the broader discourse surrounding the practice and use of accounting, thereby understanding better its fundamental nature and contribution to business, economic and social change. Their vision of widening the archival net beyond traditional books of account allows managers' letters and records, minutes of meetings, oral history, other non-accounting documentation, and the literature of the period to be incorporated into the scope of study. In seeking to penetrate the role of managerial accounting during the British Industrial Revolution, Fleischman and Parker (1990, 1991) adopted this expanded approach to the archive, finding productive sources in letters between owners and managers, managers' notebooks, minutes of manager and owner meetings, etc. In beginning to explore the interface between professional concepts of appropriate business conduct and business manager concepts, this study opted for an excursion into the published business practice literature of the 1900–55 period. The business literature sources referred to in this study are largely drawn from the author's own antiquarian accounting and business textbook collection which predominantly covers 1850–1960 and numbers in excess of 600 volumes. The texts referenced in this study comprise but a very small sample of the literature during the period. They do not set out to be representative of an undefined 'whole', but have rather been selected for their particular attention to and style of representation of issues of personal conduct in business.

As Tosh (1991) argues, historical sources encompass every kind of evidence that humans have left regarding their past activities and extend to the written word, the spoken word, material artefacts, photography and film. This study treats its selected business literature sources as virtual photographic representations of historical 'mind sets' characteristic of much business discourse in the first half of the twentieth century. Their potential relevance to contemporary ethical concerns in business and the accounting profession is supported by King (1983) who argues that the writing of any history requires the conceptualisation and selection of an idea. Ideas that can be found in historical time only have meaning for the historian or the readers of history when they exist in some sense in the present. Past ideas only resonate with us to the degree to which they can be identified in some way (by similarity or dissimilarity) with ideas of the present. This study has focused on the idea of personal business conduct, a matter of current concern right across the international business community, and seeks to reflect upon some of its historical antecedents from the immediate past.

Thus, in summary, the approach adopted by this study to its subject is rooted in the premise that accounting and business organisations, along with their practices and thinking, must be examined within their socio-cultural context. This adheres to the view expressed by Previts *et al.* (1990) that history is a cultural product that depicts human experience from a spectrum of approaches to the writing of history. The approach adopted here offers an initial exploratory enquiry into hitherto largely neglected sources in the hope of offering new alternative perspectives that may have a useful input into contemporary discourses on accounting and business ethics.

THE CONVENTIONAL ACCOUNTANTS

The internationally respected accounting historian in whose honour this book is published, has himself stated that:

> The strength of the British accountancy profession was, however, not in written rules but in successfully demonstrating to the public that accountants were men of honesty, integrity and independence.
>
> (R. H. Parker 1986: 60)

He attributed their rapid achievement of such recognition largely to their social origins. In the nineteenth century, Parker argued, those who had a choice of profession tended towards medicine, law and the Church of England and they represented a small minority of the population who had the benefit of a privileged education. Entrants to the accounting profession were religious non-conformists and Scots. They were schooled in a practical education on subjects such as mathematics, elementary science, foreign languages and bookkeeping and were instilled with the virtues of hard work, prudence, honesty and advancement. Thus, recruits to the accountancy profession tended to be from middle-class parents of modest means and instilled with the above-mentioned values. Indeed the perceived appropriate characteristics and qualities of professional accountants remained a matter of continuing comment and discussion both within the profession and by observers of it in the early part of the twentieth century.

Discussions of the required characteristics of professional accountants were to be found not only in the UK but in such countries as the USA and Australia. For example, writing in the July 1906 issue of the *Annals of the American Academy of Political and Social Science*, J. E. Sterrett (1906) of the Pennsylvania State Board of Examiners of Public Accountants argued that to function effectively as a public accountant, one must acquire a level of attainment and skill that would qualify one to be ranked as a professional person. He contended that the position of public accountant was at the time increasingly one of responsibility, dignity and influence in the community. To Sterrett, the profession offered work of dignity and great usefulness to the business community while at the same time demanding qualities of ability, tact and common sense along with a 'courageous devotion to absolute truth, honor and justice' (Sterrett, 1906: 27). He argued that, particularly in the accounting profession, high moral character was required to be combined with intelligence and training and a capacity for vigilance and hard work.

In his Foreword to a book containing a series of articles on etiquette in the accountancy profession, Sir William Plender (1927) argued that ethical professional conduct could not be derived purely by a process of study or of professional codification but rather stemmed from the attitude and caution of individual members of the profession. Such notions were echoed and amplified by Crew (1925) in his specification of the desired qualifications of a professional accountant. These included:

1 A passion for exactness and accuracy.
2 The marshalling of figures so that they speak the truth.
3 A wide outlook and a clear imagination.
4 A keen vision and an intelligent understanding of human affairs.
5 The shouldering of responsibility with intelligence and discretion.
6 A combination of knowledge, ability, judgement, experience and training.
7 A sympathetic appreciation of human nature.
8 Vision and imagination.

Such lofty ideals in the conception of the conventional accountant, apparently distanced from the cut and thrust of the world of business, were, already in the early years of the twentieth century, subject to satirical observation. One example can be found in a piece authored by Elwood S. Brown (1909), entitled 'The bookkeeper: his accuracy'. The bookkeeper is referred to as 'our loveable and confiding friend', 'bounded by a ledger, a pile of statements, a long row of figures and a worried look', with 'penetrating glance', 'long, lean hands', and 'maintaining a tremendous, intense, rapid-calculating brain' (Brown 1909: 77). In addition to these characteristics,

He is clean, immaculately clean, physically, mentally and morally, and the only creature who can handle red ink, a bad pen and a rough edged ruler without blotting the page. His cleanliness borders on the supernatural.

(Brown 1909: 77–8)

Brown goes on to expand on the bookkeeper's commitment to accuracy, and his commitment to the systematic control of and accounting for every aspect of business:

> The next feature of the bookkeeper for consideration is his system. This often borders on the marvellous .... It always paralyzes the easy-going businessman with wonder. System, system, the regulator of the universe, what a wonder it is! The competent bookkeeper usually knows more about a firm's business than the entire board of directors together. Ordinarily he has every little detail, cost, every tiny item of expense, every molecular, infinitesimal transaction at his systematic command. And he is as certain as death.

(Brown 1909: 80–1)

In reference to the moral virtues of hard work as mentioned in R. H. Parker's (1986) discussion of British accountants' social origins, Brown (1909) observes that bookkeepers are often viewed as being plodders involved in drudgery. In response, Brown satirically refers to the drudgery of a hard, honest job that is nonetheless accompanied by the 'thrill of pleasure' for a job well done and for responsibility properly borne and for the successful struggle. This is said to be the pleasure of 'a good, loyal bookkeeper' (Brown 1909: 82).

While it may be argued that, for the period under review in this study, the majority of discussions of the required qualities of an accountant conventionally reified a set of lofty attributes in somewhat splendid isolation from the business context within which accountants worked, there were nevertheless some oblique references to that wider context. Sterrett (1906) opened his discussion of the accounting profession with an outline of the business context. While some might regard it as an optimistic interpretation, he argued that business might be pursued by the individual primarily for individual private gain but that ultimately business must serve a larger purpose, namely that of providing comfort and convenience to the community. Sterrett saw the accountant as integral to the conduct and expansion of business in terms of organisation, method, control and evaluation. The potentially different motivation of those engaged in business compared with the conventionally described characteristics and motivation of the accountant is exemplified by, for example, Crew's (1925) assertion that the professional accountant is expected to risk or even sacrifice his health or very life in performing his professional duties and that this is a higher level of expectation than is ever required in business. This notion underpinned, for example, the long-standing prohibitions on advertising of accountants' professional services. Persons in business were conceded to be able to compete with each other in price, in quality and in advertising of their goods and services. Being supposedly distanced from commercial business motivations, professional accountants were seen as being restricted to gaining their livelihoods by the sole use of their professional ability (Crew 1925). Such a conceptual distancing allowed the persistence of the 'watchdog' image of professional accountants. This is delightfully exemplified by Hill-Reid in his discussion of the accountant:

> Brash, meretricious concerns arise before our eyes dazzling in their anxiety to impress, but they are cruelly ephemeral, causing distress and sometimes havoc during and after their abominable existences: and of these I warn you to beware. And because of their guilty consciences they fear the cold hand of the accountant upon them. For the Accountant is sometimes a mathematical sleuth, unearthing the wicked actions of the coming malefactor and ultimately bringing him to the punishment he so well deserves.
>
> (Hill-Reid 1953: 144)

Yet those such as Plender (1927) had already warned that, just like people in business, accountants could be seduced by taking an easy road to personal gain. In pursuing ambition and personal success, they risked the perils of injury to others and unprofessional conduct.

That the interface between business motivations and professional accounting ethics was closer than the discussants of desirable characteristics of accountants and their related ethics and professional etiquette cared to recognise, is evidenced by this author's research into the history of the Australian accounting profession's ethical pronouncements (Parker 1987) and the private versus public interest dimension evident in professional accounting body ethics (Parker 1994). The intersection between professional accounting practice and business practice was well evidenced, for example, by practitioner breaches of the advertising prohibition being adjudicated by professional bodies and discussed in the accounting literature as early as the 1920s. Indeed, this breach of one of the arguably prime differentiations between professional accounting practice and business practice occurred in Australia with increasing frequency right through until the prohibition was discontinued. Parker's (1987) study found that advertising may have been one of the prime contributors to the impetus for ethical code development in the Australian profession. It was the ethical issue that attracted the greatest attention in Australian accounting journals from the 1920s through to the 1970s and appeared to have been the prime motivator for the construction of the 1937 code of ethics and the 1950 code of ethics of the Federal Institute of Accountants. The business motivation of practising accountants appears to have been rather closer to the motivations of business managers and owners than the accounting profession may have cared to admit.

IN SEARCH OF BUSINESS PROSPERITY

As in literature relating to the accounting profession, so in the general business literature of the period, the value of hard work was promoted as a primary business ethic. So too was the notion of beginning one's career at the lowest levels of the organisation and working up the ranks. Authors advocated total commitment to the business from an employee's very beginnings with a firm and as an essential prerequisite to their gradual promotion to management status. The orientations of employer and employee are clearly depicted in the images portrayed by the following writers:

> Readiness to go cheerfully anywhere at a moment's notice and at whatever personal inconvenience, to remain absent from home for any length of time that the exigencies of business may demand, and to make the interests of the employer his own, is a most appreciated quality in an employee.
>
> (Higinbotham 1906: 13)

> You must write (personal letters) before eight or after six. I have bought the stretch between those hours. Your time is money – my money – and when you take half an hour of it for your own purposes, that is just a petty form of petty larceny.
>
> (Graham 1904: 71)

The requirement for success in business was preached to young aspiring managers in terms of their total application to business. In his series of letters to his son working within his own firm, Graham (1904) argued that the business would be harmed by the latter's immediate promotion into managerial ranks. The philosophy of learning the total business and all skills associated with it by beginning at the lowest levels of the firm were clearly espoused. Similarly, the requirement of total commitment of personal energy to business was vividly illustrated in the following statement:

> A man can't have his head pumped out like a vacuum pan or stuffed full of odds and ends like a bologna sausage, and do his work right. It doesn't make any difference how mean and trifling the thing he's doing may seem, that's the big thing and the only thing for him just then. Business is like oil – it won't mix with anything but business.
>
> (Graham 1904: 71–2)

To a far greater extent than was at least formally stated in the accounting literature of the period, practising business literature was quite unabashed in its preparedness to specify the pursuit of wealth as a primary objective of the business person. In laudatory style, Casson (1928) pointed out that personal wealth and very rich individuals were some of the rarest things in the world. At the time of his writing, he claimed that there were only about

1,000 persons in Great Britain whose income exceeded £20,000 a year and there were not more than 400 millionaires. He also argued that, while there was much talk of the vast size of companies in the USA, very few were really so and that most were quite small at the time. He stated that of 250,000 corporations in the USA, only sixty five had a capital of more than £20 million. His admiration is best reflected in his statement that those statistics proved that success in business is a very rare thing. He likened rich men to mountain peaks – conspicuous and very few.

In his extensive book on business power, Haddock (1911) defined the aim of business as being the development of wealth and listed a whole series of its aspects that contributed to powerful business. These included:

1 Money contributes to business power when it is accumulated as capital for the earning of future income.
2 The earning power of money depends on the skill with which it is handled in business.
3 In the financial world the demand for increased business skill is greater than the demand for increased capital.
4 Sacrifice for the earning of income and the abstinence of expending capital are the prices of wealth accumulation.
5 Business power is always alert for the discovery of some new way of appealing to human desires.
6 Business power is enhanced by the financial gains from exploiting the supply of those items which are limited or whose supply can be controlled.
7 Business power creates demand value as well as sells goods already in demand and seeks to create artificial values.
8 Business power seeks the best investment return consistent with general business.

The discussion surrounding such observations as listed above was couched in philosophical and economic language. The observations represented, nevertheless, a fundamentally clear and simple pursuit of wealth as the overriding objective of business and business persons. This is well reflected in the following picturesque analogy:

> The agriculturalist here must dig his ditches and in one way or another get water to his acres…. The successful farmer will be the man who knows the laws, and knows the practical application thereof, and digs the best ditches, and controls the most water– according to the rules. As a business man you are merely digging canals for money to flow your way.
>
> (Haddock 1911: 197)

That such sentiments maintained their continuity over the decades is indicated by the well-known satirical book published in the early 1950s, entitled *How to Succeed in Business Without Really Trying*. In it, the satirist lampoons the continuing focal preoccupation with wealth in the business world, at the corporate and individual level.

> You may still ask, then, 'Why make money?' as so many have. The answer is clear and ringing: *It is the American thing to do!*
>
> (Mead 1952: 84)

In their search for business prosperity, the business writers of the period under study provided the genesis of the 'bottom line' focus characteristic of much business and accounting rhetoric today. The focus on results is exemplified by the following:

> There is but one criterion by which all men in modern mercantile life are judged, and its name is Results.
>
> (Higinbotham 1906: 27)

The author went on to argue that results are the final elements on which someone in commercial life must be judged. In Higinbotham's view, reasons and excuses for less than desired results would not avail. The quantification of those results was also regarded as the fundamental basis for assessing whether desirable results had been achieved. Indeed this could be found to be represented in accounting terms:

> All I know of Jones or need to know of him, is written in the figures of my red book of balances. That tells the story every time. It tells me that Jones produces results – large ones, which are down in big figures on the right side of the ledger ... and it gives me all the facts I need to make up my mind on that score.
>
> (Higinbotham 1906: 28)

By the 1920s, we find this results focus being articulated quite specifically in terms of profit. Casson's (1928) text focused entirely on methods of making more net profit. Indeed he argued that a focus on the concept of net profit was not only essential for business prosperity but would save the Australian nation from destruction. At the firm level, he argued that a failure to make profits would lose the goodwill of the public, the confidence and loyalty of employees, and the 'nerve and dash' of its managers and directors. His discussion makes an interesting allusion to the role of accountants in computing the achieved net profit figures – presenting imagery quite the opposite from that advocated in the professional accounting literature of the day:

> 'Gross profit' is a phrase that was invented by accountants to hide the inefficiency of Managing Directors. It is an excuse. It is an attempt to make things look better than they are. It is an effort to whitewash a black situation. The fact is that few firms dare to face the facts. They

expect their accountants to cover up their mistakes and losses.

Hundreds of firms, perhaps thousands, have ultimately been wrecked because they did not wish to know the facts about their own affairs. They compelled their accountants to invent excuses; and eventually they learned the truth from official receivers.

(Casson 1928: 18–19)

Thus, in these few examples of business writing, we are presented with a conventional wisdom that dictates hard work, an aspiration to earn money and create wealth at the personal and firm level, and an intensive focus on quantifiable profits. These quite openly stated motivations are couched in terms of the individual employee, the manager, and the firm overall. They imply pressures for total commitment of time and energy to the business, acquiring the skills in every facet of the business, and the measurement of achievement at the individual employee, manager and firm level in terms of quantifiable accounting figures. Arguably the focus and mode of expression of these concepts appears somewhat removed from the assumed motivations implied in accounting literature and professional discussions of appropriate personal conduct that have already been referred to in this paper. Nevertheless, in some business comments on the role of accountants in relation to the measurement of business results, we do see some, albeit small, signs of the potentially uncomfortable interface between business motivations and accounting codes of conduct.

EMPLOYER AND MANAGER RESPONSIBILITIES

In the emerging corporate world of the early part of the twentieth century, examples can be found amongst both observers of business and business writers themselves reminding their listeners and readers of the accountability and responsibilities of corporate management towards both society and employees. Given that, for example, the first two decades of the century were breeding grounds for the popularity of scientific management approaches to the organisation of the workplace, with its accompanying emphasis on securing harder and more efficient work from the workforce (L. D. Parker 1986), such recommendations on accountability and responsibility are all the more notable.

Woodrow Wilson (1910), in an address to the American Bar Association, strenuously argued for the invoking of legal accountability of individual managers and leaders of corporations so that they could not hide behind the artificial legal entity of the company. He argued that their control over employees and whole communities was so great that, while their corporations were making positive contributions to the American economy and society, the potential for the impact of any unethical behaviour upon a great number of people was considerable. Thus, Wilson

77

argued that society could not afford to have individuals effectively wielding the power conferred by their employment of thousands, without assuming some personal responsibility for that. Focusing on the responsibility of managers for their employees, Henry Jones (1906), Professor of Moral Philosophy at the University of Glasgow, in a series of lectures addressed to the businessmen of Glasgow, argued that masters must care for their men and contribute to the ennobling of labour. He advocated the development of working conditions that would enhance employees and not destroy them and that they should seek inventions that would encourage industry, honesty and thrift among their workers. In the USA as well, Hubbard (1916) argued that big business must not grind down its employees and the public. He, too, argued that large-scale business organisations must be led by managers 'who have sympathetic hearts and are humanitarians as well as economists' (Hubbard 1916: 39). In addition he advocated the avoidance of 'Scrooge methods' and the appropriate recompense to 'men and women who give an undivided service and do their work with a minimum of supervision'.

Higinbotham (1906) devoted an entire chapter of his text to the treatment of employees. In doing so he sadly observed that:

America has very many men of great fortune who appear to have small capacity for any pleasure other than that of increasing their wealth.

(Higinbotham 1906: 87)

Recognising that some manufacturers provided halls, churches, libraries, schools, gymnasiums, theatres and clubhouses for their employees, Higinbotham argued that this was difficult for merchandising organisations which usually had employees geographically spread. He nevertheless advocated the developing of employee confidence in their long-term tenure within the organisation, maintaining close personal relationships between management and the workforce, and assuring employees that they would be looked after in times of sickness and calamity. The major potential benefit of these actions to the employer was held to be a greater degree of employee loyalty to the firm. Further suggested strategies included the introduction of an employee pension system, the payment of competitive salaries, and even the conferring of some measure of ownership of the whole enterprise upon employees. Thus against the orientation towards wealth and results already portrayed in this study, at least some writers and observers were calling for attitudes of personal conduct that accounted for the human factor:

In truth and in fact, the interests of the employer and the employed are mutual, and everything which goes to make this more apparent is to be welcomed.

(Higinbotham 1906: 95)

SAMPLING CONCEPTS OF CONDUCT

Business writers periodically expounded a variety of concepts of business conduct, some of which they recommended for cultivation and others of which they warned should be avoided. The nature and style of these portrayals smacks of a combination of homespun philosophy and ingenious invention. A sample of them is presented here.

Leadership and efficiency

The subjects of leadership and efficiency in business have remained of continuing interest throughout the twentieth century, with a resurgence in the management and accounting literatures of the 1980s and 1990s. Plentiful references to appropriate conduct in these respects can be found in the first half of the century. Typically, references and discussions reflected a moralistic stance clearly influenced by the scientific management school of thought with its devotion to hard work and efficiency. Leadership was construed in terms of the exercise of power and supervision over the work of others, with a particular focus on inducing full efficiency from each employee. The notion of the leader as a 'chief' leading by example and through the exercise of authority-based control was very much in evidence (Haddock 1911).

While the cost of supervision was regarded by some as a form of economic waste, it was nevertheless considered necessary under the assumptions that workers were prone to carelessness, inefficiency and disinterestedness. The concept of business leadership and its relationship to efficiency was very much tied to the focus on the pursuit of profit and wealth. For the employer and leader:

> The dangers of deficits, bankruptcy and disgrace are ever before him. If he pays men to do certain tasks, he is obliged to see that they do them.
>
> (Hubbard 1916: 123)

Taylor's (1947) famous management by exception principle became reflected in management thinking that has persevered right through to today (Parker and Lewis 1995). For example, Hubbard (1916: 125–6) argued:

> One man can destroy the efficiency of a dozen, and possibly a hundred. Such cases are not so very rare, as any man who employs a large number of people knows full well.

Authority-based leadership and control was also a form of conduct advocated and admired till the 1950s (and arguably beyond). Autocratic institutions such as the church and the army were admired and held out as models of formalised authority for other organisations to emulate. Responsibility, command and power all flowed from the right of authority-based leaders to manage the organisation. It was considered to be top management's prerogative to exercise centralised control and associated discipline as part of authoritative leadership (Urwick 1937; Mooney 1947; Mixter 1923; McKinsey 1921).

The strength of such convictions concerning the appropriate style of leadership in contributing to business growth and profit is best reflected in the following quotations:

> At least half of our firms need new men at the top. We need a new lot of generals and colonels and captains. Once we get them our sergeants and privates will do well enough.
>
> Thousands of our leaders are only clerks. They are nothing but routine men. They are mere habits. We have lost the hard virtues of earlier days – many of us have …. It is the fault of those who have been leading us for the last twenty years. And they must now either learn to be efficient or resign and make way for new and better leaders who are sure to arise in our time of need.

> (Casson 1928: 89–90)

Nous

In his book entitled *Nous: An Antidote for Business Inertia*, Richard Hope (1930) argued that in a period of uncertainty, the Australian businessman often followed the example of the turtle when threatened with danger – retreating into his shell and waiting for the danger to pass by. Writing just before the onset of the Depression in the early 1930s, Hope argued that the impending business situation was not as bad as people were anticipating. He advocated that business leaders could readjust and stabilise if they undertook common-sense planning and then action. Planning and action constituted his concept of nous. Thus he argued that the business manager who passively reacted to depressed business conditions would lose trade to the more energetic competitor 'who has the *nous*, to realise that the time to *go out after* new business is when business is needed most' (Hope 1930: 3).

Hope's philosophy was one of aggressive advertising, promotion and selling in order to stimulate business and increase sales volume, even in a difficult business climate. His concept of nous was in effect an aggressive approach to generating new business:

> To get your share of the new opportunities you must *go after* business in dead earnest.

> (Hope 1930: 6)

In the final page of his text, Hope argued that the reason that many businessmen could not overcome a business slump was because they lacked 'guts' which he also defined as part of nous. In his view, the aggressive pursuit of business opportunities principally by advertising was a matter of common sense.

Psychic bookkeeping

In outlining the personal requirements for developing so-called business power, a rather inventive concept of psychic bookkeeping was advanced by Frank Channing Haddock (1911). This was based on the notion of a capital account, called 'Psychic', which included increases to capital and decreases (termed 'psychic charges') which resulted from faults, weaknesses, various tenancies and habits. In psychic bookkeeping, the business person was recommended to estimate the capital value of himself and his abilities. That estimate most likely would differ from the estimate of him by the public. Thus if the individual kept an account of himself, he might discover why the public estimate of himself was less or more than his own. Haddock advocated constant comparison of the individual's psychic assets, in terms of the individual's ability and worth, with what other people perceived those assets to be. He identified three ways of raising actual assets to those perceived by the public or raising public perceptions of one's assets to their real level. These were (a) being a worthwhile individual, (b) conscious deception or (c) unconscious deception. Only the first method was recommended.

Haddock's psychic bookkeeping had three major features:

1 A single fault or deficiency more than offset the sum total of assets that would otherwise ensure success.
2 The input of labour, discipline and pains endured were to be charged against the individual account as an expense. Only the actual output or work accomplished and associated benefits to the individual were to be credited to the account.
3 As long as the labour, discipline and pains endured had been undertaken in striving for self-improvement, then the output or work accomplished would always at least equal or exceed those amounts debited to the account. Such inputs would ensure multiplied returns to the individual.

Haddock went on to represent many aspects of personal requirements for business success and business power in 'T' form. The following account represents a business illustration of the above principles (Haddock 1911: 124):

Any Successful Business

DR.			CR.		
To	Goods Bought in	x	By	Goods in Stock	x
"	Labor, time, skill	x	"	Work	xy
"	Running Expenses	x	"	Gross Returns	xyz
		$\overline{3x}$			$\overline{3x2yz}$
				Credit Balance	2yz

The credit side of the account was said to represent 'surplus cash and psychic advance'. For the employee, the following account included a mix of intrinsic and extrinsic personal outcomes on the credit side (p. 127):

Self–Employee.

DR.			CR.		
To Item:	Labor	x	By	Work	3x
"	Time	x	"	Use of Skill	y
"	Weariness	x	"	Utilization of Time	z
			"	Freedom from Responsibility	a
			"	Improvement	b
			"	Opportunity	c
			"	Expectation	d
		$\overline{3x}$			$\overline{3xyzabcd}$

For the superintendent or manager, the psychic account appeared as follows (p. 128):

Superior Department of Service

DR.				CR.		
To	Item:	Time	x	By	Work	6x
"	"	Skill	x	"	Occupation	y
"	"	Labor	x	"	Superior Position	z
"	"	Weariness	x	"	Confidence and Honor	a
"	"	Responsibility	x	"	Use of Skilled Ability	b
"	"	Results of Hazard	x	"	Large Ways of Living	c
				"	Society	d
				"	Surplus over Expenses	e
				"	Growth	f
				"	Salary	xg
				"	Expectation	h
			$\overline{6x}$			$\overline{7xyzabcdefgh}$

For the overall business, Haddock outlined the following psychic account (p. 129):

Our Successful Business

	DR. To Item			CR. By		
Personal	" Time of Self	x		Work	5x	
	" Labor, Weariness, etc.	x		Gross Returns	4x	
				Use of Skill	y	
	" Skill given	x		Occupation	z	
	" Wear and Tear of Body	x		Sustenance	a	
				Accumulation	b	
	" Responsibility	x		Development of Power	c	
Financial	" Investment	x		Realized Ambition	d	
	" Interest	x		Enjoyment of Business	e	
				Reputation	f	
	" Insurance	x		Growth of Self	g	
	" Other Expenses	x		Growth of Business	h	
		9x			9xyzabcdefgh	

He argued that the psychic income more than offsets the physical and psychic outgoings when the individual persists in multiplying the best of himself into his work in the best improving way. For the business overall, the same principle applied. Work, being defined as accomplishment of results, should be worth at least what it costs in personal debits. The financial charges are more than offset by the profits earned from the successful business. The success of the business depends on the personal requirements employed in overcoming the environment, and thus psychic income should be in excess of all charges indefinitely.

In terms of personal business conduct, Haddock went on to characterise a number of personal requirements, once more in 'T' account format. This included a list of debit and credit items for physical health, personal dress, personality and business language. Noteworthy in this extended bookkeeping exposition (Haddock 1911: 117–60) is the integration of financial and attitudinal/motivational variables. Once more this reflected the management thinking of the period – an unabashed pursuit of income, wealth and personal business success along with considerable attention to advocated values and attitudes to business practice. At both the individual and organisational levels, moral virtues of hard work, efficiency, self-improvement and wealth creation were seen to be mutually reinforcing. Some evidence of the resurgence of this type of thinking was arguably to be found in the business environments sponsored by Thatcherites in the UK and by Reaganomics in the USA.

Swank

Some types of attitude or conduct were highlighted by business writers as requiring avoidance if business success was to be achieved. Casson (1928) defined swank as the tendency of an individual to attempt to convince others that he is a more important and successful person than they currently perceive.

> Swank springs eternal in the human breast.
> Looking dignified instead of getting busy – that is swank.
>
> (Casson 1928: 82–3)

Casson argued that most business people tended to seek praise and flattery and listened only for good news. He described them as 'fair-weather' managers, preferring self-deception to the discomfort of knowing the real facts about business conditions and the state of their business. In failing to face the facts, they therefore risked the loss of the opportunity to reconstruct and develop that business.

To Casson (1928: 80), swank was 'almost as great an evil as unprogressiveness'. He argued that it caused the overstocking of inventory, the retention of unsaleable goods on retail shelves, the regarding of aggressive selling and promotion of goods as undignified, the spending of excessive time by managers in the office instead of interfacing with the customers, the failure to learn how to carry out certain tasks effectively, and a predisposition to paint a picture of oneself and one's business as bigger and richer than it is in reality. In essence, all of these weaknesses were attributed to the human tendency towards pride. In a subsequent publication, Casson (1939) argued that a firm must usually choose between pride and profit. Pride could result in a perception of arrogance by the public and potential customers, whereas an organisation and its managers perceived as friendly and sociable would maintain good customer relations. Self-conceit, Casson argued, was a defect of both firms and individuals. Thus Casson was arguing that the general attitude of swank could easily cause inefficient and ineffective working practices, poor public and customer relations, inadequate or inadequately analysed performance reports, and failures to assess realistically the business environment and devise proactive strategies in response.

Financial snobbery

A related evil to that of swank was later identified by Hill-Reid (1953) in his concept of financial snobbery. This he regarded as a virus which could develop and thrive in an individual at any age. The possession of material things to such a person was said to have no more aesthetic value than their being the visible evidence of the size of an individual's bank balance.

Financial snobbery was to be identified in the ostentatious projection of an image of wealth. Thus Hill-Reid argued that the power of money could be frightening and could alter the whole course of the future unless controlled within certain bounds. Its power could 'distort the picture and ... warp the soul' (Hill-Reid, 1953: 166).

Nevertheless, the author argued that money was not automatically the basis of evil but could be a power for the production of good. In concluding his letter warning of the perils of financial snobbery, once more, this particular author evinced the arguments of prior decades that integrated moral virtues with the production of wealth. This is well illustrated by the following concluding statement to his argument:

> Money can be a power for good; it is no longer just a medium of exchange blown hither and thither by the winds of avarice. Is it possible that it has, when wisely handled and treated with proper reverence, attained some spiritual level all its own, yet liable to link itself with the powers of darkness when invited to do so? It is far more than a medium of exchange: it is the medium through which is performed the noblest and basest in human endeavour.
>
> (Hill-Reid 1953: 167–8)

REFLECTED IMAGERY

What emerges most pronouncedly from the sampling of concepts of business and personal conduct illustrated above, is the close integration in the minds of business writers of certain moral values and wealth creation. The pursuit of business profitability and wealth accumulation through the exploitation of personal virtues, ranging from individual personality variables to the pursuit of efficiency and the avoidance of self-deception, arguably reflected at least to some degree the social and cultural values of the period. As L. D. Parker's (1986) research into the control concepts inspired by the development of scientific management in the early decades of the twentieth century found, American approaches to business management and control reflected both a general social and business psyche. In the early 1900s, Roosevelt had begun to crusade for the improvement of moral standards in the business world and a Taylorite preoccupation with business efficiency had begun to spill over into American social life in general. People were exhorted to pursue efficiency in all aspects of life as a matter of personal duty. Politicians, churches, educational institutions, reforming organisations and business organisations all advocated the pursuit of efficiency as a positive moral value. This ethos even penetrated the American home and reinforced the desirability and social acceptability of business people's ethic of competition and pursuit of profit (Allen 1952; Bagwell and Mingay 1970; Haber 1964; Wren 1979).

Hard work was a moral duty and held out to be good for the individual's moral stature. It was regarded as promoting efficiency and hence profits which by definition were seen to be good for the society as a whole. From penetrating the home (through housekeeping books and home economics books) right through to large business, efficiency and co-operation were interwoven with notions of morality and profit to produce a social and business drive for hard work, clean living and bigger profits (Haber 1964; Aitken 1960). Thus there seems to be a convincing case for regarding the business literature imagery of desired personal conduct, with its integrated pursuit of moral values and profit, as reflecting a close interaction between changing social and business values of the period.

AN OPEN VERDICT

When compared with the business practice literature of the period, it is arguable that the accounting profession's codes of conduct and related discussions were, to say the least, focused in content, restrained in style, and virtually divorced from reference to the world of business within which accounting operated. The profession's approaches to the conduct of accountants exhibited high moral tone and prescribed increasingly detailed processes for maintaining the much treasured concepts of independence, objectivity and so on. Yet we have seen that issues such as advertising of professional services gave rise to tensions between the moral virtues of a profession and the commercial motivations of a business. Such fleeting images hint at the existence of similar tensions between virtuous conduct and pursuit of profits quite regularly painted in the portraits of business practice by business literature authors.

In their descriptions and advocacy of the pursuit of business success, the business writers rendered wealth and profit as icons to be unabashedly worshipped and possessed. In doing so, they at times ignored the risks of inducing dysfunctional behaviour amongst the practitioners of business, from a social and business point of view. Yet many appeared to guard against simply promulgating a doctrine of the ends justifying the means. In their repeated attention to the exposition of moral values in business – hard work, initiative, efficiency, responsibility and accountability – they provided potential offsets and moderators to the foregoing risks.

To the business practice writers, personal business conduct and the pursuit of profit were intrinsically interrelated. The moral values listed above, both at the individual and corporate level, were considered vital components of the pursuit of business success and business profit (e.g. Anonymous 1900). In this close integration, we may indeed find some source of inspiration for grappling with the ethical issues of conducting international business today. The globalisation of many aspects of business has brought with it a multitude of cultural differences and the accompanying ethical issues that they pose as different social and business cultures struggle to reach mutual understanding and common business practices.

In sampling the variety of concepts of business conduct presented here, we have the opportunity to glimpse a small number of intermittent images rendered across a period of fifty years. Yet they paint a consistently rendered canvas that is full of light and shade, variety and commonality, as well as explicit signs and subtle nuances. These images tell as much by their style of expression and use of language as by their basic content. They are at once pragmatic and romantic, phlegmatic and melodramatic, unassuming and pretentious, transparent and veiled, naïve and sophisticated. The texture is rich and the meanings to be inferred are many. Nevertheless they communicate the depth and extent of moral underpinning to what might otherwise appear to contemporary observers as having been a naked, amoral business pursuit of monetary gain. Even so, that potentially naked amorality appears always to have threatened to emerge and overpower individual manager and business alike. In its boisterous flamboyance, the business practice literature appears unmatched in the accounting domain. Thus in its pursuit of codes of ethical conduct, the accounting profession may have missed the opportunity for grappling with the ongoing tension and at the same time integration of moral values and pursuit of profit. Yet herein lies both the pressures and potential for confronting at a deeper level the corporate and financial ethical conduct issues that have beset our contemporary business world over the last decade.

Thus the portraits painted here hint at reflections of the experiences of the past that may yet carry messages for today. Still we must record an open verdict. To what extent do the business values espoused today reflect the mutual reinforcement of social and business values of the early part of the twentieth century? Can the profession's codes of conduct contribute more realistically to the contemporary debate of business conduct issues by a more frank confrontation of the commercial as well as professional motivations of accounting practitioners themselves? To what degree do our contemporary concerns with the morals of entrepreneurial strategies, bribery as part of some national business cultures, responsibilities for whistle blowing, and financial versus environmental accountability, emerge as new issues or altered effigies of past struggles? In the face of all these weighty and daunting questions, one observation can be made with reasonable justification. There appears to be sufficient evidence to suggest that, from our wandering through the gallery of canvases displayed here, we can catch images of yesteryear that are still trying to tell us something today.

REFERENCES

Aitken, H. G. J. (1960) *Taylorism at Watertown Arsenal: Scientific Management in Action 1908–15*, Cambridge MA: Harvard University Press.

Allen, F. L. (1952) *The Big Change: America Transforms Itself 1900–1950*, New York: Bantam Books.

Anonymous (*c.* 1900) *Mercantile Morals*, London: James Blackwood.

Bagwell, P. S. and Mingay, G. E. (1970) *Britain and America 1850–1939: A Study of Economic Change*, London: Routledge & Kegan Paul.

Brown, E. S. (1909) 'The bookkeeper: his accuracy', in *Clever Business Sketches*, Detroit, MI: The Business Man's Publishing Co., pp. 75–84.

Carnegie, G. D. and Napier, C. J. (1996) 'Accounting history into the twenty-first century', *Accounting, Auditing and Accountability Journal* 9(3): 7–39.

Casson, H. N, (1928) *How to Make More Net Profit*, Sydney: Cornstalk.

—— (1939) *Courtesy in Business*, Sydney: Angus & Robertson.

Crew, A. (1925) *The Profession of an Accountant and Some Notes on the Legal Profession*, London: Gee.

Fleishman, R. K. and Parker, L. D. (1990) 'Managerial accounting early in the British Industrial Revolution: the Carron Company, a case study', *Accounting and Business Research* 20(79): 211–21.

—— (1991) 'British entrepreneurs and pre-Industrial Revolution evidence of cost management', *Accounting Review* 66(2): 361–75.

Graham, J. (1904) *Letters from a Self-made Merchant to His Son*, London: Methuen.

Haber, S. (1964) *Efficiency and Uplift: Scientific Management in the Progressive Era, 1890–1920*, Chicago: University of Chicago Press.

Haddock, F. C. (1911) *Business Power: A Practical Manual in Financial Ability*, Alhambra, CA: Power-Book Library.

Higinbotham, H. N. (1906) *The Making of a Merchant*, Chicago: Forbes.

Hill-Reid, W. S. (1953) *Letters From a Bank Parlour*, London: Falcon Press.

Hope, R. M. (1930) *Nous: An Antidote For Business Inertia*, Sydney: Angus & Robertson.

Hubbard, E. (1916) *The Romance of Business*, East Aurora, NY: The Roycrofters.

Jones, H. (1906) *Social Responsibilities: Lectures to Business Men*, Glasgow: James Maclehose.

King, P. (1983) 'Thinking past a problem', in P. King (ed.) *The History of Ideas: An Introduction to Method*, London: Croom Helm, 21–65.

McKinsey, J. O. (1921) 'Budgetary control and administration', *Administration: The Journal of Business Analysis and Control* 1(1): 73–82.

Mead, S. (1952) *How to Succeed in Business Without Really Trying*, New York: Simon & Schuster.

Millerson, G. (1964) *The Qualifying Associations: A Study in Professionalization*, London: Routledge & Kegan Paul.

Mixter, C. W. (1923) 'The general question of extent and method of control under scientific management', *Harvard Business Review* 2(1): 13–22.

Mooney, J. D. (1947) *The Principles of Organization*, New York: Harper & Row.

Parker, L. D. (1986) *Developing Control Concepts in the 20th Century*, New York: Garland.

—— (1987) 'An historical analysis of ethical pronouncements and debate in the Australian accounting profession', *Abacus* 23(2): 122–40.

—— (1994) 'Professional accounting body ethics: in search of the private interest', *Accounting, Organizations and Society* 19(6): 507–25.

—— (1996) Broad scope accountability: the reporting priority', *Australian Accounting Review* 6(1): 3–15.

Parker, L. D. and Lewis, N. R. (1995) 'Classical management control in contemporary management and accounting: the persistence of Taylor and Fayol's world', *Accounting, Business and Financial History*, 5(2): 211–35.

Parker, R. H. (1986) *The Development of the Accountancy Profession in Britain to the Early Twentieth Century*, Birmingham, AL: Academy of Accounting Historians, Monograph 5.

Plender, W. (1927) 'Foreword', in Chartered Accountant *The Etiquette of the Accounting Profession*, London: Gee.

Previts, G. J., Parker, L. D. and Coffman, E. N. (1990) 'Accounting history: definition and relevance', *Abacus* 26(1): 1–16.

Ripley, W. Z. (1927) *Main Street and Wall Street*, Boston: Little, Brown.

Sterrett, J. E. (1906) 'The profession of accountancy' in E. R. Johnson (ed.) *The Annals of the American Academy of Political and Social Science*, Philadelphia: American Academy of Political and Social Science, 28(1) 16–27.

Taylor, F. W. (1947) 'Shop management' in *Scientific Management*, New York: Harper, pp. 17–207. First published by the American Society of Mechanical Engineers, 1903.

Tosh, J. (1991) *The Pursuit of History*, 2nd edition, London: Longman.

Urwick, L. (1937) 'Organization as a technical problem', (presented 1933) in L. Gulick and L. Urwick (eds) *Papers on the Science of Administration*, New York: Institute of Public Administration, pp. 49–88.

Wilensky, H. L. (1964) 'The professionalization of everyone?', *American Journal of Sociology* 70(2): 137–58.

Wilson, W. (1910) 'Before the war: how things looked then', Annual address to American Bar Association, Chattanooga, TN, *Reports* pp. 426–34, 439. Reprinted in Ripley, W. Z. (1927) *Main Street and Wall Street*, Boston: Little, Brown.'

Wren, D. A. (1979) *The Evolution of Management Thought*, 2nd edition, New York: John Wiley.

6

THE ORIGINS OF THE NO-LIABILITY MINING COMPANY AND ITS ACCOUNTING REGULATIONS*

Richard D. Morris

INTRODUCTION

The no-liability mining company is an organisational form unique to Australia and New Zealand. This paper traces its evolution from the British cost book mining company, through the mining partnership and mining company legislation of early (1850s and 1860s) Australian gold mining. The paper shows this led to creation of the no-liability company in the colony of Victoria in 1871. It also shows that the accounting regulations for no-liability companies and their predecessors in Victoria were imposed earlier and more extensively than accounting regulations for British cost book mining companies. In both places, accounting regulations for mining companies exceeded those for limited liability companies. The no-liability mining company flourished in Victoria and within twenty years had been adopted in other Australian colonies and in New Zealand. In contrast, the cost book mining company 'died out' in the UK at the end of the nineteenth century, replaced by the limited liability company.

The chief distinguishing feature of the no-liability mining[1] company is that shareholders are not legally bound to pay calls on partly paid shares, and cannot be sued for unpaid calls. Shareholders who fail to pay a call forfeit their shares, which the company can then sell to others. In contrast, the British Companies Act of 1862 (on which early Australian Acts were based) limited shareholders' liability to the amount unpaid on their shares, a liability which extended for one year after partly paid shares were sold (section 38). Where mining companies were floated with partly paid shares – a common financing arrangement in nineteenth-century Australia (Hall 1968: 75; Ford 1986: 33) – the no-liability system reduced shareholders' financial risk, especially in speculative enterprises such as mining where demand for more capital frequently arose. In effect, the no-liability system allowed the issue of shares at a discount. No-liability companies carry the words 'No Liability' or

90

the abbreviation 'NL' after their names to distinguish them from limited liability companies. The no-liability system has remained popular in Australia: for example, 921 no-liability mining companies were registered in 1994 (Australian Securities Commission 1994: 48) and many are listed on the Australian Stock Exchange. However, proposals to abolish par value for shares in the Second Corporations Law Simplification Bill will, if adopted, make the no-liability concept redundant.[2]

I argue that creation of the no-liability mining company in 1871, its Victorian predecessors, and regulation of their accounts arose (a) from attempts to establish and enforce the law in a setting where existing British company law was unsuitable; and (b) from governmental concerns about physical and financial safety in the mining industry. Both points are consistent with Parker's (1990) model of accounting regulation. British cost book mining companies were less regulated by statute than their counter-parts in Victoria because the relevant British statutes – the Stannaries Acts of 1869 and 1887 – were, in the main, codifications and streamlining of existing case law from the Stannaries Courts of Devon and Cornwall, rather than major regulatory changes. The limited imposition of new accounting regulations in these statutes was also associated with establishing and enforcing the law and with concerns about physical and financial safety, but these were less important influences in the UK than in Victoria.

Parker argued that accounting regulation in the UK in the nineteenth century was associated with at least one of three factors, namely concerns about monopoly powers, privileges granted by the state, and physical and financial safety, with the first being the most important. Regulatory authorities were not primarily concerned with investor protection. Parker showed that often quite demanding accounting and auditing requirements for nineteenth-century British banks, electricity, gas, insurance, railway and water companies were associated with these three factors. In contrast, the three factors usually were absent in general limited liability companies, where accounting and auditing were unregulated.

Concern about the monopoly powers enjoyed by some public utilities arose because their abuse could be detrimental to the public. Similarly, privileges granted to monopolists, such as railways' rights of way or power suppliers' rights to lay down pipes and cables, were to be obtained at a price – that of having their affairs subject to regulatory scrutiny. Concerns about physical and financial safety were also grounds for regulation. With railways the concerns were accident prevention, safety of the realm and maintenance of law and order; with gas and electricity companies, accident prevention and ensuring adequate lighting of public places were paramount; while, with banks and insurance companies, long-run solvency and security of investments, savings and policies predominated.

Parker derived his model from Crouch (1967) who set out general reasons for state intervention in economic affairs during the nineteenth

91

century. In Crouch, regulations were imposed to establish and enforce the law, combat monopoly, allow for externalities, exercise unavoidable paternalism, provide a stable monetary framework, or protect the indigent. Parker discussed monopoly under that heading and under 'privileges granted by the state' while his 'physical and financial safety' subsumed externalities, paternalism and a stable monetary framework. Crouch's other factors were not immediately relevant to corporate financial reporting in the industries chosen by Parker.

Parker's model has been used by Morris (1993) to investigate profit-based dividend restrictions in nineteenth-century British regulated industries; and by Jones (1995) to examine views of nineteenth-century Parliamentary Committees' witnesses about disclosure and auditing, and their links with the Committees' recommendations and subsequent legislation.

The present paper applies Parker's model to the regulation of nineteenth-century mining companies and their accounts in the UK and Australia. At the time, British and Australian mining companies were not monopolists. However, concerns about physical and financial safety arose where mining produced externalities such as civil unrest, injuries to miners, major population shifts, and substantial effects on economic growth and the balance of payments. In the last case, mining could destabilise an economy's monetary framework. To remedy or stabilise the preceding influences, the privileges of limited liability or no liability and attendant accounting regulations were included in mining legislation. And, because of the nature of mining, unique regulations were introduced in Victoria to establish and enforce mining company law, because existing British company law was unsuitable.

The paper covers the evolution of the no-liability company from its British cost book origins through early mining company legislation in Victoria to its creation and rapid acceptance in that colony. The paper does not cover the subsequent diffusion of the no-liability system elsewhere in Australasia, a matter left for further research. Also the focus is on the statutory regulation of mining companies and their accounts, not mining companies' actual accounting practices[3] or their utility.

COST BOOK MINING COMPANIES IN THE UK

In the UK, cost book companies were unincorporated organisations, a compromise between limited liability companies and ordinary partnerships, which evolved over the centuries from the partnership system in the stannaries of Devon and Cornwall (McIlraith, 1903: 258; Burt 1984: 73–4, 79). These counties had long been major British tin producers, and Cornwall, but not Devon, remained a major producer of tin and other non-ferrous minerals during the nineteenth century (Burt et al. 1984: tables 1–10; 1987: tables 4–12).

Cost book companies acquired their name during the eighteenth century (Pennington 1973: 152), in acknowledgement of the central role played by the 'cost book' in setting up and running these enterprises. The term 'cost book' signified more than just an account book, being defined in the Stannaries Acts of 1869 and 1887 as including:

all books and papers relating to the business of a mine which are for the time being kept by a purser, or which, according to the custom of the Stannaries, or the directions of the company, ought to be kept by him.

Cost book companies were constituted by rules set down in the cost book, so that no charter, deed of settlement, partnership agreement or articles of association were needed to form one (Burt 1984: 73–4). Indeed, the Joint Stock Companies Act of 1844 (s. 63) and the Companies Act of 1862 (s. 4) explicitly excluded cost book companies.

Cost book rules evolved over the centuries as unwritten customs which were partially codified by the Stannaries Courts of Devon and Cornwall in resolutions of disputes among shareholders and other parties. Cost book rules were revised and streamlined in the Stannaries Acts of 1869 and 1887. However, a number of rules and customs in the operation of cost book mining companies remained outside these statutes (Pennington 1973: ch. 5). The Stannaries Act of 1887 followed an investigation of the Stannaries Act (1869) Amendment Bill by a Parliamentary Select Committee (BPP 1887). Cost book rules were *ad hoc*, often contradictory, and left some important questions unclear, although they were popular in practice because for a long time they worked! (Burt 1984: 74).

Several key features distinguished cost book companies from limited-liability companies and partnerships. First, unlike the limited liability company, the cost book company did not have capital fixed as so many shares of a stipulated par value, either fully paid or partly paid (Leifchild 1857: 242; St Aubyn in *Hansard* [Commons], 26 February 1869: 401; Lewis, 1924: 205). Initial capital was not raised in cash; instead, shareholders provided machinery, stores, etc., themselves for working the mine (Downing[4] in BPP 1887, Qs 160–2) – 'the adventure alone was divided into shares' (St Aubyn in *Hansard* [Commons], 26 February 1869: 402). If losses were made or amounts owed to creditors, the company made calls to raise more funds. There was no limit on the number of calls that could be made: that is, shareholders had unlimited liability. Unlike partners, cost book company shareholders were both jointly and individually liable for their company's debts (Pennington 1973: 173). In practice, shareholders' liability could be controlled, as explained shortly.

Second, cost book companies were run as short-term 'ready-money' enterprises (Tapping 1867: 3), in which periodic surpluses were fully paid out or shortfalls made good in cash (Burt and Kudo 1983: 36). Incurring debt was strictly controlled (Burt and Kudo 1983: 35). To facilitate being run as 'ready-money' enterprises, cost book companies had frequent shareholders' meetings, e.g. monthly, bi-monthly or quarterly. At these meetings, shareholders would review accounts prepared by the purser, agree to distribute all periodic profits as dividends – no reserves were kept for future outlays – or raise fresh capital via calls on shares to fund losses (Pennington 1973: 165; Leifchild 1857: 243). Periodic calling of capital for specific objectives had the advantage – over fully subscribing capital in advance – of making frauds less attractive (Morrison 1980: 16).

The third key feature was that, unlike partners, shareholders of a cost book company could sell their shares without the consent of other shareholders (Tapping 1867: 8; Lewis 1924: 205; Pennington 1973: 152).

Fourth, unlike members of either limited liability companies or partner-ships, cost book company shareholders who wished to cut their losses could relinquish their shares to the company, and not be liable for any future calls made. Relinquishment entailed the purser calculating whether the mine had a surplus or a deficit, based on a valuation of net assets on hand, and the relinquishing shareholders were paid their share of the surplus or were liable for their share of any deficit made before the surrender (Downing in BPP 1887: Qs 4–7, 17, 71–2; Pennington 1973: 183–9). Relinquished shares would then be absorbed proportionately by the other shareholders or sold on the market (Lewis 1924: 205; Burt 1984: 78).

Fifth, all transactions were entered in the cost book (Tapping 1867: 3) in single-entry journal form (Neimark and Tinker 1988: 6). In essence, a fund accounting system was used in which all capital receipts, mineral sales and other income as well as all running expenses, capital expenditure and dividends were recorded, with capital expenditure being treated as an operating cost (Morrison 1980: 40). Thus periodic dividends or calls, and settling up with relinquishing shareholders, were based on periodic calculations of surplus or deficit of income over all expenditure.

The purser was required by custom to keep accurate records of receipts and payments and of stocks of unsold ore (Pennington 1973: 169), a requirement codified in the Stannaries Act of 1869, section 9, and extended therein to include recording all receivables, debts and liabilities, a list of all adventurers, as well as all calls on shares paid and unpaid during the accounting period, now defined as being at least every four months (s. 9). Section 23 of the 1887 Stannaries Act shortened the maximum reporting period to sixteen weeks. The accounts could be audited where a call was to be made on shareholders (Stannaries Act 1869: s. 10). Section 13 of the 1887 Stannaries Act required that mine club funds (miners' provident funds) be separately accounted for and separately shown in the balance sheet (the only time this term was used in the Act) that was presented to shareholders. Miners could appoint two of their number to audit the mine club.

The purser's books or accounts were laid before shareholders at each periodic meeting (Williams 1891: 248; Pennington 1973: 169) and, when the accounts were signed by a majority of shareholders, all were bound to pay their share of any deficit (Pennington 1973: 167). A custom not codified by the Stannaries Acts gave shareholders, but not creditors, the right to inspect their company's cost book, accounts and papers (Pennington 1973: 157; Rich[5] in BPP 1887: Q. 550) and the mine itself (Tapping 1867: 10). There was no established custom for the purser to send copies of accounts to shareholders before or after meetings, but such an obligation to shareholders (and to mineral landowners[6]) was introduced in the Stannaries Act 1887, section 26 (Pennington 1973: 170). Section 23 of that Act allowed shareholders to specify the details that the purser's accounts should contain (Pennington 1973: 169). However, unlike the regulations for public utilities such as railways, the Stannaries Acts did not specify any model accounts or formats that should be followed by pursers in preparing their companies' periodic accounts.

The key person in the day-to-day running of a cost book company and in preparing its accounts was the purser (Lewis 1924: 206) who could sue or be sued on behalf of the company (Pennington 1973: 153–4). In some larger companies, the role of purser was filled by a 'managerial committee' of 'in adventurers' (local shareholders) (Burt 1984: 75). Next in importance was the chief captain or manager who supervised the workings of the mine (Lewis 1924: 206).

Cost book companies became popular in mining outside Devon and Cornwall during the nineteenth century. By the early nineteenth century, shares in such companies traded on the London share market (Burt 1984: 76). Cost book companies were used in North and South Wales, the Isle of Man and Ireland and in the formation of British gold mining companies to operate in Australia, but they rarely appeared outside non-ferrous mining (Burt and Kudo 1983: 32–3). However, expansion of the cost book system created a problem: companies not mining tin in Devon and Cornwall were outside the jurisdiction of the Stannaries Courts and so, perhaps, were illegal. The Stannaries Courts' jurisdiction was extended to all metalliferous mines (rather than just tin mines) in South West England in 1834; but cost book companies outside the South West remained a problem legally, and were abolished by the Joint Stock Act of 1856. Thereafter, cost book companies outside Devon and Cornwall were at law simply ordinary partnerships (Burt and Kudo 1983: 33).

A feature of the cost book company system was its adaptability to changing economic circumstances. Even though it had originated in small mining ventures, the cost book company structure was flexible enough to finance and operate large mines (Burt et al. 1987: xviii). For instance, to facilitate expansion in successful mines, shares were sometimes split into multiples of 8 or 16 – 32, 64, 128, etc. (Morrison 1980: 40) – and then sold to new shareholders, if existing shareholders were unable to supply new capital. Mines with as many as 6,000 or 7,000 shares, with shareholders widely scattered, were floated by mid-century (Lord Portman in *Hansard* [Lords], 1 June, 1869: 1084; Burt and Kudo 1983: 32). To regulate the liability of shareholders among themselves for a company's debts, some companies assigned nominal values to their shares, although the limitation was not effective against creditors (Pennington 1973: 173–4). Also, creditors' actions in the Stannaries Courts against the company purser came to be directed at companies' assets and not at shareholders (Burt and Kudo 1983: 35). Retention of profits to facilitate capital investments, creation of reserve funds to maintain dividends and making capital calls to finance expenditure several months ahead (the latter codified in the Stannaries Act 1869: s. 11) had all evolved by the end of the nineteenth century (Burt and Kudo 1983: 37–9; Burt 1984: 81).

However, the cost book company system also had limitations which its adaptability could not completely overcome. Control by management committees of 'in adventurers' created substantial agency costs because 'in adventurers' supplied materials, food, lodgings, etc., to the mines and miners often at inflated prices (Burt 1984: 80). Where mines were financed only by 'in adventurers' the agency problem was contained, and Burke and Richardson (1983: 197) have argued that these outside activities by 'in adventurers' contributed to the longevity of the cost book system, because they spread risks and profits from mining and served as a means of social interaction and cohesion. However, raising capital from 'out adventurers' (non-local shareholders) as mines expanded meant that these agency problems grew more serious. Such shareholders, living at a distance from the mine, could not take advantage of the frequent shareholders' meetings to supervise the management properly. Timely relinquishment or sale of shares by shareholders possessing inside knowledge about a mine's ill fortunes could leave remaining shareholders facing substantial losses, and it created further tension between 'in adventurers' and 'out adventurers' (Morrison 1980: 41). The practice of fully distributing all surpluses and the short-termism of cost book companies' financing created incentives for exploiting easily won mineral deposits and for inadequate long-term planning which often left such companies vulnerable to economic downturns (Burt 1984: 80).

Cost book companies were popular in Cornwall until the end of the nineteenth century, even after passage of the Companies Act of 1862. Burt *et al.* (1987: x) estimate that at least 1,500 mining ventures operated in Cornwall between 1845 and 1913. Before 1862, all were cost book companies (Downing in BPP 1887: Qs 19, 158; Lewis 1924: 20). Limited liability mining companies became increasingly important from the 1870s, but until the 1890s were confined to smaller, risky mines; most of the larger producers remained cost book companies (Burt *et al.* 1987: xviii–xix).

However, by the end of the 1890s, the cost book mining company was in sharp decline in Cornwall, replaced by the limited liability company. Its fate outside the South West is unknown, but was probably similar. In 1888 there were eighty-eight cost book mining companies working in Cornwall; by 1897, only twenty three of these remained; and by 1912, only one company of any importance continued to operate under cost book principles (Burke and Richardson 1981: 3, 15).

It has been argued (Burke and Richardson 1981: 4) that the decline was due to weaknesses of the cost book company organisational structure, in particular excessive profit distributions, inadequate reserve funds and unlimited liability which discouraged new capital investment. These structural problems of cost book companies coupled with long-term decline in ore grades of Cornish tin, large-scale emigration of miners from Cornwall, and increasing international competition in the tin market led to the demise of the cost book company in Cornwall during the 1890s (Burke and Richardson 1981: 5–6).

However, these contentions have been disputed. Burt and Kudo (1983) argued that the adaptability of the cost book system made it preferable to the limited liability company for most of the nineteenth century. The demise of the cost book system only occurred because of the superiority of the limited liability company in facilitating the large capital requirements of the Cornish mines, especially in meeting capital market demands for limited liability and increased security because of the then uncertain future of the Cornish tin industry (Burt *et al.* 1987: xviii). Burt and Kudo (1983) argued that, even so, the superiority of the limited liability company remained a marginal one. Similarly, Mathews (1990: 32) argued that the increased expense and risk of finding new tin reserves as existing ore bodies were exhausted made the cost book system in Cornwall 'untenable'.

Whatever the reasons, the demise of the cost book company in Cornwall at the close of the nineteenth century is clear enough. In contrast, derivatives of the cost book company flourished in Australia during the nineteenth century, and into the twentieth.

THE DEVELOPMENT OF GOLD MINING IN COLONIAL VICTORIA

The first major gold rushes in Australia occurred during the 1850s, commencing in 1851 at Ophir and other sites in New South Wales and at several locations in Victoria including Ballarat and Bendigo (Blainey 1993a: chs 1–2). Thereafter, gold mining occurred throughout Victoria at many centres, large and small.[7] Victoria was the premier gold mining colony in Australia (see Table 6.1, columns 2 and 3), although important gold discoveries were made elsewhere:[8] for example, Hill End and Hawkins Hill (1870s) in New South Wales; Gympie (1867), Mt Morgan (1880s),

Table 6.1 Economic importance of gold production in Australia, 1851–99

(1)	Victorian gold production (tonnes) (2)	Victorian gold as percentage of total Australian gold production (%) (3)	Value of Australian gold production (£'000) (4)	Gold as percentage of Australian total mineral production (%) (5)	Mining as percentage of Australian gross domestic product (%) (6)	(Rank[a]) (7)	Gold as percentage of Australian exports (%) (8)	(Rank[b]) (9)
1851–4	218.84	83.7	n/a	n/a	24.1	2	n/a	n/a
1855–9	399.75	92.6	n/a	n/a	20.7	1	n/a	n/a
1860–4	272.59	80.6	46,185	91.7	15.0	1	48.8	1
1865–9	231.09	82.1	30,744	69.3	11.7	3	44.6	1
1870–4	183.73	71.1	35,847	79.4	9.1	6	33.8	2
1875–9	127.66	64.3	27,155	68.6	6.0	8	23.2	2
1880–4	119.67	66.4	24,579	62.9	4.7	8	16.5	2
1885–9	95.42	52.7	24,309	55.1	4.3	9	14.9	2
1890–4	93.95	42.6	30,110	51.3	6.2	7	14.9	2
1895–9	118.62	31.4	51,573	67.4	8.7	6	26.0	2

Sources: Columns 2–5: Saddler (1987); columns 6–7: Butlin (1987); columns 8–9: Loughed (1987)
[a] Rank out of eight economic categories 1851–9, out of thirteen economic categories 1860–99.
[b] Rank out of thirteen categories, interpolated from data in source.

Palmer River (1873–6) and Charters Towers (1872) in Queensland; parts of the Northern Territory (after 1872); and Coolgardie (1893) and Kalgoorlie (1893) in Western Australia (Blainey 1993b; Lockwood 1984: 63–5). Gold was by far the most valuable mineral extracted in Australia during the nineteenth century,[9] even though other important minerals were found, e.g. copper at Burra Burra in South Australia (1840s), and silver at Broken Hill (1880s) (Table 6.1, columns 4 and 5).

At first, gold could be extracted by simple alluvial methods close to the surface, and the easy riches won by some sparked a wave of immigration, particularly to Victoria, that brought thousands to the new gold fields during the 1850s (Serle 1977: appendix 2). As one economic historian put it: 'Gold mining was initially a primitive labour-intensive industry where average returns were not startlingly high but where the uneven distribution of income and the hope of striking it rich proved a sufficient inducement to diggers' (Jackson 1977: 61). Subsequent rushes brought further migration from abroad and between colonies.

Gold mining played a major role in the economic and social development of nineteenth-century Australia, especially Victoria (Maddock and McLean 1984). Apart from immigration, the economic effects of gold mining included a substantial upward shift in gross domestic product, massive export earnings (because Australian gold was sold in the UK), increased imports, and a demand for infrastructure such as water supply, roads and railways. Social effects included the establishment of major regional towns and other settlements away from the coastal cities.

Interest in gold mining had been sparked partly by men returning from the Californian gold rushes of 1849 bringing with them gold mining expertise previously scarce in Australia. Also prominent among those rushing to the Victorian gold fields in the 1850s were Cornish miners (or Cousin Jacks as they became known) who had migrated to South Australia and had used their skills in the development of copper mining there during the 1840s (Barton 1968: 67–92; Payton 1984: ch. 2). In South Australia, Cornish mining customs including the cost book company system were soon adopted (Payton 1984: 32). Cousin Jacks, whether migrating from South Australia or direct from Cornwall,[10] were to have an important influence on gold mining in Victoria because they brought with them their mining laws, customs and expertise. Their influence was also to be felt later in other colonies (Payton 1984: part 2).

To regulate mining activities and the flood of prospectors in the 1850s, both New South Wales and Victoria developed mining laws, with Victoria at first following the lead of New South Wales. Miners had to purchase a mining licence and pay a fee, set initially in New South Wales and then in Victoria at thirty shillings per month (Blainey 1993a: 21; Hodge 1974: 40). Injustices in the scheme and its administration led to an armed revolt by miners at Ballarat in 1854 (the Eureka Stockade incident) which was forcibly put down by troopers. Following that incident, the Victorian government initiated a Goldfields Commission of Enquiry whose report in 1855 influenced subsequent regulation of mining in Victoria, including regulation of mining companies, as discussed in the following section.

After the Goldfields Commission Report, the unpopular licence fee was replaced by a 'miner's right', allowing miners to vote in elections for Parliament;[11] while the management of gold fields, including dispute resolution, was turned over to the miners themselves via local mining courts (later, mining boards) whose members were elected by the miners. To replace revenue lost by abolition of the licence fee, the Victorian government levied a duty on gold exports, which fell on successful mining ventures, and not, as the licence fee had done, on the unsuccessful (La Croix 1992: 214). The new mining laws of Victoria were adapted from the tinners' rights of Cornwall, and evolved from 1855 to 1880 via decisions of local courts on the gold fields, via by-laws derived from customs and usages of miners and framed by mining boards (Moore 1934: 192). The mining statute of 1865 in Victoria removed inconsistencies among these local laws, provided uniformity, and became a cornerstone of subsequent Australian mining law (Moore 1934: 192; Castles 1982: 467–8).

In the early 1850s, because of the comparative ease with which gold could be found, mining was conducted by individual diggers or by small partnerships of miners. However, as the alluvial gold ran out, miners found it necessary to search underground for deep leads. Deep lead mining occurred within a few years at Ballarat and Bendigo in Victoria, because of the unusual geological features of these areas, but arrived later at other gold fields. Factors facilitating deep mining were the expertise of Cornish mining captains at Ballarat and Bendigo (Blainey 1993a: 74) and the liberality of Victorian government and mining courts in permitting individuals to accumulate adjoining small claims (Hall 1968: 17).

Deep mining required the co-ordination of labour and capital, encouraging the creation of mining companies or syndicates, which began to appear in Victoria about 1854 (Serle 1977: 73). For instance, by the mid–1850s, syndicates of about twenty-four persons controlled Ballarat deep mining (Salsbury and Sweeney 1988: 25).[12] The Goldfields Commission Report (1855: paragraph 146) observed:

Deep-sinking soon introduced complexities.... The expense and delay of these sinkings rendered necessary a larger number in the co-partnery, for the sake both of larger means and a more effective staff. These undertakings soon assumed the form of companies, with a 'stock', consisting, besides the chance of gold, of some little plant, as slabs, windlass, &c., and divisible into a fixed number of shares. These shares were transferable, and to meet the circumstances of all, were sub-divisible. As the sinking proceeded the stock gradually acquired value, and becoming marketable, was the subject of constant traffic.

The pattern of alluvial mining followed by deep lead mining and company formation experienced in Victoria also prevailed in later gold rushes around Australia.[13] In general, after the 1870s, most gold mining across Australia was conducted by companies (Fitzpatrick 1969: 178). However, the number of gold mining companies in Victoria exceeded those elsewhere in Australia. At the turn of the century, there were 489 gold mining companies in Victoria, a greater number than in any other Australian colony (Table 6.2). At one major centre, Bendigo, at least 829 mining companies operated at various times from the earliest days to the closure of the last mine there in 1954 (Palmer 1976). Gold mining companies were the main source of corporate dividends in Victoria for many years. Table 6.3 shows that dividends from Victorian gold mining companies exceeded dividends of non-mining companies until 1885, often by large margins.[14]

However, most gold mining companies were short-lived ventures with highly variable returns. Some were fraudulently or incompetently run and soon came to grief, but even honestly managed ones were very speculative investments. Butlin (1962: 420)[15] estimated that, for a sample of 200 Australian mining companies between 1856 and 1889, average life expectancy was 3.87 years, subscribed capital was fully called up in 2.7 years on average, and dividend returns ranged from zero to 200 per cent of paid-up capital. For years after 1880, adequate data are available to allow the calculation that the weighted average dividend yield on paid-up capital fluctuated between 9 and 11 per cent.

Gold mining company formation in Victoria during the nineteenth century was punctuated by episodes of boom and speculation in the shares of gold mining companies. The first began in 1859 and focused on 200 companies formed that year and the next – 'the culmination of years of transition' in company formation (Serle 1977: 224, 255). These companies differed from their predecessors in having substantial numbers of non-mining men among their promoters (Serle 1977: 225, Strahan 1955: appendix B). Similar booms occurred in the other colonies.[16]

Table 6.2 Mining companies in Australia, 1902

	New South Wales	Queensland	South Australia	Tasmania	Victoria	Western Australia	Total
No-Liability	70	12	12	31	448	65	638
Other	33	145	6	6	41	246	477
Total	103	157	18	37	489	311	1,115

Source: Nash (1902)

101

Table 6.3 Dividends from public companies in Victoria, 1867–98 (£'000)

| | | Gold mining | | Total | |
	Non-mining	Quartz	Alluvial	mining	Total
1867	288.1	226.0	597.4	823.4	1,111.5
1868	299.3	224.3	572.6	796.9	1,096.3
1869	321.8	295.7	352.4	648.1	970.0
1870	280.7	470.8	232.3	703.1	983.8
1871	281.3	690.3	241.7	932.0	1,213.3
1872	285.1	889.1	180.3	1,069.3	1,354.4
1873	288.7	841.9	119.0	960.8	1,249.5
1874	321.4	807.0	45.0	852.1	1,173.5
1875	351.6	572.3	83.6	655.8	1,007.4
1876–80	1,980.5	2,302.8	429.0	2,731.9	4,712.4
1881–4	2,067.9	2,100.6	953.1	3,053.7	5,121.6
1885	834.8	461.4	326.0	787.4	1,622.2
1886–90	2,592.9	1,569.5	892.2	2,461.8	5,054.7
1891–5	4,885.6	n/a	n/a	2,374.4	7,260.0
1896–8	1,749.7	n/a	n/a	1,483.1	3,232.8

Source: Hall (1968: appendix 4)

Speculation in the shares of mining companies facilitated, and in turn was facilitated by, the development of stock exchanges at mining centres such as at Ballarat (from 1858) (Salsbury and Sweeney 1988: 25) and Bendigo in Victoria. The Ballarat Exchange during the 1860s was more important than the Stock Exchange of Melbourne (formed 1861) (Hall 1968: 59, 107).[17]

REGULATION OF MINING COMPANIES IN VICTORIA

With the discovery of gold, the governments of Victoria and New South Wales were soon faced with the problem of creating a legal framework to regulate the companies being formed by groups of miners. In a break from English law, both colonies passed legislation, in 1853, to extend limited liability to partnerships (Salsbury and Sweeney 1988: 29). Until that legislation, mining ventures could only be formed as ordinary partnerships (with unlimited liability) or incorporated by private Act of Parliament, the latter being beyond the means of small mining ventures.

The Victorian and New South Wales Acts of 1853 distinguished between general and special partners. General partners had unlimited liability, special partners had limited liability (clause 2). The general partners were to account to the special partners for how they had managed the business (clause 13) although no details of how this was to occur were specified.

Special partners could dissolve the partnership if the general partners did not keep 'regular books of account' or if they did not grant the special partners access to those books (clause 15). The special partners were bound to ensure that books of account were kept and, if they were kept incorrectly, contained false or deceptive entries, or were not kept at all, the special partners would have their limited liability privilege removed (clause 16). These partnerships had a life limited to seven years (clause 7). They also had a capital maintenance requirement (clause 9): the 'certified capital' of the partnership could not be withdrawn, and no profit could be distributed which would reduce capital.

These 1853 Acts had close similarities with the Irish Anonymous Partnership Act of 1782 (described in French 1990) (Pyke in *Victorian Hansard*, Legislative Assembly, 29 May 1860: 1237). Like the Irish Act, the Australian legislation seems not to have been a success (Moore 1934: 193; Baxt 1974: 17) – in Victoria only two partnerships were formed under it by 1860 (Pyke in *Victorian Hansard*, Legislative Assembly, 29 May 1860: 1237) – and the Acts were soon overtaken by later legislation.

Victoria thereafter took the lead in enacting mining company legislation. The Goldfields Commission Report (1855), which followed the Eureka Stockade incident, led to Australia's first mining companies' legislation (Hall 1968: 14–15). The Report (paragraph 154) recommended that the cost book system of mining organisation be adopted for the numerous small mining enterprises then in existence in Victoria. It was envisaged that the cost book organisation would be suitable for individual and puddling machine mining (alluvial mining) enterprises which were small and of limited duration (paragraph 153). Each company could be registered for a small fee and it was to keep a book of expenditure and receipts (paragraph 154). Interestingly, the Commission thought that such organisations were 'aided by a legal protection to the association from liabilities which any of the proprietors might contract with the general public' (paragraph 152). If that meant limited liability, the Report was incorrect as the discussion in section 2 showed that the shareholders of British cost book companies actually had unlimited liability.

Haines' Act, 1855

Australia's first mining company legislation, the Victorian Mining Companies Act 1855 (18 Vic. No. 42), known as Haines' Act (after W. C. Haines, then Premier of Victoria (Wright 1992: 244)), reflected the recommendations of the Goldfields Commission Report (1855). The legislation (preamble and section 2) adopted the cost book system of organisation. Mining companies formed under the Act were to have a maximum life of seven years. As in British cost book companies, shares had no par value. Each company's rules were to contain provisions for transfer or relinquishment after payment of all calls (section iii [5]). The company manager was to keep a book showing details of shareholders' names, addresses, shareholdings and share transfers, and a list of shareholders' names and addresses, open for inspection on payment of one shilling, was to be prepared monthly (section iii [6]). The book was also to show 'a debtor and creditor account of all disbursements and receipts of the company and of all sums owing to it or by it' (section iii [6]). Shareholders could inspect the company's book, and managers were to prepare balance sheets and reports every two months for submission to shareholders at company general meetings. There was no audit requirement.

Unlike British cost book companies, shareholders were granted limited liability. Was this a result of the misunderstanding about limited liability in British cost book companies expressed in the Goldfields Commission Report? Clause xi of the Act stated that 'no shareholder ... shall be personally liable for any debt obligation contract or other matter incurred for by or on behalf of any such company beyond the amount subscribed on all calls made'. Here was a major alteration to the British cost book system, although a clumsily drafted one (Salsbury and Sweeney 1988: 35).

The 1855 legislation was not a success. In the words of Mr Ireland (Solicitor-General in the government of John O'Shanassy, March 1858 to October 1859 (Wright 1992: 244)), the legislation had 'the very important defect of over legislation. It required too many preliminaries' (*Victorian Hansard*, Legislative Assembly, 8 May 1858: 442), i.e. extensive administrative machinery to set up a mining company (see also Pyke in *Victorian Hansard*, Legislative Assembly, 15 March 1860: 784; Moore 1934: 193).

As Hall (1968: 15–16) notes, important too was the prevailing political view that claims should be shared among as large a number of diggers as possible. Companies, even those of the cost book type, smacked of capitalism and subservience to a boss, factors which many diggers opposed. Also, most mining companies, even those with deep leads, were then still relatively small ventures which did not require extensive capital, so there was no great demand for complicated legislation like the 1855 Act. Nevertheless, the statute was a harbinger of things to come.

Ireland's Act, 1858

Haines' Act was amended in 1858 (21 Vic. No. 56) to require a compulsory audit where the number of shareholders exceeded twenty, as well as compulsory publication of standardised quarterly accounts, using a model format appended to the Act, in the *Government Gazette* and in one local newspaper if the number of shareholders exceeded fifty. As the 1858 Act, known as Ireland's Act after its proposer, was an amendment to Haines' Act, it too adopted the cost book form of organisation for mining companies. However, Ireland's Act prohibited mining companies from borrowing money, which became an impractical rule (Ireland in *Victorian Hansard*, Legislative Assembly, 12 December 1862: 239). And its drafting created doubt about whether shareholders really had limited liability (Pyke in *Victorian Hansard*, Legislative Assembly, 15 March 1860: 784), a doubt removed by Pyke's Act of 1860 (Hall 1968: 18).

Pyke's Act, 1860

Mining partnerships legislation in Victoria in 1860 (24 Vic. No. 109), known as Pyke's Act (after the Commissioner of Trade and Customs in the government of William Nicholson, October 1859 to November 1860 (Wright 1992: 244)), was similar in general structure to Ireland's Act (Hall 1968: 18). The intention behind the legislation was to create 'facilities for the introduction of capital into mining enterprise, and for the protection of that capital when so introduced' (Pyke in *Victorian Hansard*, Legislative Assembly, 29 May 1860: 1236). However, Pyke's Act differed from Haines' and Ireland's Acts in some important respects. Under Pyke's Act companies would be incorporated. The Act limited the liability of shareholders in the same way as the British Companies Act of 1856 (*Victorian Hansard*, Legislative Assembly, 1 May 1860: 1028; 29 May 1860: 1236). Shares had a stated par value, as in the British Companies Act, but, unlike that Act, had no specified minimum par value (Salsbury and Sweeney 1988: 35).

Pyke's Act required managers of mining companies to publish full and correct half-yearly accounts of assets and liabilities in the *Government Gazette*. However, unlike Ireland's Act, the contents of these accounts were not specified, despite the matter being raised in the Legislative Assembly (*Victorian Hansard*, 12 June 1860: 1307). Nor was an audit required. Proposals to require that mining company managers keep books showing all receipts and expenditure, as well as debts owing to and by the company, these books to be open for inspection by interested parties, were passed in the Legislative Assembly but rejected by the Legislative Council (the Upper House) (*Victorian Hansard*, Legislative Assembly, 12 and 13 June 1860: 1306–7, 1316; 18 July 1860: 1554).

In New South Wales, identical legislation was enacted in 1861 (24 Vic. No. 21) (*Sydney Morning Herald* 16 March 1861, Parliamentary Reports). Salsbury and Sweeney (1988: 36) commented that 'the ease with which companies could be started under this legislation surpassed "democratic" corporation laws passed by Massachusetts and Connecticut and exacerbated the wild mining-company boom-and-bust which New South Wales experienced in the 1870s'. Identical accounting requirements to Pykes' Act appeared in the New South Wales legislation, of which Salsbury and Sweeney (1988: 199) observed: 'The act allowed the kind of balance sheet that many English companies were still providing to their shareholders and the stock exchanges in the 1920s and which led to the famous Royal Mail

Steamship scandal'. Presumably these remarks would also apply to Pyke's Act.[18]

Frazer's Act, 1864

In Victoria, Pyke's Act was accidently repealed in 1864 when that colony enacted its first General Companies Act, based on the British Companies Act of 1862. However, mining interests in Victoria thought the British statute unsuited to mining, and soon agitated for the 1860 Act to be reinstated, which was quickly done via the Victorian Mining Companies Limited Liability Act (27 Vic. No. 228, 1864) (Hall 1968: 43), known as Frazer's Act (after its proposer, a minister in the first government of James McCulloch, June 1863 to May 1868 (Wright 1992: 244)).

Frazer's Act was a continuation and refinement of Pyke's Act (Hall 1968: 43). As well as granting limited liability to shareholders (clause 3), mining companies were to be incorporated (clause 12). Frazer's Act (clauses 18–19) required managers to keep books of account which could be inspected by shareholders, a provision not in Pyke's Act, and required publication of half-yearly accounts of assets and liabilities in the *Government Gazette* (clause 17). There was still no audit requirement, nor was the form of accounts specified, and the compulsory accounting rules could be altered by majority decision of shareholders. The legislation was also adopted in Tasmania from 1864 to 1884 (Morris and Barbera: 1990), but not in other colonies.

After 1864, several anomalies arose in the operation of Frazer's Act. First, in response to a growing tendency for non-payment of mining companies' calls, the forfeit of shares had become a widespread industry practice by the late 1860s (Hall 1968: 76). This was a perfectly reasonable market response. However, the Sandhurst (Bendigo) Court of Mines in *Nolan vs Annabella Company* in 1869 decided that share forfeiture was inconsistent with the 1864 Mining Companies Limited Liability Act. The decision greatly disturbed the mining community (Hall 1968: 76) and led to pressure for Parliament to reverse the decision by amending Frazer's Act.

Second, the limited liability provisions in Frazer's Act had become subverted by the practice of 'dummyism', whereby shares in mining companies were held in the names of fictitious persons. If companies' fortunes were good, calls would be paid, but if bad they would not, and attempts to sue the dummies would be useless. Honest shareholders then had to bear a disproportionate share of these companies' debts, so that for them, mining companies' shares could be riskier investments than the mines themselves (Blainey 1993a: 95–6). Creditors could not rely on companies' uncalled capital to reduce their risks in lending to mining companies. Dummyism represented a breakdown in the bureaucratic machinery used to enforce Frazer's Act – the inability to verify the accuracy of companies' share registers (McQueen 1991: 66). Data on the extent of dummyism in the 1860s are not available. However, its inequities were frequently mentioned in Parliament as attempts were made to reform Frazer's Act (see *Victorian Hansard*, Legislative Assembly, 11 May 1871: 143; 19 May 1871: 279, 292, 294).

Third, winding-up provisions had become inefficient. Frazer's Act required the appointment of a mine agent as liquidator, but experience showed that these agents' fees plus legal fees absorbed much of the funds obtained in making calls on shareholders (the latter already reduced by dummyism) leaving little to pay creditors. For example, it was reported to Parliament that in the case of 114 mining company windings-up, £10,392 was recovered from shareholders, of which only £4,335, less than half, went to creditors after all legal and agents' fees had been paid (*Victorian Hansard*, Legislative Assembly, 11 May 1871: 144).

THE NO-LIABILITY SYSTEM

After three Bills, extensive debate in both Houses of Parliament, examination by a Select Committee, and a change of government,[19] the Victorian Parliament passed the Mining Companies Act of 1871 (35 Vic. No. 409) which replaced Frazer's Act. The 1871 Act created no-liability mining companies.[20] As already mentioned, the key feature of such companies is that shareholders' liability to pay calls on shares was removed, once the initial purchase sum had been paid (clause 117). Shares were to be forfeited for non-payment of calls, sold at public auction and any surplus resulting from the sale, after allowing for the unpaid calls, returned to the forfeiting shareholders (clause 118 [v]). In the third Bill, a proposal that no-liability companies were to have two-thirds of their capital paid up at incorporation was reduced by the Legislative Council to the requirement in the Act (clause 118 [i]) that 5 per cent be initially paid up (*Victorian Hansard*, Legislative Council, 8 November 1871: 1777). Directors could only pay dividends out of profits, arising from the business of the company,[21] although the term 'profits' was not defined, and heavy financial penalties or a prison term awaited those who wilfully violated this requirement (clause 49). No dividends could be paid on shares on which calls were unpaid (clause 117). The words 'No Liability' were to be added to the name of each such company registered under the Act (clause 118 [iii]).

The reforms in the 1871 Act had several attractions. Since no liability for calls attached to a share, all investors were placed on an equal footing and the incentive for dummyism disappeared. The no-liability system also facilitated efficient transfers of shares: brokers and investors were no longer faced with the problem, common during speculative booms, of share sales being made with new holders later discovering they were liable to pay calls in arrears owed by previous holders (Salsbury and Sweeney 1988: 145). The

1871 Act codified industry practice on share forfeiture for non-payment of calls. The 1871 Act also reformed winding-up procedures by having the mine agent appointed by the courts. However, whether this increased the net payouts to creditors is doubtful, since the no-liability system meant that smaller amounts were received from calls on shareholders.

The 1871 Act contained accounting requirements. Managers were to keep true accounts of their companies' affairs and transactions (clause 36). The third Bill had the Governor-in-Council specifying the form of these books (*Victorian Hansard*, Legislative Assembly, 24 October 1871: 1650), one member noting that the requirement was desirable 'in order that a uniform system of keeping accounts should be adopted by all mining companies' (Vale in *Victorian Hansard*, Legislative Assembly, 24 October 1871: 1650). However, this role for the Governor-in-Council was dropped later by the Legislative Council (*Victorian Hansard*, Legislative Council, 7 November 1871: 1761). Directors were to prepare half-yearly statements of accounts and a report, but there was no compulsory audit.

Shareholders and creditors could inspect books of account, half-yearly statements and reports before companies' general meetings (cost one shilling) (clauses 25, 38), or they could purchase a copy of the accounts covering the previous three months (cost 10 shillings) (clause 39). Companies could adopt the optional disclosure rules in schedule 7 of the Act (clause 132), which stipulated the tabling of quarterly balance sheets at shareholders' meetings and publication of half-yearly balance sheets in the *Government Gazette*.

Unlike Ireland's, Pyke's and Frazer's Acts, there was no compulsory disclosure of accounts in the *Government Gazette*. In introducing the second Bill, the new Attorney General, R. Walsh, noted that:

> in practice, the former half-yearly balance sheets have been perfectly useless. The old plan of advertising the value of the claim, plant, and machinery at £20,000 or £30,000 ... has been found completely valueless. I propose, under this Bill, to compel the preparation of a proper balance-sheet, from examination of which any man of business may be able at once to ascertain the exact financial position in which the company is.
>
> (*Victorian Hansard*, Legislative Assembly, 17 August 1871: 917–18).

Walsh originally intended that these balance sheets be published half-yearly in 'one Melbourne and two country newspapers' (p. 918), but was influenced by the heavy cost of publication on small mining companies to modify his proposal so that the accounts, verified by the mine manager, were to be 'lodged with the clerk of the Court of Mines nearest to the office of the company' and open for inspection by shareholders and creditors on payment of one shilling (p. 918). Walsh's proposals were changed as his Bill passed through Parliament so that printed copies of each Directors' Statement were to be filed with the Victorian Registrar-General who had the power (not exercised until 1902) to specify its format (section 37).[22]

The above accounting requirements in the no-liability legislation were more demanding than those of the Companies Act of 1864 in Victoria, or the British Companies Act of 1862, Similar requirements were not enacted for companies in general until 1896 in Victoria and well into the twentieth century in other states. There were also penalties for various omissions and misstatements in relation to keeping accounts and other records (sections 133–42). These, plus the penalty for wrongly paying dividends, were also in advance of those in the contemporary general company law of the UK or Australia (Waugh 1992: 380).

Subsequent adoption of the no-liability system

The no-liability system was immediately popular among Victorian mining companies. Despite the experimental nature of the legislation, its success in Victoria led all the other Australian colonies and New Zealand to adopt similar mining company legislation within twenty years. In 1889, the Melbourne Stock Exchange refused to list any mining company (other than coal) not registered under the No Liability Act (Hall 1968: 194–5). A similar rule was passed by the Sydney Stock Exchange (Salsbury and Sweeney 1988: 146). By the turn of the century, no-liability mining companies were to be found across Australia, as shown in Table 6.2, but were most popular in Victoria. The diffusion of the no-liability system from Victoria to other parts of Australasia is the subject of ongoing research.

ANALYSIS

The no-liability mining company evolved in Victoria from the British cost book company in a process that began with Cornish miners bringing the cost book system to Australia, continued with the Goldfields Commission Report, Haines', Ireland's, Pyke's and Frazer's Acts, and culminated in the Mining Companies Act of 1871 with subsequent rapid adoption of the no-liability system in practice.

There are four striking differences between regulation of the no-liability mining company and its predecessors in Victoria on the one hand and regulation of the British cost book company on the other. First is the exclusive use made of statutory regulation in Victoria versus its relatively limited use in the UK.

Second, in Victoria, a concerted effort was made to reduce the liability of shareholders, resulting in creation of the no-liability system. In the UK, cost book company shareholders faced unlimited liability, although there were some market-based attempts to restrict it.

Third, the no-liability mining companies, their predecessors in Victoria, and British cost book companies had accounting requirements in advance of those in the general company law in Victoria before 1896 and in the UK before 1929. However, British cost book companies' rules arose partly from custom, partly from Stannaries Courts' decisions and partly from the Stannaries Acts. It may fairly be said that the Stannaries Acts imposed fewer new accounting regulations than were imposed by custom or by Stannaries Courts' decisions. Moreover, mining company legislation in Victoria from 1858 required compulsory publication of accounts in the *Government Gazette* or their lodgement with the Registrar-General. In the UK, compulsory publication of cost book companies' accounts did not occur until 1887. No-liability mining companies in Victoria had statutory penalties for misstatements and for wrongly paying dividends, British cost book companies had none.

Fourth, the no-liability mining company was very popular in Victoria and remained so into the present century. In contrast, the popularity of the cost book company in the UK fell sharply at the end of the nineteenth century, with British mining companies reorganising as limited liability companies.

Whether these four differences can be explained by Parker's (1990) model will now be considered.

Establishing and enforcing the law

Some attempts to regulate mining companies by statute in Victoria and in the UK are examples of Crouch's (1967) 'establishing and enforcing the law'. British cost book companies were already regulated by the customs[23] of centuries and by the decisions of the Stannaries Courts. The Stannaries Act of 1869 largely revised and streamlined existing rules for cost book companies to bring them into line with legislation for incorporated companies (Pennington 1973: 65). In contrast, Australian mining companies, and mining generally, began in an unregulated setting. Although Cornish miners brought their customs, including the cost book company, to Australia with them, in Victoria during the 1850s these customs would not have been well established, and there was no equivalent of the Stannaries Courts. The Goldfields Commission Report (1855) recommended the cost book system as a means of forming mining companies, and also recommended the establishment of mining courts.

Parker (1990) did not include establishing and enforcing the law in his model, as it was not relevant for his purpose. Nevertheless, his model, being derived from Crouch (1967), is consistent with establishing and enforcing the law.

Physical and financial safety

However, establishing and enforcing the law is not a necessary and sufficient reason for the regulation of mining companies and their accounts. The early general Companies Acts in the UK and Australia also established and enforced the law (such as it was), yet these Acts left accounting and auditing unregulated, and did not permit the no-liability system. Something more is needed to explain the differences in the regulation of Australian and British mining companies, which I argue is Parker's factor of 'physical and financial safety'. I will discuss the factor under the headings of physical safety, externalities and establishing a stable monetary framework.

Physical safety

In the UK, the Stannaries Act of 1887 followed the Report of a Parliamentary Select Committee (BPP 1887). The Committee primarily investigated problems of miners' health and safety, and it recommended improvements in the system of miners' provident funds. The accounting reforms included in the Stannaries Act of 1887 can be seen as a secondary benefit arising out of concerns with miners' physical safety evident in the Select Committee's proceedings.

In Victoria, Haines' Act of 1855 arose from the recommendations of the Goldfields Commission Report (1855) which in turn had been a response to the Eureka Stockade incident. The Victorian Parliament was concerned that civil unrest on the gold fields should cease. A simple and efficient way of forming mining companies – the cost book system – was part of the proposals to achieve that goal (Goldfields Commission Report, 1855, paragraphs 146–55). However, later mining company legislation in Victoria was not directly aimed at curbing civil unrest.

Externalities

As previously stated, the discovery of gold led to a massive wave of migration to Australia, which was at its peak in Victoria during the 1850s and 1860s (Butlin 1964: 27; Serle 1977: appendix 2). Many immigrants went straight to the gold fields but others took up less adventurous pursuits in the cities and towns. Because of its large economic impact, gold mining also had substantial multiplier effects not only on the gold fields but also in the main cities. Table 6.1, column 6, shows mining production – in which Victorian gold predominated – as a percentage of Australian gross domestic product in five-year subperiods from 1851 to 1899; while column 7 shows the rank of the mining sector in each subperiod. From 1851 to 1854, mining contributed almost one-quarter of Australia's gross domestic product. Thereafter, the contribution of mining slowly declined to 9.1 per cent of gross domestic product in the early 1870s, and to less than 5 per cent during the 1880s, with a small revival in the 1890s from gold discoveries in Western Australia. Mining ranked in the top three sectors of the Australian economy from 1851 to 1869. After 1870, mining was always just above or just below middle ranking in the thirteen economic categories making up Australia's gross domestic product. As mentioned above, gold mining companies were the main source of dividends from Victorian public companies until 1885, and remained an important source thereafter (Table 6.3).

Although British mining output was more valuable absolutely than Australian mining output, mining was *relatively* less important to the British economy than to the Australian. Table 6.4 shows British mining output – of which mining in Devon and Cornwall was only a part – as a percentage of gross domestic product at five-yearly intervals from 1855 to 1900. Except in 1900, mining output fluctuated around 5 per cent of gross domestic product. The shares of British mining companies – including mines outside Devon and Cornwall – made up less than 1 per cent of the nominal value of shares quoted on the British stock exchanges at each ten-yearly interval from 1853 to 1903 (Morgan and Thomas 1962: table V).

Crouch (1967) describes how substantial positive externalities arising from risky investments were seen by classical economists such as Adam Smith as grounds for granting concessions, such as monopoly rights for an overseas trading venture, to those making the investments. Similarly, with Australian gold mining, the prospect of substantial benefits to a fledgling economy would have been a powerful incentive to provide relief from liability to shareholders and to provide information via accounting reports to reduce risk, in order to encourage investment in the industry. The incentive was not

Table 6.4 Mining output and gross domestic product in the UK 1855–1900

	Gross domestic product (at factor cost) (£m)	Mining output (current prices) (£m)	%
1855	707	30	4.2
1860	761	34	4.5
1865	975	41	4.2
1870	1,079	46	4.3
1875	1,236	65	5.3
1880	1,297	84	6.5
1885	1,228	60	4.9
1890	1,373	101	7.4
1895	1,439	77	5.4
1900	1,794	161	9.0

Sources: Gross domestic product: Mitchell (1988: 832–3);
mining output: HMSO (1867, 1884, 1886, 1901)

as powerful for British mining. Table 6.3 shows that dividends from Victorian alluvial mining companies were supplanted by dividends from quartz (i.e. deep) mining companies during the 1870s. Quartz mining required much more capital than alluvial mining, and initiatives such as the no-liability company would have encouraged such investment.

Establishing a stable monetary framework

A key feature distinguishing Australian from British mining during the nineteenth century was that Australian mining was predominately for gold. At the time, both countries were on the gold standard, so that major gold discoveries would have effects on Australia's balance of payments. Most Australian gold was sold in the UK. Columns 8 and 9 of Table 6.1 show gold production (the majority of which was from Victoria) as a percentage of Australian exports from 1861 to 1900 and its rank as an export. Gold was Australia's most important export until 1870, replaced thereafter by wool, and remained the second most important export to the end of the century. Gold made up more than 40 per cent of Australian exports during the 1860s, and although the percentage slowly declined after that, it still had a substantial impact on exports. During the 1890s, there was a resurgence in gold exports due to the discoveries in Western Australia, so that in 1899 gold made up 26 per cent of total exports.

Gold's importance as an export was two-fold. Because of the gold standard, gold fetched a stable price per ounce, so that it produced a less variable stream of export earnings than wool, provided that gold supply could be maintained. Second, the abundance of gold exports meant that the Australian colonies could sustain imports of consumption and investment goods at levels impossible before the gold discoveries.

Therefore, because of the impact of gold production on the monetary framework of Victoria, it is understandable that the Victorian government was anxious to regulate the gold mining industry and to encourage investment to maintain gold production. Their attempts to limit shareholders' liability and to provide compulsory accounting disclosures are consistent with these objectives.

Conclusions on physical and financial safety

The reduction of shareholders' liability in Victorian mining companies was a 'privilege granted by the state' but flowed as a consequence of 'physical and financial safety'. That is, limited liability and no liability for Victorian mining companies do not seem to be privileges for which the government extracted a price – that of having their accounts compulsorily disclosed – as was the case with British railway and gas companies (Morris 1993: 166). Rather, liability reduction and compulsory disclosure are better thought of as complementary devices both promoting investment in gold mining. The same may be said of the various penalties included in the 1871 no-liability legislation.

Finally, the popularity of the no-liability system among Victorian mining companies after 1871 in contrast with the demise of the cost book company in the UK at the turn of the century appears to be linked to the retention of shareholder liability in the British cost book company and its abolition in the no-liability company. Creation of the no-liability company was associated with Parker's physical and financial safety factor. However, other issues are also relevant. From the earliest days, shareholders in Victorian gold mining companies tended to be local miners, speculators or citizens of Melbourne, sometimes small businessmen (Blainey 1993a: 94–5). Relatively little British capital was invested in Australian mining until the late 1880s (Blainey 1993a: 97) after which British capital went mainly into Queensland and Western Australian gold mining (Lougheed 1983, 1990; McCarty 1961–2; Appleyard and Davies 1988). The widespread practice in Australia of issuing mining shares partly paid, when coupled with no-liability, made investment in mining companies more affordable and attractive to small investors, as the shares were paid for in instalments. Capital sums raised by Victorian mining companies typically were not large in comparison, say, with those required to fund banking, railway or gas companies. Indeed the combination of the no-liability system and partly paid shares was criticised because it acted as a disincentive to raising large capital sums (De Lissa 1894: 193–4). No liability, small local investors, modest capital raisings, and partly paid shares made the no-liability mining company popular in Victoria.

In contrast, the cost book company in the UK was not favoured by the London capital market as an adequate vehicle for Cornish mines because, by the 1890s, the riskiness in Cornish mining had increased sharply, the sums required for exploration had risen steeply, and shareholders' liability was still unlimited. Because of the increased risk, investors demanded limited liability and got it by market processes rather than by statutory regulation since physical and financial safety issues were not as compelling in Cornish mines after the 1880s as they were in Victorian gold mines to 1871.

So, Parker's model provides some, but not a complete, insight into the differing degree of popularity of British cost book companies and Victorian no-liability mining companies.

Having evaluated the significance of Parker's model, a number of alternative explanations for the differing regulation of British cost book mining companies and Victorian mining companies are now considered.

Agency theory

Could the Stannaries Acts of 1868 and 1889 in the UK and the Mining Companies Acts in Victoria have been intended to reduce agency costs arising from conflicts of interests between mining company managements and outside shareholders? For regulations to reduce agency costs, they would tend to codify market-determined practices.

In the UK, streamlining existing customs and case law in the Stannaries Acts might codify agency-cost-reducing arrangements. Also, the agency problems of 'in adventurers' versus 'out adventurers' in British cost book companies were mentioned earlier. These problems increased when Cornish mining companies tried to raise capital in London and led to a market solution – the abandonment of the cost book company and its replacement by the limited liability company.

In Victoria from the late 1850s, shareholdings in mining companies were widespread, suggesting the presence of agency problems. It is likely that some provisions of the early Mining Companies Acts codified market-determined practices, such as requiring companies to keep books of account. However, it is difficult to accept that the compulsory disclosure in the *Government Gazette* or lodgement of accounts with the Registrar-General were market-based solutions. Moreover, all the Victorian statutes attempted (with varying success) to reduce shareholders' liability, at a time when the prevailing private contracting model was the cost book company in which shareholders' liability was unlimited.

Therefore, agency theory does not provide a satisfactory explanation of regulation for Victorian mining companies, although it may with British cost book companies. Since Parker's model explains the differing regulations in both countries, it is preferred on grounds of parsimony.

Investor protection

In Parker's model, investor protection is secondary to the factors of monopoly, privileges granted by the state and physical and financial safety. An alternative explanation is that investor protection was the primary aim of regulating mining companies. Investor protection is an imprecise term, which could mean codifying the provisions of private contracting arrangements between companies and their shareholders, or reducing the risk of investing in mining companies. As the former has already been covered under agency theory, the latter only will be considered here. Mining company legislation in Victoria did reduce shareholders' liability because of the riskiness of mining, so perhaps investor protection was its primary objective. However, mining company legislation followed the discovery of gold but not of other minerals or coal. Parliamentary debates during the passage of Victorian Mining Companies Bills referred almost exclusively to gold and not other mining. In contrast, industries such as wool and other agricultural endeavours involved risk because of Australia's climate, yet these were not regulated as gold mining was. And in the UK, the regulation of Cornish mining did not increase at the end of the nineteenth century when its riskiness increased. Therefore, investor protection as a primary goal does not satisfactorily explain the regulation of mining companies in either country.

Regulatory capture

The capture theory of regulation asserts that regulations are provided to serve the interests of the industry regulated, so that the industry 'captures' the regulator. The Stannaries Act of 1867 in the UK and Frazer's Act of 1864 in Victoria resulted from mining industry pressure (Pennington 1973: 65; Hall 1968: 43). The no-liability legislation of 1871 arose partly from mining industry pressure to overturn the *Nolan vs Anabella* case. However, it is less clear that the other British and Victorian legislation arose directly from mining industry pressure. It is also unclear whether the mining industry got what it wanted in these other Mining Companies Acts. Therefore, the capture theory appears not to be a satisfactory explanation of mining company regulation.

CONCLUSION

It seems that Parker's factor of physical and financial safety coupled with Crouch's factor of establishing and enforcing the law (with which Parker's model is consistent) can be used to explain the statutory regulation of British cost book mining companies and the no-liability mining company and its predecessors in Victoria during the nineteenth century. Agency theory, investor protection and the capture theory do not. Parker's model provides an incomplete explanation of the popularity of the no-liability mining company in Victoria and the demise of the cost book company in the UK in the late nineteenth century. Whether Parker's model can explain the diffusion of the no-liability company from Victoria across Australia and New Zealand after 1871 is an interesting matter for future research.

NOTES

* Funding for this research was provided by a UNSW Faculty of Commerce and Economics special research grant. The research assistance of Eva Law is gratefully acknowledged. Research on British cost book companies was conducted while the author was on a Special Studies Programme at the University of Exeter, November 1992–January 1993.

1 Apart from a short-lived extension to trading companies in the Victorian Companies Act of 1896, the no-liability system has only applied to mining companies.

2 I thank my colleague A. E. F. Rofe, a member of the Corporations Law Simplification Programme Committee, for this information.

3 Some evidence of mining companies' disclosure practices in nineteenth-century Australia appears in Morris (1984).

4 Samuel Downing, a witness before the Select Committee, was a barrister,

resident in Cornwall, who had over thirty years of experience of the Stannaries Court.

5 William Rich, a witness before the Select Committee of 1887, was a mine agent of Redruth, Cornwall.

6 Ownership of mineral lands in Devon and Cornwall rested with landlords who granted mining rights or setts to miners, who, in turn, formed mining companies to work them (Pennington 1973: 111).

7 See Blainey (1993a: ch. 3) and Lloyd (1978, 1982).

8 Blainey (1970) argued that major mineral discoveries in nineteenth-century Australia were not random events, but rather were more likely when the price (e.g. of gold) was *relatively* high, the economic cycle in a trough, unemployment high and interest rates low. Blainey's theory sparked a controversy among economic historians (see Morrissey and Burt 1973; Blainey 1973; Davies 1985; Mathews 1990).

9 Australian gold production was also large by international standards. After 1851, Victoria kept pace with Californian gold production (Castles 1982: 466). In one year during the period 1898–1907, Australia's annual total gold output exceeded that of South Africa, which was generally the world leader (Blainey 1995).

10 Victoria was the prime destination for emigrant Cornish miners during the 1850s, replacing South Australia and California (Payton 1984: 117).

11 Victoria had been granted self-government in 1851.

12 Deep mining also meant that many diggers were forced to work for a mining syndicate. Resentment among diggers at their loss of independence was somewhat mollified by introduction of the Cornish tribute system of payment which allowed diggers to retain a little of their former independence (Payton 1984: 129).

13 In New South Wales, extensive formation of mining companies occurred in the 1870s (Salsbury and Sweeney 1988: 75). At Gympie, in Queensland, company formation occurred in 1868, one year after the discovery of gold there, as deep gold deposits were found requiring more funds than were available to individual miners: seventeen of the twenty companies registered in Queensland that year were for gold mining and/or quartz crushing in Gympie and Rockhampton (Lougheed 1984a: 11). At gold mining sites in the Northern Territory fifty companies held claims by early 1873 (Lockwood 1984: 65). At Kalgoolie, in Western Australia, company formation followed almost immediately gold was discovered in the early 1890s (Blainey 1993b: 13–14).

14 Indeed, the rate of company formation in industries other than mining was very slow in Australia until the 1880s because of the comparatively small-scale nature of Australian manufacturing firms, and the public ownership of capital-intensive industries such as railways (McQueen 1991: 65). Some firms of reasonable size, such as gas, shipping and banking companies, were incorporated by private Acts of Parliament (Morris 1984).

15 It is unclear how many of Butlin's companies came from Victoria, although probably most did, given the large numbers of mining companies in that colony.

16 For example, the first gold mining company boom in New South Wales centred on Hill End and Hawkins Hill during the 1870s; in just one year, 1872, 589 gold mining companies were formed (Salsbury and Sweeney 1988: 76). Other examples are the boom in Gympie gold mining shares in Queensland during 1881 in which 114 companies were floated (Lougheed 1984b),

and the boom in Kalgoorlie mining shares on the London Stock Exchange in the 1890s during which over 700 companies were floated (Lougheed 1990).

17 Similarly, stock exchanges operated in Sydney (from 1871), at mining centres such as Broken Hill (1888–9), Silverton and Hillgrove (Morris 1984: 61) in New South Wales; at Brisbane (1883), Gympie (1884) and Charters Towers (1885) in Queensland (Lougheed 1984a: 20, 27); and at Kalgoorlie and Coolgardie (1890s) in Western Australia (Blainey 1993b: 30).

18 Morris (1984: 79–81) details the poor quality of accounting disclosures in the New South Wales *Government Gazette* by companies registered under the New South Wales legislation of 1861.

19 James McCulloch's second government was replaced by that of C. G. Duffy in June 1871 (Wright 1992: 244).

20 The Act also created the prepayment company, in which mining ventures would estimate expenditure for a month ahead, call capital to that amount and spend the money on the proposed works. This system did not prove popular in Australia. Initially, while the three Bills were going through Parliament, no-liability companies were called share-warrant companies, but this title was soon discarded.

21 This was very similar to clause 73 of Table A in the British Companies Act of 1862, and to a comparable requirement in Table A of the Victorian Companies Act of 1864.

22 Originally, the Governor-in-Council was to have this power, but the proposal was rejected by the Legislative Council (*Victorian Hansard*, Legislative Council, 8 November 1871: 1776). In 1902, the Victorian Registrar-General specified that half-yearly accounts of no-liability mining companies in that state were to consist of a balance sheet, statement of receipts and disbursements, and a profit and loss account (Godden and Robertson 1902: appendix B).

23 Some might argue that rules deriving from custom are not regulations because they are self-imposed. If so, then cost book companies' regulations came only from Stannaries Courts' decisions and from the Stannaries Acts.

REFERENCES

Appleyard, R. T. and Davies, M. (1988) 'Financiers of Western Australia's goldfields', in R. T. Appleyard and C. B. Schedvin (eds) *Australian Financiers: Biographical Essays*, Melbourne: Macmillan, ch. 8.

Australian Securities Commission *Annual Report 1993/94*.

Barton, D. B. (1968) 'Cornishmen and Australian copper', in D. B. Barton (ed.) *Essays in Cornish Mining History*, vol. 1, Truro: D. Bradford Barton.

Baxt, R. (1974) *Second Australian Supplement to the Third Edition of Gower's Modern Company Law*, Sydney: Law Book Company.

Blainey, G. (1970) 'A theory of mineral discovery: Australia in the nineteenth century', *Economic History Review*, 2nd series, vol. 23.

—— (1973) 'A rejoinder', *Economic History Review*, 2nd series, vol. 26.

—— (1993a) *The Rush That Never Ended: A History of Australian Mining*, 4th edition, Melbourne University Press.

—— (1993b) *The Golden Mile*, St Leonards, NSW: Allen & Unwin.

—— (1995) 'The 1850s were Australia's richest era of gold', Myth 4 of 'The twelve great myths of Australian history', *Sydney Morning Herald* 10 June.

British Parliamentary Papers (BPP) (1887) *Special Report and Reports from the*

Select Committee on Stannaries Act (1869) Amendment Bill; Together with Proceedings of the Committee, Minutes of Evidence, and Appendix, July.

Burke, G. and Richardson, P. (1981) 'The decline and fall of the cost book system in the Cornish tin mining industry, 1895–1914', *Business History* March.

—— (1983) "The adaptability of the Cornish cost book system", a response, *Business History* July.

Burt, R. (1984) *The British Lead Mining Industry*, Redruth: Dyllansow Truran.

Burt, R. and Kudo, N. (1983) 'The adaptability of the Cornish cost book system', *Business History* March.

Burt, R., Waite, P. and Burnley, R. (1984) *Devon and Somerset Mines: Metalliferous and Associated Minerals 1845–1913*, University of Exeter.

—— (1987) *Cornish Mines: Metalliferous and Associated Minerals 1845–1913*, University of Exeter.

Butlin, N. G. (1962) *Australian Domestic Product, Investment and Foreign Borrowing 1861–1938/39*, Cambridge University Press.

—— (1964) *Investment in Australian Economic Development 1861–1900*, Cambridge University Press.

—— (1987) 'Australian national accounts', in W. Vamplew (ed.) *Australians: Historical Statistics*, Broadway, NSW: Fairfax, Syme & Weldon Associates, ch 8.

Castles, A. C. (1982) *An Australian Legal History*, Sydney: Law Book Company.

Crouch, R. L. (1967) 'Laissez-faire in nineteenth century Britain: myth or reality?', *Manchester School* September.

Davies, M. (1985) 'Blainey revisited: mineral discovery and the business cycle in South Australia', *Australian Economic History Review* 25 (2).

De Lissa, A. (1894) *Companies' Work and Mining Law in New South Wales and Victoria*, Sydney: George Robertson.

Fitzpatrick, B. (1969) *The British Empire in Australia 1834–1939*, London: Macmillan.

Ford, H. A. J. (1986) *Principles of Company Law*, 4th edition, London: Butterworths.

French, E. A. (1990) 'The origin of general limited liability in the United Kingdom', *Accounting and Business Research* Winter.

Godden, D. and Robertson, W. N. (1902) *Australian Mining Companies' Accounts*, London: Gee.

Goldfields Commission Report (1855) *Report From the Commission Appointed to Inquire into the Condition of the Goldfields*, 1978; reprinted by Red Rooster Press, Melbourne.

Hall, A. R. (1968) *The Stock Exchange of Melbourne and the Victorian Economy 1852–1900*, Australian National University Press.

Her Majesty's Stationery Office (1867) *Statistical Abstract for the United Kingdom in each of the Last Fifteen Years from 1852 to 1866*, fourteenth number, London: HMSO.

—— (1884) *Statistical Abstract for the United Kingdom in each of the Last Fifteen Years from 1869 to 1883*, thirty-first number, London: HMSO.

—— (1886) *Statistical Abstract for the United Kingdom in each of the Last Fifteen Years from 1871 to 1885*, thirty-third number, London: HMSO.

—— (1901) *Statistical Abstract for the United Kingdom in each of the Last Fifteen Years from 1886 to 1900*, forty-eighth number, London: HMSO.

Hodge, H. (1974) *The Hill End Story – Book 2*, 2nd revised edition, Forestville, NSW: Hill End.

Jackson, R. V. (1977) *Australian Economic Development in the Nineteenth Century*, Australian National University Press.

Jones, S. (1995) 'A cross-sectional analysis of recommendations for company financial disclosures and auditing by nineteenth-century parliamentary witnesses', *Accounting, Business and Financial History* 5: September.

La Croix, S. J. (1992) 'Property rights and institutional change during Australia's gold rush', *Explorations in Economic History* 29.

Leifchild, J. R. (1857) *Cornwall: Its Mines and Miners*, London: Longman, Brown, Green, Longmans, and Roberts; Reprinted by Frank Cass, London, 1968.

Lewis, G. R. (1924) *The Stannaries: A Study of the English Tin Miner*, Harvard University Press.

Lloyd, B. (1978) *Gold at the Ten Mile: The Jamieson Goldfield*, Wangaratta: Shoestring Bookshop.

—— (1982) *Gold at Harrietville*, Wangaratta: Shoestring Press.

Lockwood, D. (1984) *The Front Door: Darwin 1869–1969*, Adelaide: Rigby.

Lougheed, A. L. (1983) 'British company formation and the Queensland mining industry, 1886–1890, *Business History* March.

—— (1984a) *The Brisbane Stock Exchange 1884–1984*, Brisbane: Boolarong Publications.

—— (1984b) 'The first major share market boom in Queensland – Gympie, 1881', University of Queensland, Department of Economics Working Paper no. 46.

—— (1987) 'International transactions and foreign commerce', in W. Vamplew (ed.) *Australians: Historical Statistics*, Broadway, NSW: Fairfax, Syme & Weldon Associates, ch. 11.

—— (1990) 'The London Stock Exchange boom in Kalgoorlie shares, 1895–1900', University of Queensland, Department of Economics Discussion Paper no. 41.

Maddock, R. and McLean, I. (1984) 'Supply-side shocks: the case of Australian gold', *Journal of Economic History* 44(4).

Mathews, D. (1990) 'Serendipity or economics? Tin and the theory of mineral discovery, 1800–1920', *Business History* July.

McCarty, J. W. (1961–2) 'British investment in Western Australian gold mining, 1894–1914', *University Studies in History* 4(1).

McIlraith, J. R. (1903) 'Cost-book companies', in G. Lisle (ed.) *Encyclopaedia of Accounting*, vol.2, Edinburgh: William Green.

McQueen, R. (1991) 'Limited liability company legislation: the Australian experience 1864–1920', in S. Corcoran (ed.) *Law and History in Australia*, Adelaide Law Review Association.

Mitchell, B. R. (1988) *British Historical Statistics*, Cambridge University Press.

Moore, W. H. (1934) 'A century of Victorian law', *Journal of Comparative Legislation and International Law*, series 3, vol. 16.

Morgan, E. V. and Thomas, W. A. (1962) *The Stock Exchange: its history and functions*, London: Elek.

Morris, R. D. (1984) 'Corporate disclosure in a substantially unregulated environment', *Abacus* June.

Morris, R. D. (1993) 'Distributable profit in nineteenth-century British regulated industries', *Accounting, Business and Financial History* 3(2).

Morris, R. D. and Barbera, M. R. (1990) 'A Chronology of the development of corporate financial reporting in Australia 1817 to 1988', in R. H. Parker (ed.) *Accounting in Australia: Historical Essays*, New York: Garland.

Morrisey, M. J. and Burt, R. (1973) 'A theory of mineral discovery: a note', *Economic History Review* 2nd series, vol. 26.

Morrison, T. A. (1980) *Cornwall's Central Mines: The Northern District 1810–1895*, Penzance: Alison Hodge.

Nash, R. L. (1902) *Australasian Joint Stock Companies Year-Book*, Sydney: R. L. Nash.

Neimark, M. and Tinker, T. (1988) 'The social transformation of accounting practice: from cost book to joint stock company recording in the Cornish tin mining industry'. Revised version of paper in *Proceedings of the Second International Conference on Interdisciplinary Perspectives in Accounting, Manchester, July*, vol. 3.

Palmer, A. V. (1976) *The Gold Mines of Bendigo*, Hawthorn, Victoria, Craftsman Press.

Parker, R. H. (1990) 'Regulating British corporate financial reporting in the late nineteenth century', *Accounting Business and Financial History* 1(1).

Payton, P. J. (1984) *The Cornish Miner in Australia (Cousin Jack Down Under)*, Redruth: Dyllansow Truran.

Pennington, R. R. (1973) *Stannary Law: A History of the Mining Law of Cornwall and Devon*, Newton Abbot: David & Charles.

Saddler, H. (1987) 'Minerals and energy', in W. Vamplew (ed.) *Australians: Historical Statistics*, Broadway, NSW: Fairfax, Syme & Weldon Associates, ch 6.

Salsbury, S. and Sweeney, K. (1988) *The Bull, the Bear and the Kangaroo: The History of the Sydney Stock Exchange*, Sydney: Allen & Unwin.

Serle, G. (1977) *The Golden Age: A History of the Colony of Victoria 1851–1861*, Melbourne University Press.

Strahan, F. (1955) 'The growth and extent of company mining on the Victorian goldfields in the 1850s', Unpublished Honours Thesis, University of Melbourne.

Tapping, T. (1867) 'The principles of the cost-book system practically considered', *Mining Journal, Railway and Commercial Gazette*.

Waugh, J. (1992) 'Company law and the crash of the 1890s in Victoria', *University of New South Wales Law Journal* 15(1).

Williams, R. H. (1891) 'Cornish mining and the cost book principle', *The Accountant* 28 March.

Wright, R. (1992) *A People's Counsel: A History of the Parliament of Victoria 1856–1990*, Oxford University Press.

7

ANOTHER LOOK AT THE DEPRIVAL VALUE APPROACH TO DEPRECIATION

Philip W. Bell and Ken Peasnell

INTRODUCTION

This essay examines the logic underlying the deprival value approach to the computation of depreciation. Much has been written about depreciation during the last hundred years, but the topic is seldom discussed today. As far as most accountants are concerned, depreciation is simply a technique, largely devoid of theoretical or economic content, for assigning cost (whether historical or current) to products or periods. Deprival value depreciation is not a new concept and we make few claims to originality in what we have to say on the subject in the following pages. Nevertheless, we believe the time is opportune to resurrect an idea which never made much impact on accountants' thinking about depreciation. What is new is that we provide a model connecting deprival values with implicit pricing in a used-asset market.

Our purposes are four-fold: first, to draw a new generation's attention to the deprival value depreciation model; second, to clarify certain issues which have been the cause of difficulty; third, to highlight some of deprival value's most interesting properties; and finally, to indicate ways in which this approach to depreciation might be of relevance in financial reporting.

We are particularly pleased to be able to offer this contribution to the Festschrift in honour of Professor Robert H. Parker. While Bob is best known for his work on accounting history and international accounting, his reader on accounting theory, Parker and Harcourt (1969), has played an important role in the teaching of accounting theory to generations of accounting students. Indeed, the introduction to that book has justly received wide recognition as a notable contribution to accounting theory in its own right. It is a sobering reflection on the work of accounting researchers in the quarter century following the book's publication that a number of the most important papers ever published on depreciation had already appeared in print and were reprinted by Parker and Harcourt. They did not shrink from going back almost fifty years to select Hotelling (1925)

122

as a work on depreciation worthy of the attention of a later generation. We trust the accounting historian in Bob will approve of similar foraging in earlier literature by ourselves. It seems particularly appropriate that our offering should be concerned with the very idea Parker and Harcourt did so much to promote.

'Deprival Value' is the name William Baxter (1971, 1975, 1981) devised for the 'Value to the Owner' concept generally attributed to Bonbright (1937) and popularised by Parker and Harcourt. This valuation basis was subsequently renamed 'Value to the Business' and as such played a key role in the Current Cost proposals in the Sandilands Report (1975) and subsequently in the various Anglo-American standards on the subject: FASB's SFAS 33 (1979), SSAP 16 (1980) in the UK, New Zealand's Current Cost Accounting Standard No. 1 (1980), 'Reporting the Effects of Changing Prices' (1982) in Canada and Australia's SAP 1 (1983).

We prefer Baxter's label to either of the other two alternatives because it seems to us to capture better the thinking that underlies the basic concept involved. *When owned*, an asset's 'value to the owner' or 'value to the business' is likely to be thought of intuitively as the higher of use value (PV) and sale value (NRV), involving essentially the only two choices an owner or business has with respect to an asset currently owned, at least until near the end of the asset's economic life. But these are only two of the three alternatives bound up in the notion of 'deprival value'. The deprival principle shows that current replacement cost (RC) does play a role, along with PV and NRV, in measuring the market value of an enterprise's net worth: leaving aside problems of aggregation, the advantage to the firm of owning an asset worth replacing in the event of loss is equal to RC (or equivalently, is its 'edge' over a potential entrant to the industry lacking such an asset).

These considerations lead us to prefer Baxter's 'Deprival Value' label for our central concept rather than 'Value to the Owner' (or the Sandilands variant, 'Value to the Business'). But as we shall see, Bonbright's term, 'Value to the Owner', may well be a useful way of describing the higher of NRV and PV.[1]

The remainder of this paper is organised as follows. The next section explains why we think depreciation warrants renewed attention. After that, a summary of the logic of asset valuation in accordance with deprival value thinking is provided. We then apply deprival reasoning for two very different settings: a single replacement cycle with unequal horizons; and identical, infinitely recurring replacement cycles. Our last substantive section presents the key step in our analysis, which is to show how the insights obtained from the infinite-replacement case might be applied in a single-replacement setting by treating the deprival value depreciation formula as a model of used-asset pricing. Conclusions appear in the final section.

WHY BOTHER WITH DEPRECIATION?

Seldom do textbooks on accounting theory today devote more than a couple of pages to depreciation measurement issues. A notable exception is Hendriksen and van Breda (1992), which has a complete chapter on the subject. Various ways of thinking about depreciation are considered by Hendriksen and van Breda, including the internal-rate method, but the deprival value approach is ignored. Their conclusion is a fair summation of current opinion (Hendriksen and van Breda 1992: 547):

> None of these solutions is perfect. The conclusions of most observers, therefore, is to use the simplest depreciation method for financial reporting purposes whenever possible. That is usually the straight-line method.

Few attempts to suggest better depreciation methods have appeared in the research literature in recent years.

What can explain this dismal state of affairs? After all, it is not as though depreciation expense is a trivial item. Chambers *et al.* (1995: table 3) report that, during the period 1983–92, reported historical cost depreciation accounted on average for 70 per cent of net income in their sample of 3,286 American manufacturing firms. Large numbers of research papers were published on depreciation in the 1950s and 1960s. A number of factors appear to have combined in causing this supply to dry up, and it is worth pausing to consider them before getting down to the main business of the paper.

One factor seems to have been the major shift in focus of intellectual effort in accounting research which started in the late 1960s. Normative research increasingly appeared to some to be fraught with methodological difficulty and came under attack as 'unscientific' (Watts and Zimmerman 1978; Beaver and Demski 1979), mainly because it was often lacking in empirical evidence. Positive investigations into the association of accounting numbers with stock prices, the motives of management in choosing accounting methods and the role of regulation in accounting captured the imagination of the new generation of accounting scholars in leading American universities. At the same time, the search for 'better' depreciation methods came to be regarded by many as a pointless exercise after the devastating critique of accounting allocations by Thomas (1969, 1974). In retrospect, it can be seen that the symposium held at Rice University in May 1978 constituted the last major academic effort mounted by accounting researchers to address the depreciation problem (Sterling and Thomas 1979).

There are practical reasons, too, underlying the current neglect of depreciation. One of these has been the recognition that, when attention is shifted from the single depreciable asset case to the more realistic situation where a firm possesses a portfolio of similar assets of different vintages, income is less likely to be affected by the choice of depreciation method. In the unlikely situation where the buying price of assets is constant through time and the firm has a balanced portfolio of similar assets of different vintages, depreciation expense is invariant to choice of depreciation pattern (Ijiri 1967).[2] Another factor accounting for the neglect of depreciation in the professional literature seems to have been the practical problem of forecasting benefits, allied to the arbitrariness involved in allocating joint benefits to separate assets.

However, conditions have changed and there are increasing signs of a desire to address valuation and income measurement issues put to one side in the past two decades. Dramatic shifts in economic conditions involving 'down sizing' and the restructuring of some of our mightiest corporations make reliance on the 'seasoned asset stock' argument for ignoring depreciation look more like a wild act of faith rather than a reasonable working hypothesis.[3] Increased regulatory pressure to depreciate property assets in the UK (*Company Reporting* June 1995) has also created renewed interest in the issue (Hastie 1995).

The interest of standard setters in the application of 'fair value' principles is on the increase, particularly in countries such as the UK where the revaluation of fixed assets is commonplace, but also in the USA where the Securities and Exchange Commission is no longer so wedded to historical costs as it once was. The deprival value concept is accorded considerable prominence in the Accounting Standards Board's draft *Statement of Principles* (ASB 1995). In a different arena, CCA data are playing an important part in the regulation of prices of privatized utilities in the UK (Whittington 1994), as they are in the regulation of government trading enterprises in Australia (Churchill 1995).

The academic community is likewise exhibiting a stirring of interest in measurement issues. One way this has manifested itself is through a willingness to apply the techniques of capital-markets-based accounting research to the measurement of assets and liabilities. Examples include the valuation of pension assets and liabilities (Barth 1991), stock option expense (Rubinstein 1994), corporate debt (Barth *et al.* 1995) and depreciation (Chambers *et al.* 1995). Equally encouraging, interest in measurement and valuation issues at the theoretical level appears to be on the increase (Beaver 1991; Beaver and Demski 1994; Ohlson 1995).

The main obstacle to a renewal of interest in depreciation as a researchable policy issue appears to be the belief that it necessarily involves arbitrary allocations. This is clearly a problem with depreciation methods that allocate cost in proportion to revenues or by reference to changes in book value expressed as the discounted present value of future revenues. The internal-rate method, widely regarded as *the* economic depreciation method, is open to this objection since it depends on the identification of the internal rate of return by reference to future revenues. We show in this paper how deprival value depreciation is innocent of this particular charge.

Baxter (1971, 1981) provides extremely clear explanations of the logic of deprival value which even non-accountants should have little difficulty in understanding. His ideas have received very little attention, however, in the professional accounting community. Even in the 1970s, when interest in CCA was at its highest, Baxter's ideas were largely ignored in professional quarters. The recent study by Anthony Carey (1993), a member of the secretariat of the Institute of Chartered Accountants in England and Wales, calling for the reform of depreciation accounting practice on deprival value lines, is therefore a particularly encouraging event.

Notwithstanding the thoughtful, clear expositional efforts of Baxter, as well as those by Carey and others, the deprival value concept involves subtle issues which our experiences suggest are little understood by most accountants. Some of the more important aspects are indicated in the following pages.

DEVELOPING THE BASIC CONCEPTS

The value to the owner of an asset depends on the loss the firm would suffer if 'deprived' of the asset (DV), conventionally expressed in the following succinct rule (Solomons 1966; Parker and Harcourt 1969: 17):

$$DV = \min[RC, \max(NRV, PV)] \qquad (7.1)$$

where RC is the replacement cost, NRV is the net realisable value and PV is the discounted present value of the future cash flows attributable to the asset. The rule can also be represented in the form of Baxter's widely known diagram, shown below in Figure 7.1.

Application of the DV rule is straightforward in principle if an active second-hand market exists in which a replacement asset of the same age and in the same condition can be acquired. Even if deprival would lead to the purchase of a new asset, the prices of similar used assets can still be utilised (Bell and Johnson 1979). The rule allows us to determine value at a point

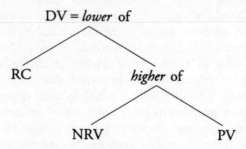

Figure 7.1 The deprival value rule

in time. The absence of an active second-hand market complicates matters, since we have to make allowance for the decline in the asset's efficiency.

In its most general form, the DV of an asset must equal the amount by which the value of the firm with the asset exceeds what the firm would be worth without it. Baxter (1971, 1981) expresses this in terms of comparing HAVE and HAVE-NOT budgets. This shift from values to budgets is potentially confusing, given that budgets are 'flow' statements, whereas the DV parameters in equation (7.1) (i.e. RC, NRV and PV) are 'stocks' or values at a point in time. Nevertheless, the shift is essential to a proper understanding of deprival value depreciation. Baxter solves the problem by converting both the HAVE and HAVE-NOT budgets to values at the balance sheet date through the process of discounting, and we follow him here. To see what is involved for the non-depreciating asset, or the depreciating asset which can be traded in active markets, we rewrite equation (7.1) as

$$DV = VO - \max[(VO - RC), 0)]$$ (7.2)

For the reasons given earlier, we use the term 'Value to the Owner' (VO for short) to refer to the maximum amount recoverable by an *existing* owner of the asset through sale or use (i.e. the greater of PV and NRV).

Consistent with Baxter's terminology and framework, the first term on the right-hand side of equation (7.2) is the value of the benefits associated with the asset which is currently owned – the HAVE budget – while the second term in the equation, max [(VO – RC), 0)], represents what a non-owner or anyone who has been deprived of the asset *would gain* from purchasing or replacing it – the HAVE-NOT budget. The HAVE-NOT budget has a lower bound of zero, to reflect the fact that the non-owner has an option (but no obligation) to buy or replace the asset and would not exercise this option if it were unprofitable to do so (i.e. if VO < RC).

A proper understanding of the shift in the formulation of the DV rule, from the way it is conventionally understood, as represented by equation

Table 7.1 A numerical example of the comparative budgets approach to deprival value

Cases	Valuation parameters			Value to current owner HAVE budget	Gain from replacing, if deprived HAVE-NOT budget	Deprival value
	RC	PV	NRV	VO	max[(VO – RC), 0]	DV
(a)	6	10	4	10	4	6 (=RC)
(b)	8	7	5	7	0	7 (=PV)
(c)	8	4	5	5	0	5 (=NRV)

(7.1) or Figure 7.1, to the budgeting formulation provided in equation (7.2), is essential to the following analysis of depreciation. To see what is involved, we ignore all cash flows common to both the HAVE and HAVE-NOT budget scenarios since these will be eliminated when the latter is subtracted from the former to arrive at DV. Table 7.1 contains a numerical example illustrating that the budgeting approach yields the same answers as the conventional method in cases where no allowance has to be made for depreciation. In case (a), the value of the replacement investment (PV – RC) is deducted from the benefit value of the existing asset (PV), leaving DV = RC. In cases (b) and (c), so long as RC > NRV (the normal case for a plant asset), the HAVE-NOT budget is automatically zero and equation (7.2) yields DV = NRV when NRV > PV, while DV = PV if PV > NRV. These are exactly in accord with conventional application of the DV rules.

In the normal case where NRV < RC, equation (7.2) can usefully be rewritten as follows:

$$DV = VO - \max[(PV - RC), 0)]\qquad(7.2a)$$

Equation (7.2a) indicates that the DV of an existing asset is equal to the excess of the asset's VO over any net PV attributable to replacement. According to equation (7.2a), the HAVE-NOT budget plays a role in the calculation of DV if and only if PV > RC, i.e. when an owner 'deprived' of the asset would wish to replace it. If replacement is worthwhile, VO = PV and DV = RC. Notice, however, that equation (7.2a) is wrongly specified if replacement takes the form of a new asset with a longer life to run (not to mention lower operating efficiency) than the existing used depreciable asset: the PV that comprises VO in the HAVE budget will be less than the PV in the HAVE-NOT budget.

To make the two budgets comparable, it will be necessary to adopt a common horizon date for both. This will mean that each budget will have to reflect the financial pay offs of events at more distant points in time. In the limit, it requires consideration of the cash flows associated with successive replacements in perpetuity. Before addressing this daunting possibility, it is helpful to examine a situation where attention is restricted to one replacement cycle.

DVD IN A SINGLE REPLACEMENT CYCLE SETTING

Suppose a firm purchases a depreciable asset for K_0 at $t = 0$ with an economic life of n years. The present value of the future cash flows, X_t, associated with this investment can be written as:

$$PV_0 = \sum_{t=1}^{n} v^t X_t \qquad(7.3)$$

where $v = 1/(1 + i)$ is the one-period discount factor and i is the (assumed constant) cost of capital. The decision to purchase the asset is based on the firm having a favourable investment opportunity, with $PV_0 > K_0$. It is further assumed that the buying price of the asset will remain constant thereafter $(K_0 = K_1 = K_2 = ...)$, although revenue will decline through pressure of competition such that for $t \geq 2$ the return will be just sufficient to pay for replacement investment $(NPV_t = PV_t - K_t = 0)$.[4] Cash flows are independent of asset vintage – unless the asset is held for longer than its economic life of n years, after which repair costs increase sharply. There is no second-hand market for the asset (so $NRV_t = 0$, $t = 1, ..., n$), because of the considerable expense involved in dismantling and transferring it to another user. In this and all subsequent examples, there are no surprises, in the sense that expectations are realised.

In this setting, since NPV_n is zero, we can omit from the HAVE budget the revenues generated by the replacement at time n. In the case of the HAVE-NOT budget, replacement in the event of deprival will be worthwhile at $t = 1$ but not thereafter. Applying equation (7.2a), $DV_0 = K_0$, as expected for a newly acquired asset. One year later, the equation yields a deprival value for the one-year-old asset of

$$DV_1 = \left(\sum_{j=2}^{n} v^{j-1} X_j \right) - \left(\sum_{j=2}^{n+1} v^{j-1} X_j - K_0 \right)$$

which reduces to

$$DV_1 = K_0 - v^n X_{n+1} \tag{7.4}$$

In other words, the deprival value of the asset is equal to the cost of a new asset minus the present value of the extra cash flow offered by a new asset $n + 1$ periods later. The cash flow is for the year following the end of the economic life of the original asset.

From $t = 2$ onwards, the replacement is simply a break-even proposition. The deprival value of the asset can therefore be set equal to PV_t (which is equal to K_t in the special case considered here):

$$DV_t = \sum_{j=t+1}^{n} v^{j-t} X_j \quad (t = 2, ..., n-1) \tag{7.5}$$

Alternatively, equation (7.2a) can be used:

$$DV_t = \left(\sum_{j=t+1}^{n} v^{j-t} X_j \right) - \left(\sum_{j=t+1}^{n+t} v^{j-t} X_j - K_0 \right) \tag{7.6}$$

Since the second parenthetical term on the right-hand side of (7.6) nets to zero, (7.5) and (7.6) must yield the same answer. Equation (7.6) also reduces to

$$DV_t = K_0 - \sum_{j=n+1}^{n+t} v^n X_j \qquad (7.7)$$

The valuation basis for $t \geqslant 2$ can therefore be viewed as either RC (equation (7.7)) or PV (equation (7.6)), since the value obtained is the same by either route. Note, moreover, that equation (7.4) is simply a special case of (7.7), indicating that the valuation formula is the same for all t.

In this example, deprival value *depreciation* is simply the decline in asset value during the period: $DVD_t = V_{t-1} - V_t$. It is straightforward to develop from equation (7.7) a recursive relationship for the pattern of depreciation through time of the following form:

$$DVD_{t+1} = (1 + i)DVD_t + v^n(X_{n+t+1} - X_{n+t}) \quad (t = 1, ..., n-1) \quad (7.8)$$

The assumptions of this model imply that revenues are constant from period $n + 3$ onwards; in which case, for $t + 3$, the second term on the right-hand side of equation (7.8) drops out and depreciation charges grow at the rate of interest through time. In other words, depreciation takes the form of an annuity – a feature of deprival value measurement that we will encounter again.

It is worth pausing at this juncture to compare the deprival value depreciation model we have developed with the standard internal-rate method. It has been our personal experience that while most academic accountants know something of internal-rate depreciation (IRD), many, particularly in the USA, are unaware of the deprival value approach. Both are grounded in the logic of capital budgeting, but there are subtle differences.

To see what is involved, we replace the cost of capital rate, i, in equation (7.3) by the internal rate of return (IRR):

$$PV_0 = \sum_{t=1}^{n} X_t / (1 + IRR)^t \qquad (7.3a)$$

Then we set $PV_0 = K_0$, and solve for IRR. IRD is then defined as the pattern of allocations of K_0 that yields profit equal to the IRR times opening book value in a period. The easiest way to calculate IRD is as follows. If opening book value of the period is multiplied by IRR, a figure for income is obtained which can be deducted from revenues (net of costs other than depreciation) to yield a residual figure equal to IRD. From a balance sheet perspective, the book value of the asset is equal to the present value of remaining revenues discounted at the IRR:

$$BV_t = \sum_{j=t+1}^{n} X_j / (1 + IRR)^{j-t} \quad (t = 1, ..., n-1) \qquad (7.5a)$$

IRD as computed above is then simply the change in book value: $IRD_t = BV_{t-1} - BV_t$. Anton (1956) shows that IRD can be represented as a recursive relation similar in form to equation (7.8):

$$\text{IRD}_{t+1} = (1 + \text{IRR})\text{IRD}_t + (X_{t+1} - X_t) \quad (t = 1, \ldots, n-1) \quad (7.8a)$$

A comparison of equations (7.8a) and (7.8) reveals that there is indeed a *mathematical* similarity between IRD and our initial stab at developing a version of deprival value depreciation (DVD) in this section. In both cases, the pattern of depreciation charges is a function of both the discount rate and the pattern of revenue. IRD depends on IRR and the change in current revenue; DVD charges have the same general functional form, except that the IRR is replaced by the cost of capital and the (discounted) change in revenue n periods hence takes the place of current revenue. Nevertheless, the similarity between these two models is more apparent than real and stems largely from the way DVD in a single-cycle setting is dependent on revenues – see equation (7.5) – whereas it is not when multi-period replacement possibilities exist. In the more general settings that we consider later, DVD and IRD may lead to quite different patterns of depreciation expense.

Notice that, at this stage, we have derived in equation (7.8) a formula for DVD from first principles that involves looking no further into the future than was presumably undertaken in the original decision to acquire the existing asset (plus the equivalent forecasting for a 'similar' asset which would have to be acquired now in the event of deprival). To our knowledge, this is the first time this particular formulation has appeared in the literature. The equation is simple in form, including a term for an extra period's revenue associated with the replacement asset n years hence. Therein lie two problems, however. Are we paying inadequate attention to the future? And, more important, how are we to assign an appropriate amount of revenue to the asset over future periods without making arbitrary allocations? This model of DVD appears to be plagued by the same kind of allocation problem as that of the internal-rate method.

The solution offered by Baxter to the revenue-allocation problem is to concentrate on the costs side of the story. There is no obvious way of doing this with the internal-rate method, but deprival value reasoning offers a way forward. As explained below, his approach deals with the unequal horizons issue in the same manner as it has been traditionally handled in the capital budgeting literature.

DVD IN AN INFINITE IDENTICAL REPLACEMENT CYCLES SETTING

We continue to assume that replacement of the asset will ensure that revenue is unaffected by loss of the asset. This time we pass to the opposite extreme and imagine that budgets are prepared stretching out infinitely far into the future, incorporating successive replacement cycles, on the assumption that each cycle is a profitable investment opportunity. In this way it will be possible to omit revenues completely from both the HAVE and HAVE-NOT budgets, on the ground that they are common to both, restricting budget entries to costs alone.[5] In addition to the capital costs, allowances will be made in this scenario for differences in maintenance, repairs and other operating outlays between the existing asset and its replacement; these allowances will have to include *all* costs associated with the ageing of the asset, including obsolescence.

In order to fix ideas, we follow Baxter and Carrier (1971) in considering an example in which economic conditions are completely static such that the firm buys a new replacement asset with an identical operating cost time profile every n years; see also Peasnell (1984). Repairs and other vintage-related costs amount to R_t in period t. (Whether these costs are caused by use or time-related decay is ignored in the following analysis.) At the time of acquisition of a new asset, the present value of these anticipated 'servicing' costs (S_0) is

$$S_0 = \sum_{t=1}^{n} v^t R_t \qquad (7.9)$$

The cost burden associated with acquiring a new asset is therefore $K_0 + S_0$. In the event of deprival, it is assumed that the firm will immediately acquire a new asset.

We can now apply deprival reasoning. Revenue can be ignored. In the HAVE-NOT budget will be the costs associated with the indefinite number of successive replacement cycles, the present value of which at t is

$$(K_0 + S_0)(1 + v^n + v^{2n} + \ldots) = \frac{K_0 + S_0}{1 - v^n} \qquad (7.10)$$

The costs included in the HAVE budget will consist of the servicing costs associated with the existing asset, the burden of which is worth

$$S_t = \sum_{j=t+1}^{n} v^{j-t} R_j \qquad (7.11)$$

plus the costs associated with the next replacement cycle delayed $n - t$ periods:

$$S_t + v^{n-t}(K_0 + S_0)(1 + v^n + v^{2n} + \ldots) = S_t + v^{n-t}\left(\frac{K_0 + S_0}{1 - v^n}\right) \qquad (7.12)$$

The deprival value of the asset is the excess of equation (7.10) over (7.12)

$$DV_t = \left(\frac{K_0 + S_0}{1 - v^n}\right)(1 - v^{n-t}) - S_t \qquad (7.13)$$

This model of deprival value can be better understood if the investment outlay, K_0, and the servicing burden, S_0, are each written as a function of their 'equivalent annual cost' (EAK and EAR, respectively):

$$K_0 = P_{n,i}\text{EAK} \quad \text{and} \quad S_0 = P_{n,i}\text{EAR} \tag{7.14}$$

where $P_{n,i} = (1 - v^n)/i$ is the value of an n-year annuity of £1 discounted at rate i. Substituting equations (7.14) and (7.11) into (7.13) and rearranging, the value of the existing asset can be written as a function of EAK and an adjustment to reflect differences in the costs of operating new and used assets:

$$\text{DV}_t = P_{(n-t),i}\text{EAK} - \sum_{j=t+1}^{n} v^{j-t}(R_j - \text{EAR}) \tag{7.15}$$

where $P_{(n-t),i} = (1 - v^{n-t})/i$ is the value of an annuity of £1 for $n - t$ years. It follows from equations (7.9) and (7.14) that when repairs do not vary with asset vintage (i.e. $R_1 = R_2 = \ldots = R_n$), they must equal EAR in every period; in which case, the second term on the right-hand side of equation (7.15) disappears.[6] The core element in the formula is therefore the first term in equation (7.15): ownership of a t-year-old asset is equivalent to saving an outlay on an annuity of EAK for the remaining $n - t$ years of life. In the more realistic scenario where servicing costs increase as the asset gets older, equation (7.15) reduces the value of the asset to reflect the lower operating efficiency of the existing used asset to that of a new replacement.

The capital cost of using the asset in a period consists of depreciation ($\text{DVD}_t = V_{t-1} - V_t$) plus the opportunity cost of funds tied up in the asset (iV_{t-1}):

$$\text{DVD}_t + i\text{DV}_{t-1} = (1 + i)\text{DV}_{t-1} - \text{DV}_t \tag{7.16}$$

Substituting equation (7.15) for DV_{t-1} and DV_t in equation (7.16) and rearranging, we obtain

$$\text{DVD}_t + i\text{DV}_{t-1} = \text{EAK} + \text{EAR} - R_t \tag{7.17}$$

The total cost of operating the asset is therefore simply the sum of the two annuities,

$$R_t + (\text{DVD}_t + i\text{DV}_{t-1}) = \text{EAK} + \text{EAR} \tag{7.18}$$

This model has a number of interesting properties. One is that the total cost of operating the asset is constant in every period. We shall use this feature to show below how the resultant book values can be treated logically as proxies for used-asset prices in the absence of a second-hand market for the asset. In the present infinite-replacement context, the model also provides a simple basis for determining the optimal economic life of the asset. Continuing to ignore revenue, since it does not affect total operating

133

cost, which is constant each year, the optimal replacement time is that n for which EAK + EAR, or average cost, is a minimum.[7] The two elements pull in opposite directions: EAK is a decreasing function of n (with EAK approaching iK_0 from above as $n \to \infty$), whereas EAR must eventually increase with n.

The following recursive relationship for depreciation can be obtained straightforwardly from equation (7.17):

$$DVD_{t+1} = (1 + i)DVD_t - (R_{t+1} - R_t) \qquad (7.19)$$

Certain features of this relationship are worth noting. If repairs are constant through time, DVD behaves in exactly the same way as annuity depreciation.[8] On the other hand, the annuity-growth effect is abated if repairs are increasing through time. The same effect is observed with IRD in equation (7.8a) since, other things being equal, net cash flows will decline if repairs increase. This structural similarity between the time series patterns of DVD and IRD charges, while interesting from a mathematical perspective, should not be misunderstood. The two methods will give the same answers only if the following three conditions are met: (a) the internal rate of return is equal to the cost of capital (i.e. the initial investment barely breaks even); (b) any period-to-period changes in cash flows over the life of the existing asset are wholly attributable to what we have called 'repairs' (i.e. vintage-related differences between used and new versions of the asset); and (c) replacement in the event of deprival would be with an asset with an identical lifetime repair profile. DVD and IRD have different foundations and can be expected to yield different answers.[9]

Another interesting feature of the deprival value model is its relationship with excess (or residual) income. It was proved many years ago that the net present value of the cash flows associated with an investment also equals the present value of the excess income stream where this is defined as revenues minus all costs including interest on the beginning book value of the investment each year.[10] These costs are shown in equation (7.18) to be constant each year. We can therefore write excess income (EI) in year t as

$$EI_t = X_t - (EAK + EAR) \qquad (7.20)$$

In the simple case where net revenue is constant through time, so is excess income. The more interesting situation is where revenue varies with the age of the asset, in which case the change in revenue will have to be included in what we have called 'repairs', leaving a 'core' revenue which will be constant in every period. Since X_t will be unchanged from period to period, so will excess income. In short, excess income on a deprival value basis will, in certain circumstances, conform to Hicks' (1946) income concept number 2, as a constant amount that can be spent in this and successive periods.

However, our model of excess income assumes the maintenance of deprival value, here cost (K_0), rather than the present value of future receipts (PV_0), as is the case with Hicksian income. Moreover, should revenue change over the life of the asset for economic reasons not associated with the ageing of the asset – for example increasing as a new product becomes more widely accepted and later decreasing as new competitors enter the field – excess income will change by exactly the change in revenue. Reporting in this fashion will be useful in evaluating performance in a way that Hicksian income cannot (and was never designed to) be.[11]

A problem with the model used to derive equations (7.18) and (7.19) is that it was based on the highly implausible assumption that the firm operated in a completely static environment where identical replacements could and would occur for ever. Numerical versions of the model have been used by Baxter and others mainly as a pedagogic device to illustrate the forward-looking character of deprival value reasoning, whereby depreciation reflects the worsening of a cash prospect, as outlays on replacement, repairs, etc., are brought nearer in time. When it comes to implementation, Baxter (1971: 53) notes:

Thus the cash flows stretch out far into the future, in a somewhat repetitive pattern. ... the owner can make allowance for predicted change in the size of items and the length of cycles. But in general he has no alternative to treating the cycles as a perpetuity.

This illustrates very nicely the value of a precisely formulated model and the reluctance in all disciplines to set it aside, no matter how great its imperfections, in the absence of anything better to put in its place. Nevertheless, perpetual replacement with assets identical to the initial investment is obviously a very strong assumption. What is needed is a deprival value model that retains the cost focus of the perpetual-replacement model but which has less demanding forecasting requirements and assumptions. This we try to provide in the next section.

A USED-ASSET PRICE VIEW OF DVD

As we noted at the outset, the ideal way to determine DVD is to let the market do the job. This is a straightforward exercise when there is an active market for the asset. In reality, used-asset prices will reflect many demand and supply factors, both short and long term in nature (Edwards and Bell 1961: 175–80; Beidleman 1973); these will include margins to protect traders from the risks of loss due to asymmetries in information (Akerlof 1970) and to cover the costs of transacting (Williamson 1985), either of which, if great, are sufficient to prevent such markets forming in the first place. In the spirit of the genre, we ignore such complications in the following analysis in order to build a theoretical model of asset pricing that can be applied to settings where used-asset markets are thin or non-existent.

Consider again equation (7.18). This formula shows that the total cost of operating the asset is the same in every period in an infinite-replacement setting. What we want to be able to do is to replace the services of our existing used asset, which has $n - t$ years of good wear left, with the services of one or more assets over the next $n - t$ years. Buying a similar t-year-old used asset would do the job nicely since we would not have to consider anything beyond the working horizon of our existing asset. Alternatively, we could consider putting into service a succession of assets over the next $n - t$ years, with the final one in the sequence ceasing to be economic at time n. The problem with this alternative, though, is that it would expose us to the risk of used-asset prices moving against us in the intervening period.[12] We sidestep such complications by assuming that the firm is willing and able to enter into firm 'future' transactions which remove all uncertainty regarding 'spot' buying prices in later periods.

In our hypothetical market, there are many buyers and sellers. Our firm is 'representative' of buyers in this market, in the sense of incurring similar operating expenses (again referred to as 'repairs') to those of other buyers. Supply conditions are stable, in that traders possess stocks of all vintages of used (but technologically unchanged) versions of an asset which can be purchased new for K_0; this situation has prevailed unchanged in the recent past and is expected to persist for at least the next n periods.

Suppose we are at time $t = 0$ and are considering whether to buy a new asset or a succession of second-hand ones capable of rendering the same service. Either way, our planning horizon is restricted to n years, the life of the new asset. The new asset provides a benchmark: we will be unwilling to buy any succession of used assets which costs more to operate, in present value terms, than the burden of $K_0 + S_0$ that we will incur with the new asset. The market will be in equilibrium if the present value of the costs of all feasible buying plans equals this amount.

To fix ideas, set n equal to four years. The cost of a new asset and outlays on repairs are K_0 and $R_t(t = 1, ..., 4)$, respectively, as before, and are determined by external factors. A used asset costs K_t, where the subscript $t = 1, ..., 3$ indicates the asset's age (and hence how much of its services have been used up). A four-year-old asset is worthless: $K_4 = 0$. These prices apply now and are expected to be held steady during the planning period.

To cover four years of use, the firm has a choice between buying a new four-year-life asset for an outlay K_0 or any one of seven possible sets of used assets whose remaining combination of lives sums to four years. With only three unknown second-hand buying prices to be determined, it is sufficient to select any three of these seven buying plans which 'span' the price space, in order to obtain prices for assets with one, two and three years of life remaining. We could:[13]

(i) buy a one-year-old asset for K_1 now and a three-year-old replacement for K_3 in three years' time;

(ii) buy two two-year-old assets for K_2 each, one now and a replacement two years later; and

(iii) buy a three-year-old asset for K_3 and replace it with a one-year-old one at a cost of K_1 at the end of the year.

The market will be in equilibrium if the total cost of operations under each of these three buying plans equals the cost of operations with a new asset. In the case of plan (i), this equilibrium condition can be represented in present value terms as:

$$K_1 + vR_2 + v^2R_3 + v^3(K_3 + R_4) + v^4R_4 = K_0 + S_0 \qquad (7.21a)$$

Likewise with plans (ii) and (iii):

$$K_2 + vR_3 + v^2(K_2 + R_4) + v^3R_3 + v^4R_4 = K + S_0 \qquad (7.21b)$$

and

$$K_3 + v(K_1 + R_4) + v^2R_2 + v^3R_3 + v^4R_4 = K_0 + S_0 \qquad (7.21c)$$

In each of these plans, repairs are purely a function of the vintage of the asset purchased.

The equilibrium market prices can be determined from this system of equations in the following manner. If the (discounted) repairs are transferred to the right-hand side of equation (7.21), the result can be expressed in matrix form as

$$\mathbf{VK} = \mathbf{Z} \qquad (7.22)$$

where $\mathbf{V}$ is a 3×3 matrix of valuation factors, $\mathbf{K}$ is a 3×1 column vector of asset prices and $\mathbf{Z}$ is a 3×1 column vector representing the net cost of the asset acquisition plans. Equation (7.22) can be written out in full as the following system of equations:

$$\begin{bmatrix} 1 & 0 & v^3 \\ 0 & 1+v^2 & 0 \\ v & 0 & 1 \end{bmatrix} \begin{bmatrix} K_1 \\ K_2 \\ K_3 \end{bmatrix} = \begin{bmatrix} Z_1 \\ Z_2 \\ Z_3 \end{bmatrix} \qquad (7.23)$$

where

$$\begin{bmatrix} Z_1 \\ Z_2 \\ Z_3 \end{bmatrix} = (K_0 + S_0) \begin{bmatrix} 1 \\ 1 \\ 1 \end{bmatrix} - \begin{bmatrix} v & v^2 & v^3 + v^4 \\ 0 & v + v^3 & v^2 + v^4 \\ v^2 & v^3 & v + v^4 \end{bmatrix} \begin{bmatrix} R_2 \\ R_3 \\ R_4 \end{bmatrix} \qquad (7.24)$$

Since the determinant of $\mathbf{V}$ is non-zero, equation (7.22) can be inverted:

$$\mathbf{K} = \mathbf{V}^{-1}\mathbf{Z} \qquad (7.25)$$

137

and Cramer's rule employed to solve for **K** in equation (7.25):

$$\begin{bmatrix} K_1 \\ K_2 \\ K_3 \end{bmatrix} = \left(\frac{1}{1-v^4}\right) \begin{bmatrix} 1 & 0 & -v^3 \\ 0 & 1-v^2 & 0 \\ -v & 0 & 1 \end{bmatrix} \begin{bmatrix} Z_1 \\ Z_2 \\ Z_3 \end{bmatrix} \qquad (7.26)$$

Substitute equation (7.24) into (7.26), collect and cancel terms:

$$\begin{bmatrix} K_1 \\ K_2 \\ K_3 \end{bmatrix} = \left(\frac{K_0 + S_0}{1-v^4}\right) \begin{bmatrix} 1-v^3 \\ 1-v^2 \\ 1-v \end{bmatrix} - \begin{bmatrix} v & v^2 & v^3 \\ 0 & v & v^2 \\ 0 & 0 & v \end{bmatrix} \begin{bmatrix} R_2 \\ R_3 \\ R_4 \end{bmatrix} \qquad (7.27)$$

Using equation (7.14) to substitute equivalent annual costs for K_0 and S_0 in equation (7.27), the following expression for the equilibrium market price for a t-year-old used asset is obtained:

$$K_t = P_{(4-t),i}\text{EAK} - \sum_{j=t+1}^{4} v^{j-t}(R_j - \text{EAR}) \quad (t = 1,\ldots,3) \qquad (7.28)$$

Notice that equations (7.15) and (7.28) yield exactly the same answers, so $K_t = V_t$ for $n = 4$. The same result has been obtained for other sample values of n. Proof of the general validity of this result has eluded us to date, since the variety of ways in which used assets can be successively employed expands dramatically with increases in n. We conjecture that the same relationship holds for all n and therefore, in the following discussion, we generalise equation (7.28) as:

$$K_t = P_{(n-t),i}\text{EAK} - \sum_{j=t+1}^{n} v^{j-t}(R_j - \text{EAR}) \quad (t = 1,\ldots,n-1) \qquad (7.28a)$$

The following numerical example illustrates what we have demonstrated mathematically above. The example is drawn from Bell (1996: table 1) and the interested reader is advised to refer to that work for further arithmetical illustrations and comparisons with alternative depreciation methods. Suppose a firm buys an asset for £100,000 in the prospect of receiving cash revenues of £75,000 in each of the following four years. Maintenance and repair costs will increase through time as the asset wears out, starting at £5,000 in year 1, rising to £19,000 in year 2, £32,000 in year 3 and £44,000 in year 4. The situation is of the 'static' form assumed in our mathematical analysis, in the sense that buying a replacement asset at a later date would result in the same pattern of maintenance and repair costs. The cost of capital for an investment of this risk is 15 per cent per annum. The net present value of the investment is positive (£49,211), so valuation at replacement cost is justified.

The deprival value calculations for this example are shown in Table 7.2. Panel A of the table contains the summary income statement and book value of the asset in each year. The figure for depreciation can be obtained either by taking the difference between the opening and closing book values, each obtained directly using equation (7.28), or from the difference between the HAVE and HAVE-NOT budgets for the period, reported in panel B of the table. This latter approach can be understood by turning to equation (7.18), whose right-hand side corresponds with the HAVE-NOT budget given in row 10 in the table. Likewise, the HAVE budget figure is the sum of the repair cost and interest expense elements in this equation, the numerical values for which are shown in row 9. This method bears a striking similarity to the leasing perspective we discuss below. Finally, panel C reports that the payoffs from using assets of different vintages are the same for all combinations, if the assets can be purchased at deprival prices.

We have shown that the deprival value of a used asset (V_t) is equal to what logically should be its market buying price (K_t), if such a market existed. This is a striking result, given that different assumptions were employed in each case. Whereas our deprival value formula assumes identical replacement in perpetuity, all that is needed to get the buying price is a limited amount of stability before and after the four-year period in question, coupled with the assumption that the total costs of operating assets must be the same in equilibrium, regardless of the vintages of the assets involved, for the 'representative' buyer.

Viewed this way, deprival value has a lot going for it. It is no longer necessary to have recourse to dubious assumptions about infinitely repeatable replacement cycles. Instead, we can restrict our attention to a single replacement or set of replacements over the asset's life, without getting caught up in the planning horizon 'missing revenue' problem we identified in our initial treatment of the single replacement cycle setting. In effect, by taking a 'simulated market' perspective we have been able to collapse Baxter's many-cycle model into a single-cycle one without having to change the valuation formula!

The components of equations (7.28a) and (7.15) can best be understood by taking a slightly different market perspective. Suppose that, instead of buying the used asset, we leased it.[14] In equilibrium, there will be no opportunities to arbitrage between the new market, the second-hand market, or the leasing market. The cost K_0 of a new asset will be equal to the present value of n lease payments of EAK each. The present value of the lease payments should also equate to the relevant vintage-adjusted buying price, K_t, in the second-hand market. For a t-year-old asset, the charge must equal $n - t$ potentially varying lease payments of amount

$$L_j = \text{EAK} - (R_j - \text{EAR}) \tag{7.29}$$

That this is indeed the equilibrium pattern of lease payments is demon-

Table 7.2 Numerical example of depreciation, book values and excess incomes computed according to deprival value principles

	Year 0	Year 1	Year 2	Year 3	Year 4	NPV0
Panel A: financial results						
1 Net revenue (X_t)		75,000	75,000	75,000	75,000	
2 Maintenance and repair costs (R_t)		−5,000	−19,000	−32,000	−44,000	
3 = 1 − 2 Net cash flows	−100,000	70,000	56,000	43,000	31,000	49,211
4 Depreciation (DVD_t)		−37,763	−29,427	−20,842	−11,968	
5 = 3 − 4 Operating income		32,237	26,573	22,158	19,032	
6 Interest (= 15% × K_{t-1})		−15,000	−9,336	−4,921	−1,795	
7 = 5 − 6 Excess income		17,237	17,237	17,237	17,237	49,211
8 Asset book value (K_t)	100,000	62,237	32,810	11,968	0	
Panel B: deprival value budgets						
9 = 2 + 6 HAVE budgets		20,000	28,336	36,921	45,795	
10 HAVE-NOT budgets (= EAK + EAR)		57,763	57,763	57,763	57,763	
11 = 10 − 9 Benefit of owning (= depreciation)		37,763	29,427	20,842	11,968	
Panel C: asset buying plans						
12 NPV of cash flows of using one one- + one three-year-old asset						49,211
13 NPV of cash flows of using two two-year-old assets						49,211
14 NPV of cash flows of using one three- + one one-year-old asset						49,211

strated by the fact that their discounted sum equals the market price for the used asset:

$$K_t = \sum_{j=t+1}^{n} v^{j-t}L_j \quad (t = 1, \ldots, -1) \tag{7.30}$$

where K_t is defined in equation (7.28a). Notice that each lease payment as in equation (7.29) is adjusted to allow for the extent to which repairs and maintenance in a particular year are expected to differ from the overall annual average of EAR on a new asset.

This notional leasing perspective provides additional insight into the connection between accounting valuations and the income recognition process. The approach is applicable to the historical cost accounting framework as well as to a current cost approach. To see this, it is helpful to employ the distinction between 'initial recognition' and subsequent 're-measurement' which appears in the ASB's draft *Statement of Principles* (ASB 1995).

Under both historical cost and current cost, an asset is initially shown at the amount paid for it (K_0 in our notation). Historical cost accounting can be thought of as a special case of current cost accounting in which the replacement cost of the asset in new condition is assumed not to change during the life of the asset. In which case, historical cost book value corresponds to the used-asset price of an asset of that vintage. The trouble with expressing the measurement process in this way, of course, is that it appears to conflict with the 'matching' perspective traditionally adopted for historical cost accounting. A way round this difficulty is to think of allocation in terms of the capital component in the charges that the firm would have had to pay if it had leased rather than bought the asset.

We assume the historical cost of the asset is to be allocated to periods according to the forecast notional lease payments avoided by reason of ownership of the asset. The notional lease payments will include an element representing interest on capital, which will have to be deducted from the charge shown in equation (7.29) to arrive at the charge for historical cost depreciation:

$$D_t = L_t - iB_{t-1} \tag{7.31}$$

where B_{t-1} is the historical cost book value of the asset at the beginning of period t. Equation (7.31) corresponds exactly with what we have called 'benefit from owning' in our numerical example; see panel B of Table 7.2. Substituting equation (7.29) into (7.31) and rearranging, we obtain a formula for the total historical cost of operating the asset:

$$R_t + (D_t + iB_{t-1}) = EAK + EAR \tag{7.32}$$

which has the same structural form as equation (7.18). Since $B_0 = K_0 = V_0$,

141

it follows that $B_t = V_t$ throughout; hence $D_t = DVD_t$, in every period. As expected, depreciation is allocated on a deprival value basis. To repeat, the result will be a pattern of written-down book values for the asset which can be interpreted either:

(a) as the result of a process of matching costs according to the pattern of outlays which would have been incurred if the firm had leased rather than purchased the asset; or

(b) as approximations of the replacement cost of the used asset, under the assumption that the cost of the corresponding new asset remains the same throughout the life of the asset.

The deprival value approach can be used without difficulty to deal with cases where 're-measurement' is deemed appropriate. The model is therefore suitable for the computation of current cost depreciation. Since this application has been dealt with at length by Baxter, we limit ourselves here to a few brief remarks on the used-asset interpretation of current cost depreciation.

To simplify matters, we assume that estimates of repairs remain unchanged throughout, but that immediately after the end of period $t-1$ the cost of a new asset rises by Δ_t from K_0 to $K_0 + \Delta_t$. The asset is still considered worth replacing and the cost of the asset remains unchanged for the remainder of period t. If the firm were deprived of the asset at this point, it would spend $K_0 + \Delta_t$ and thereby obtain an asset with $n - t + 1$ more years of useful operating life than the existing one. It will therefore be necessary to assume that the firm plugs the gap at time n, when the existing asset expires, with another used one (or succession of used ones) with only $n - t + 1$ years of life left to run. This will ensure that we can restrict the comparison between our HAVE and HAVE-NOT budgets at time t to a common horizon of n years, ending at time $n + t$. In a time of rising prices, it will be necessary to make allowance for the likelihood of cost of a replacement asset at time n being greater than it would be at time t. As with repairs, we will ignore such complications for the purposes of analysis.

Plugging the new cost figure into equation (7.28a), we obtain a revised estimate of the asset's value. Subtracting from this the value currently shown on the books, we obtain the realisable cost saving (or holding gain). This period t benefit, denoted here as RCS_t, is equal to the present value of the additional annualised cost of the increased purchase price of a new asset:

$$RCS_t = P_{(n-t+1),i}(\Delta_t / P_{n,i}) \qquad (7.33)$$

In other words, the firm has gained through holding an asset which has increased in value by an amount equivalent to the value of the $n - t + 1$ incremental lease payments avoided by reason of ownership of the asset.

Current cost depreciation in period t can be obtained by using equation (7.28a) to compute beginning and ending values for the asset using the new cost figure, $K_0 + \Delta_t$. Henceforth, depreciation has to be uplifted by an amount equal to the extra lease payment for one year, discounted $n - t + 1$ years:

$$\Delta DVD_t = v^{n-t+1}(\Delta t / P_{n,i}) \qquad (7.34)$$

A comparison of equations (7.33) and (7.34) indicates that the increase in depreciation, which is the realised cost saving for the period, is the last of the $n - t + 1$ additional lease payments which go to make up the realisable cost saving figure. Use or the passage of time brings the time of replacement nearer (Baxter and Carrier 1971).

Finally, it is worth noting that the deprival value approach to depreciation can be used to develop rough rules of thumb of the kind familiar to accountants. In practice, cost–benefit considerations dictate that depreciation charges be estimated in a routine manner and without undue delay. Rules of thumb are therefore bound to be widely employed, under both historical cost and current cost accounting regimes. Equation (7.19) provides a useful means of establishing the relative accuracy of various methods commonly encountered in practice. Since we have shown previously that our formula has the same structural form as the one Anton (1956) devised for internal-rate depreciation, such that his results can be applied with only minor amendment, it will suffice to show how a rule of thumb can be obtained in a straightforward manner from the model in two widely understood situations.

We have already noted the simple case where repairs are constant through time. In this situation, the annuity method should be used, which will result in the charge for depreciation increasing on a compound basis at a rate equal to the cost of capital. The annuity method is sometimes graced with the title 'economic depreciation', presumably in acknowledgement that an allowance is being made to reflect the cost of finance. It is, however, a very special case, applicable only in a constant-efficiency setting. An obvious case where the annuity method can be (and is) used is in the amortisation of the discount on a low-coupon bond. In the more general setting, where repairs are likely to increase from one period to the next, the upward drift in depreciation caused by the interest-growth effect will be offset by a downward pull to reflect the loss in operating efficiency in older assets. The relative strength of the two forces will determine the time series pattern of depreciation charges (Baxter 1971: ch. 8).

An interesting limiting case is where repairs increase linearly at a rate just sufficient to offset the interest effect:

$$DVD_{t+1} = (R_{t+1} - R_t)/i = DVD_t \quad (t = 1, \ldots, n - 1)$$

In this situation, the depreciation charges are constant through time and the ubiquitous straight-line method is appropriate:

$$DVD_t = K_0/n$$

As a first approximation, this might well serve as the working hypothesis for most depreciable assets in practice. At any rate, the economic justification given here is stronger than the limp defence of the method provided in the quotation from Hendriksen and van Breda given earlier in the chapter.

CONCLUSIONS

The ideas we discuss in this paper are not new. The concept of deprival value was clearly understood by Canning (1929); and Wright (1964) outlined the broad principles of deprival value depreciation over thirty years ago. The neglect of the concept seems to have been due to a number of factors, including widespread acceptance of the idea that all depreciation methods are inherently arbitrary.

The starting point of our analysis is that replacement cost is best defined by reference to the price obtainable from the relevant used-asset market. However, it has to be recognised that used-asset markets are likely to be thin or non-existent when transaction costs are large or there are difficulties in determining asset quality. We have tried to show how an estimate of replacement cost can be obtained in such situations by using an extended version of the deprival value calculus, previously expounded by Baxter in homely terms of HAVE and HAVE-NOT budgets. For this purpose, we set to one side the cases where an asset might have to be written down to a lower recoverable amount and concentrate on exploring the properties of cost-based measurements. This has the additional attraction of avoiding the problem of having to allocate the firm's revenue across different assets. Attention is focused instead on costs associated with the use and ageing of the asset, such as repair and maintenance costs, which appear likely to be less intertwined with the other costs of the business and can therefore be identified without recourse to arbitrary allocations.

The deprival value approach is forward looking. In principle, this poses nothing new for the accountant, in that all depreciation allocations involve forecasts of future events. Where Baxter's method is likely to cause unease is that it explicitly involves peering into the very distant future, beyond the economic life of the existing asset, to consider successive replacement cycles. Our contribution has been to show how Baxter's many-cycle model can be collapsed into a single-cycle one by interpreting the resultant book values as used-asset prices (or, equivalently, the depreciation charges as the capital elements of notional lease payments).

A virtue of the deprival value approach to depreciation and asset measurement is that it provides a schema for accounting for the many and various kinds of future events which are currently causing difficulty for accountants. Examples are provided in the conceptual study of future events carried out jointly by the International Accounting Standards Committee and the standards boards in the USA, Canada, the UK and Australia, summarised in Johnson (1994) and discussed by Baxter (1996) from a deprival value perspective. These future events include the treatment of lumpy maintenance and refurbishment expenditures which any really satisfactory theory of depreciation must be capable of handling. Our analysis shows how deprival value can handle such complications in ways which both make good economic sense and are capable of rationalising conventional rules of thumb as special cases.

Limitations of space prevent our providing comparisons of the arithmetical properties of deprival value depreciation with those of alternative approaches which have appeared in the literature. These appear in a companion paper (Bell 1996). We end with the usual plea of the researcher: more work needs to be done on what we hope we have succeeded in demonstrating is a promising approach to an important practical problem which has been neglected for too long.

NOTES

1 Bonbright used 'Value to the Owner' sometimes to mean 'Deprival Value' and elsewhere restricted it to mean PV. Since there is no good term to refer to the higher of PV and NRV, the label 'Economic Value' preferred by some being too broad for our liking, 'Value to the Owner' seems appropriate for our purpose. See MacDonald (1974) and Fraser (1988) for further discussion of the uses made of these terms.

2 This does not mean that firms should be indifferent to choice of depreciation method. Anton and Brief (1987) show that in such static conditions depreciation will have an expansionary effect on financial capital whenever book depreciation is computed on a more accelerated basis than the economic depreciation method. This can have implications for the financial management of the firm.

3 For sophisticated early analyses of some of the issues involved, see Preinreich (1938, 1939).

4 Since the outlay remains constant at K_0, this implies revenues remain constant after $n + 2$: $X_{n+3} = X_{n+4} = \ldots.$ The alternative is to allow the outlay to change from $t = 2$ onwards, keeping the assumption of zero net present value. The following analysis abstracts from the problems of changing prices, in order to avoid the complications involved in accounting for cost savings (holding gains).

5 Recall that in the previous single-cycle setting we had to allow for the fact that the existing asset would generate revenues for a shorter period than the replacement asset and this difference in revenues had to be incorporated into the analysis.

6 Put differently, servicing costs are the same in both the HAVE and HAVE-NOT budgets and can be left out of the analysis in the same way that revenues are.

7 A graphical analysis using deprival value depreciation which takes this into account is provided by Bell (1996). This paper also contains a number of arithmetical examples comparing deprival value depreciation with other depreciation procedures, the measures of deprival value depreciation all being

consistent with the algebra of equations (7.18) and (7.19), as well as other formulae presented in this section.

8 It is important to remember that we are using the term 'repairs' to refer to all cash flows which are a function of the age of the asset.

9 Note also that any IRD calculation inevitably involves future revenues, which limits its usefulness as an *ex post* performance measure.

10 See Edwards and Bell (1961): Appendix B to Chapter 2 and Peasnell (1982). An historical treatment is provided in Brief and Peasnell (1996).

11 Limitations of space preclude our discussing the many attractive features of deprival value as a basis for developing an income concept which can be used as a measure of financial performance. See Bell (1996), particularly table 6 and the discussion on pp. 131–4 for numerical demonstrations of how deprival value depreciation yields the correct signals about changing economic circumstances, whereas these can be masked when other procedures, including the internal-rate method, are used.

12 A similar problem arises for the investor in the bond markets, who has to choose between a long-dated bond or a succession of short-maturity bills.

13 The other four buying plans, stated here for brevity in terms of remaining lives, entail the following combinations: (iv) two and one and one; (v) one and two and one; (vi) one and one and two; and (vii) one and one and one and one.

14 Strictly speaking, the contract would have to be on a finance (or capital) lease basis, whereby all risks of ownership were borne by the lessee. An operating lease is formally equivalent to a finance lease but with the added benefit for the lessee of having an embedded option to 'put' the asset back to the lessor if circumstances dictate. The lease charge will therefore contain a premium to reflect the value of such a put. We ignore such complications in our analysis.

REFERENCES

Accounting Standards Board (1995) *Exposure Draft: Statement of Principles for Financial Reporting*, London: ASB.

Akerlof, G. A. (1970) 'The market for "lemons": qualitative uncertainty and the market mechanism', *Quarterly Journal of Economics* 84 (August): 488–500.

Anton, H. R. (1956) 'Depreciation, cost allocation and investment decisions', *Accounting Research* 2 (April): 117–34. Reprinted in T. F. Keller and S. A. Zeff (eds) *Financial Accounting Theory II: Issues and Controversies*, New York: McGraw-Hill, 287–309.

Anton, H. R. and Brief, R. P. (1987) 'An index of growth due to depreciation', *Contemporary Accounting Research* 3 (Spring): 394–407.

Barth, M. E. (1991) 'Relative measurement errors among alternative pension asset and liability measures', *Accounting Review* 66 (July): 433–63.

Barth, M. E., Landsman, W. R. and Rendleman, R. J. Jr (1995) 'Accounting for financial instruments: an option pricing-based approach to measuring corporate debt components', working paper, Stanford University and University of North Carolina at Chapel Hill.

Baxter, W. T. (1971) *Depreciation*, London: Sweet & Maxwell.
—— (1975) *Accounting Values and Inflation*, London: McGraw-Hill.
—— (1981) *Depreciating Assets: An Introduction*, London: Gee.
—— (1996) '"Future events – a conceptual study of their significance": a review article', *Accounting and Business Research* 26 (Spring): 171–6.

Baxter W. T. and Carrier, N. H. (1971) 'Depreciation, replacement price, and cost of capital', *Journal of Accounting Research* 9 (Autumn): 189–214.

Beaver, W. H. (1991) 'Problems and paradoxes in the financial reporting of future events', *Accounting Horizons* 5 (December): 122–34.

Beaver, W. H. and Demski, J. S. (1979) 'The nature of income measurement', *Accounting Review* 54 (January): 38–46.

—— (1994) 'Income measurement and valuation', working paper, Stanford University and Yale University.

Beidleman, C. R. (1973) *Valuation of Used Capital Assets*, Sarasota, FL: American Accounting Association.

Bell, P. W. (1996) 'Depreciation accounting and evaluation of decisions and performance', in E. Steiner, F. Gjesdal and A. Sandmo (eds) *Analyser og Perspectiver I Bedriftsøkonomi*, Bergen: Fagbokforiaget Vigmostad & Bjørke.

Bell, P. W. and Johnson, L. T. (1979) 'Current value accounting and the simple production case: Edbejo and other companies in the taxi business', in R. R. Sterling and A. L. Thomas (eds) *Accounting for a Simplified Firm Owning Depreciable Assets: Seventeen Essays and a Synthesis Based on a Common Case*, Houston: Scholars, pp. 95–130.

Bonbright, J. C. (1937) *The Valuation of Property: A Treatise on the Appraisal of Property for Different Legal Purposes*, New York: McGraw-Hill (reprinted Michie Company, 1965).

Brief, R. P. (ed.) (1996) *A Landmark in Accounting Theory: The Work of Gabriel A. D. Preinreich*, New York: Garland.

Brief, R. P. and Peasnell, K. V. (eds) (1996) *Clean Surplus: A Link Between Accounting and Finance*, New York: Garland.

Canning, J. B. (1929) *The Economics of Accountancy*, New York: Ronald Press.

Carey, A. (1993) *Depreciation: The Time for Change*, London: Institute of Chartered Accountants in England and Wales.

Chambers, D., Jennings, R. and Thompson, R. B. II (1995) 'Evidence on the usefulness of alternative depreciation measures', working paper, University of Texas at Austin and University of Maryland at College Park.

Churchill, M. (1995) 'GTEs: closing the value gap', *Australian Accountant* 65 (August): 23–6.

Edwards, E. O. and Bell, P. W. (1961) *The Theory and Measurement of Business Income*, Los Angeles and Berkeley: University of California Press.

Fraser, I. A. M. (1988) 'Deprival Value or Value to the Owner – a clarification', *Abacus* 24 (March): 86–9.

Hastie, L. (1995) 'A matter of appreciating depreciation', *Accountancy* 116 (December): 97.

Hendriksen, E. S. and van Breda, M. F. (1992) *Accounting Theory*, 5th edition, Homewood, IL: Irwin.

Hicks, J. R. (1946) *Value and Capital*, 2nd edition, Oxford: Oxford University Press.

Hotelling, H. (1925) 'A general mathematical theory of depreciation', *Journal of the American Statistical Association* 20 (September): 340–53. Reprinted in R.e H. Parker and G. C. Harcourt (1969) (eds) *Readings in the Concept and Measurement of Income*, Cambridge: Cambridge University Press, pp. 261–75.

Ijiri, Y. (1967) 'On the convergence of periodic reinvestments by an amount equal to depreciation', *Management Science* 13 (January): 321–5.

Johnson, L. T. (1994) *Future Events – A Conceptual Study of their Significance*, Stamford, CT: Financial Accounting Standards Board.

MacDonald, G. (1974) 'Deprival Value: its use and abuse', *Accounting and Business Research* 4 (Autumn): 263–9.

Ohlson, J. A. (1995) 'Earnings, book values, and dividends in equity valuation', *Contemporary Accounting Research* 11 (Spring): 661–87.

Peasnell, K. V. (1982) 'Some formal connections between economic values and yields and accounting numbers', *Journal of Business Finance and Accounting* 9 (3): 361–81.

—— (1984) 'Technological change and other aspects of the definition of replacement cost for managerial purposes', in J. Klaassen and P. Verburg (eds) *Replacement Costs for Managerial Purposes*, Amsterdam: North-Holland.

Parker, R. H. and Harcourt, G. C. (eds) (1969) *Readings in the Concept and Measurement of Income*, Cambridge: Cambridge University Press.

Preinreich, G. A. D. (1938) 'The principles of public-utility depreciation', *Accounting Review* 13 (June): 149–65. Reprinted in R. P. Brief (ed.) (1996) *A Landmark in Accounting Theory: The work of Gabriel A. D. Preinreich*, New York: Garland, pp. 135–51.

—— (1939) 'The practice of depreciation', *Econometrica* 7 (July): 235–65. Reprinted in R. P. Brief (ed.) (1996) *A Landmark in Accounting Theory: The Work of Gabriel A. D. Preinreich*, New York: Garland, pp. 157–89.

Rubinstein, M. (1994) 'On the accounting valuation of employee stock options', working paper, University of California at Berkeley.

Sandilands, F. E. P. (1975) *Report of the Inflation Accounting Committee: Inflation Accounting*, Cmnd. 6225, London: Her Majesty's Stationery Office.

Solomons, D. (1966) 'Economic and accounting concepts of cost and value', in M. Backer (ed) *Modern Accounting Theory*, Englewood Cliffs, NJ: Prentice Hall.

Sterling, R. R. and Thomas, A. L. (eds) (1979) *Accounting for a Simplified Firm Owning Depreciable Assets: Seventeen Essays and a Synthesis Based on a Common Case*, Houston: Scholars.

Thomas, A. L. (1969) *The Allocation Problem in Financial Accounting Theory*, Sarasota, FL: American Accounting Association.

—— (1974) *The Allocation Problem: Part Two*, Sarasota, FL: American Accounting Association.

Watts, R. L. and Zimmerman, J. L. (1978) 'The demand for and supply of accounting theories: the market for excuses', *Accounting Review* 54 (April): 273–305.

Whittington, G. (1994) 'Current cost accounting: its role in regulated industries', *Fiscal Studies* 15 (October): 88–101.

Williamson, O. E. (1985) *The Economic Institutions of Capitalism*, New York: Free Press.

Wright, F. K. (1964) 'Towards a general theory of depreciation', *Journal of Accounting Research*, 2 (Spring): 80–90.

8

THE END OF THE CURRENT COST REVOLUTION

*David Tweedie and Geoffrey Whittington**

INTRODUCTION

In 1984, we published *The Debate on Inflation Accounting*, which attempted to provide a comprehensive international and historical survey of the development of the theory and practice of accounting for changing prices. It is important to note that the topic is actually *changing prices* rather than simply *inflation*. The former allows for changes in the *relative* prices of particular assets and liabilities as well as changes in prices due to pure inflation, i.e. to the decline of the general purchasing power of money. In accounting terms, this distinction is reflected in the difference between CPP (Constant Purchasing Power), which adjusts historical cost for pure inflation, and CCA (Current Cost Accounting), which replaces historical costs by the current costs of particular assets, and is therefore concerned with specific price changes.

Our 1984 work found that, in the English-speaking world, the initial reaction of accountants (particularly professional bodies and standard setters) to the rising inflation rates of the late 1960s and early 1970s was to embrace pure inflation accounting systems of the CPP variety. Later, as inflation continued and the debate on price change accounting was protracted by the intervention of governments, there took place what we characterised as the Current Cost Revolution (Tweedie and Whittington 1984: ch. 11), in which CCA became the price change accounting system favoured by standard setters. By 1980, both the USA and the UK had adopted accounting standards which required supplementary disclosure of CCA information by leading companies, under SFAS 33 (of 1979) and SSAP 16 (of 1980) respectively. Similar proposals followed in Australia, New Zealand and Canada, and the Current Cost Revolution seemed to be complete. By 1987, both SFAS 33 and SSAP 16 had been withdrawn, and CCA disclosures were not majority practice anywhere in the world. The purpose of this paper is to trace this remarkable decline, concentrating on the UK and the USA, which led international practice in the field and provided the main focus of our earlier study, but also commenting upon the distinctive experience of other countries during the same period. Notable

149

among these are the Netherlands, in which substantial minority practice of replacement value accounting (which can be regarded as a variant of CCA) had developed long before the Current Cost Revolution occurred elsewhere, and several countries of Latin America, where CPP was adopted as a response to the pressures of hyperinflation, and which did not experience a subsequent switch to CCA.

BACKGROUND

Our book adopted an inductive approach: the historical experience was described and a subsequent attempt was made to derive general propositions about the factors which determined the evolution of accounting standards and practice in relation to changing prices. In this paper, therefore, we have the comparative luxury of being able to start with general propositions about the main causal factors, derived from our previous work (Tweedie and Whittington 1984: ch. 13). This listed five main factors:

1 Economic events (notably inflation rates).
2 Self-interest (such as how certain groups might be affected by the tax consequences of a particular form of price change accounting).
3 Ideas (including not merely the supply of new theoretical insights, but also their dissemination amongst standard setters and practitioners).
4 International influences (the development of practice in any particular country will tend to be informed or influenced by developments in others, particularly if there are close economic ties between countries).
5 Accidents of history (there are historical factors additional to those described above, which will influence developments in a particular country, such as the influence of individuals, committees or reports that are especially persuasive).

All of the above factors will be seen at work in our account of the decline of CCA in the 1980s. In the UK and the USA, which were leaders both in the introduction of current cost and in its subsequent withdrawal, the first two factors were particularly important. In both countries, inflation rates were high in 1979–80, when the two new price change accounting standards were introduced, but there was subsequently a sharp reduction in the inflation rate. Moreover, in both countries the decline in the inflation rate was a consequence of changes of government economic policy, associated with Prime Minister Thatcher in the UK and President Reagan in the USA. These new political regimes were also in favour of regulation by the market rather than regulation by government, and this took away some of the self-interest incentives for the adoption of price change accounting: not only was the impact of price changes reduced (as a consequence of lower inflation rates) but the possibility of price controls and penal taxation (the

150

Table 8.1 Inflation rates in various countries

	1973–9 (average)	1980	1981	1982	1983	1984	1985	1986
USA	8.5	13.5	10.3	6.1	3.2	4.3	3 5	1.9
UK	15.6	18.0	11.9	8.6	4.6	5.0	6.1	3.4
Australia	12.1	10.2	9.7	11.1	10.1	3.9	6.8	9.1
New Zealand	13.8	17.2	15.4	16.2	7.3	6.2	15.4	13.2
Canada	9.2	10.2	12.4	10.8	5.8	4.3	4.0	4.2
Netherlands	7.2	6.5	6.7	5.9	2.7	3.3	2.3	0.1

Source: OECD (1992) *Historical Statistics*, OECD Economic Outlook, Paris, Table 8.11.
Note: The numbers are year-to-year percentage changes in consumer price indices

impact of which might be minimised by the use of price change accounting) was also much reduced. Thus, in retrospect, SFAS 33 and SSAP 16 were introduced too late: the threats of inflation, and its adverse consequences for business, were about to recede. Table 8.1 provides background data on inflation rates during this period.

We now turn to the experience of individual countries in attempting to implement various forms of CCA. Following the pattern of our 1984 book, we give primacy to the experience of the UK and the USA, which tended to lead international developments during this period. We shall then review the experience of the other English-speaking countries which attempted, with much less success in terms of compliance, to follow the implementation of CCA, and we shall also consider the continuing Dutch experience of replacement value accounting, and the Latin American application of CPP accounting in conditions of extreme inflation.

THE UK EXPERIENCE SINCE 1980

SSAP 16, issued in March 1980, was the result of many years of debate and fourteen years of hard work by the Accounting Standards Committee's (ASC's) Inflation Accounting Steering Group (IASG), chaired by Sir Douglas Morpeth. The evolution of the new standard, and its predecessor, the Hyde Guidelines (a voluntary recommendation which proposed some similar disclosures), was described in Tweedie and Whittington (1984: chs 4 to 6). Inevitably, the result of such a long debate was an accounting standard marked by compromise. There were three important compromises in SSAP 16, each of which was to continue to be subject to controversy. First, although SSAP 16 required current cost disclosures based on specific price changes, a compromise with inflation (as opposed to price change) accounting was made in the gearing adjustment and the monetary working capital adjustment, which attempted to reflect the inflationary gain on borrowing and loss on holding monetary assets (albeit using specific rather

151

than general indices). Second, the standard applied only to large companies, not to all companies. Third, current cost adjustments were not required to be made in the main accounts, although this was an option.

Despite its painful birth and the marks of compromise, SSAP 16 was at first a success, in so far as it achieved very high compliance rates. In 1981, the first year in which it was mandatory for all accounting dates, 95 per cent of the companies surveyed in *Financial Reporting* produced current cost data (see Table 8.2). However, three years later this had fallen to 34 per cent, and by 1985 it was only 6 per cent, and SSAP 16 ceased to be a mandatory standard.

The salient facts of this decline are recorded in Table 8.2, which is taken from Pong and Whittington (1996), a paper which examines the events of

Table 8.2 UK inflation rates, compliance rates, and price-level events, 1977–88

Year	% increase in average RPI[3]	% of companies producing price-level statements[1,2,3]	Price-level accounting events of the year
1977	12.1	45	Hyde Guidelines
1978	8.4	56	
1979	17.2	58	ED 24 (April)
1980	15.1	78	SSAP 16 (March)
1981	12.1	95	
1982	5.4	81	Green Paper on Corporation Tax (March) Keymer Haslem resolution (July) Stock Exchange stops requiring CCA interim accounts (December)
1983	5.3	61	Neville Reports (April and September) Carsberg Report (November)
1984	4.6	34	ED 35 (July)
1985	5.7	6	SSAP 16 no longer mandatory (June)
1986	3.7	3	Handbook (October)
1987	3.7	3	
1988	6.8	—	SSAP 16 withdrawn (April)

Notes:

1 Based on accounts circulated to shareholders during the year to 30 June of the following year. Hence, 1980 is the first year in which SSAP 16 was universally applicable (SSAP 16 applied to accounting periods commencing after March 1980).

2 The first four years include methods other than the ED 24/SSAP 16 system. The methods were nearly all simplified CCA adjustments consistent with the 1977 Hyde Guidelines. The percentages of companies using these methods were 35, 51, 46 and 6 in 1977, 1978, 1979 and 1980 respectively.

3 *Sources*:

(a) % increase in RPI for the year (year to December) – Datastream. This differs from Table 8.1 figures which are based on a comparison of averages for the final quarter of each year.

(b) % of companies producing price-level statements – Skerratt and Tonkin (eds). Annual Surveys of *Financial Reporting*, published by the ICAEW, summarised by Hanson (1989; tables 4 and 6).

the period in some detail, using data from the ASC's archives. Although most of the interesting developments in the standard setting occurred from 1983 onwards, following the publication of the first Neville Report, it seems likely, in retrospect, that much of the support for SSAP 16 had already eroded. Reference has been made to the change of economic policy following the change of government in 1979. Table 8.2 shows that inflation dropped from 12.1 per cent in 1981 to 5.4 per cent in 1982, as a result of the new government's anti-inflationary fiscal and monetary policies. Thus, price changes were a much less pressing issue than they had been up to 1981. Moreover, the potential advantages of CCA as a means of defence against government interventions were also reduced. The Prices and Incomes Board, together with the associated threat of government-enforced price controls, was abolished, and in 1982 the Green Paper on Corporation Tax made it clear that CCA was unlikely ever to be used as a base for corporation tax, because it was too subjective. Thus, two of the potential practical benefits to business of producing CCA information were removed before 1983. An empirical study by Lemke and Page (1992) suggests that regulatory and tax considerations were important factors in encouraging firms to withdraw support from SSAP 16. If this was the case, support may have been damaged irreparably even before the ASC's committees started their review of the future of the standard.

There were two other events in 1982 which support this view. First, Messrs Keymer and Haslam, who had earlier been successful in proposing a resolution of members of the Institute of Chartered Accountants in England and Wales (ICAEW) which led to the withdrawal of the first current cost exposure draft (ED 18 of 1976), proposed a similar resolution to ICAEW members (in July 1982) calling for withdrawal of SSAP 16. This time, their resolution was rejected, but by a narrow margin; 48.5 per cent of those voting supported the resolution. This caused much anxiety to the Council of the ICAEW, the biggest of the professional bodies in the Consultative Committee of Accountancy Bodies (CCAB), the parent organisation of the ASC.

Second, in December 1982, the Stock Exchange withdrew the requirement that CCA disclosures should accompany interim statements. This was a clear signal that one of the guardians of the users of accounts did not consider that current cost accounts were important. Moreover, this view was later supported substantially by the results of the ICAEW research study (Carsberg and Page 1984), which found that current cost information was only of secondary importance, relative to historical cost. Similar empirical results were obtained from the studies of the use of the SFAS 33 disclosures in the USA.

Against this background, the ASC took no immediate action. When issuing SSAP 16, it had committed itself to a three-year experimental period in which no revisions would be made but during which the implementation of SSAP 16 would be monitored by its Inflation Accounting Subcommittee

(IAS) and its working parties. The first outcome of this process was the publication of the interim report of the Monitoring Working Party in 1983, exactly three years after SSAP 16 had been issued. This report was known as the Neville Report (after the Chairman of the group, Tom Neville) and the final report, published later in the same year, identified widespread discontent with SSAP 16 amongst preparers of accounts, particularly those in small businesses, but little consensus about how it should be replaced. The Report made some recommendations, notably that SSAP 16 should be replaced by a less demanding standard which did not require a current cost balance sheet and allowed choice of method, but which nevertheless applied to all companies. These recommendations had little direct support from the empirical evidence that had been gathered (e.g. small businesses seemed strongly opposed to CCA and might be expected to oppose universality of application).

Later in the same year, 1983, a four-volume collection of academic studies appeared (later published as Carsberg and Page 1984), containing a variety of empirical studies of the application and use of SSAP 16. Benefits to users (e.g. evidence of use by analysts and commentators) were found, but these were generally small, although some of the studies suggested that the costs of implementing SSAP 16 were also small, so that the standard should not necessarily be ruled out on cost–benefit grounds. The first volume consisted of a survey by Bryan Carsberg ('The Carsberg Report'), which summarised the results and made recommendations. In contrast with the Neville Report, the Carsberg Report concluded that CCA had been shown to be worthwhile and that the CCA experiment should therefore continue, albeit in a form modified in the light of the research results. In contrast to Neville, Carsberg proposed that CCA should continue (whereas Neville supported the much greater choice of price change adjustment method) and that the universality principle espoused by Neville should be rejected in favour of continuing to confine CCA disclosure requirements to large companies, on cost–benefit grounds. He proposed that simplified methods of calculation, such as the use of price indices, should be allowed, on cost–benefit grounds, in cases of difficulty.

The conclusions of the Carsberg Report were controversial. Messrs Archer and Steele, the authors of a substantial survey which comprised the fourth volume of the Carsberg and Page study, felt that proper weight had not been given to their results which, like the Neville Report, showed that there was strong opposition to CCA amongst preparers of accounts. As with the Neville Report, there was an inevitable degree of difficulty in drawing conclusions from diverse and sometimes contradictory evidence. However, in retrospect, it is clear that there was not really strong evidence in support of the usefulness of SSAP 16; the substantial effort to evaluate the effects of SFAS 33 reached much the same conclusion, and the first major conference to evaluate this evidence took place in 1983.

The empirical evidence in both the UK and the USA was essentially indecisive. At best, small benefits from using current cost data could be detected, but this was at an early stage in the experiment, before users and preparers had become fully accustomed to the new systems. Additionally, it could be argued that the possible deficiencies of the systems as implemented (such as the confusion generated in the UK by the gearing and monetary working capital adjustments) prevented the experiment from being a proper test of the general usefulness of current cost disclosures. Furthermore, relatively simple adjustments had probably been made previously by analysts, and in both the USA (under the SEC's 1975 requirements) and in the UK (under the 1977 Hyde Guidelines) current cost data were published before the full standards were promulgated, so that the market had probably already absorbed much of the initial impact of CCA disclosures.

It now fell to the IAS and the ASC to fulfil the ASC's original (1980) promise that SSAP 16 would be reviewed after the three-year experimental period. There was considerable debate between supporters of what might be loosely characterised as the Neville view (universality of application but freedom of choice as to method) and the Carsberg view (current cost methods required but with application restricted to large companies). To aid the debate, the ASC took two legal opinions (Hoffman and Arden 1983 and 1984) which suggested first that it would be appropriate for the ASC to require current cost disclosures as part of the 'true and fair view' requirement for the main accounts, and second that the true and fair view could incorporate a cost–benefit test, i.e. small companies could be excluded from a requirement on the ground that its cost was high in relation to its benefit to them.

Armed with the Hoffman and Arden opinions, the ASC produced ED 35 in July 1984. This came down broadly in favour of the Carsberg view. CCA would continue to be required, but by way of notes to the main accounts (which would be audited) rather than, as previously, in supplementary unaudited statements. Application would be to public companies only, on the ground that these were the most likely to offer the greater benefits (owing to their wider range of potential users of accounts), and 'value based' companies (such as investment trusts and property companies) were to be exempt. Alternative methods of calculating the gearing adjustment were to be allowed (including general indexation) and the methods of assessing the current costs of assets were simplified, allowing greater use of price indices and putting less emphasis on the need to estimate recoverable amounts.

The responses to ED 35 were overwhelmingly negative: three-quarters of the 119 respondents were opposed to its being developed as a standard (Pong and Whittington 1996). Not only were companies strongly opposed, as might have been expected in the light of the Neville Report and the study by Archer and Steele, but so were audit firms and the CCAB professional accounting bodies which issued the standards prepared by the ASC. The only significant message of support came from the Society of Investment Analysts; other users of accounts remained substantially silent on the issue.

Following the analysis of these responses, early in 1985, the Department of Trade and Industry was approached about possible government backing for a CCA standard, but no offer of support was forthcoming. The Stock Exchange was also unenthusiastic about supporting CCA. Thus, in March 1985, ED 35 was abandoned. Then, in June 1985, the mandatory status of SSAP 16 was removed, so that it became merely a recommendation. This effectively marked the end of the CCA experiment in accounting standards in the UK.

Remarkably, the ASC continued its attempt to develop some sort of standard on accounting for changing prices. It drafted an abortive exposure draft, ED 38, which was never formally issued. This was to apply only to listed companies and required a simple one-line adjustment to profit to reflect changing prices, on a basis to be chosen by the preparer of the accounts. Even this very weak proposal was not supported by the Stock Exchange or government bodies. Thus, in December 1985, the ASC recommended the withdrawal of SSAP 16. In 1986 the ASC published a *Handbook on Accounting for the Effects of Changing Prices*, which merely summarised the alternative methods that had been developed in the debate, as a guide to those who might wish voluntarily to report the effects of price changes (see later). SSAP 16 was now redundant, but it was not formally withdrawn until April 1988, owing to the insistence of one CCAB body (the Chartered Association of Certified Accountants) that the ASC should have some formal recommendation on price change accounting.

The collapse of SSAP 16 and the inability to replace it meant that the ASC's longest-running, most controversial and most time-consuming project had failed, owing to opposition and non-compliance by preparers of accounts. This blow to the authority of the ASC proved to be fatal. When faced with the problems of creative accounting, which flourished in the middle and late 1980s (Griffiths 1986), the ASC could not act decisively because of the fear that its constituency would fail to support it. In 1987, the CCAB appointed the Dearing Committee to investigate the accounting standard-setting process and as a result of its report (Dearing Report 1988), the ASC was replaced by a new body, the Accounting Standards Board (ASB), which had greater independence from the accounting profession, greater resources and some support from company law.

Although 1985 effectively saw the end of CCA as part of UK accounting standards, it did not see the end of CCA in practice. CCA or similar systems had, for some time, been used by nationalised industries, and this was endorsed by the Byatt Report (1986), a report of a Treasury Committee. In the 1980s and early 1990s, a number of important nationalised undertakings were privatised, and most of these adopted CCA for regulatory purposes. Of the major utilities, British Gas still produces its main accounts on a CCA basis, which is also used for regulatory purposes. The electricity distribution and water companies also use CCA for regulatory purposes and make the regulatory accounts available to the public, although their main accounts are on the widely used historical cost basis (including some revaluations). The airports company, BAA, follows a similar practice. However, it has to be said that the use of CCA for regulatory purposes has not been without difficulty. In particular, the valuation concepts of recoverable amount and modern equivalent asset give rise to practical difficulties in some cases (Whittington 1994).

Apart from the survival of CCA as a complete system in regulated utilities, piecemeal revaluation on a current value basis has continued to be practised in the UK and, if anything, its popularity has increased, e.g. in the case of marking to market of commodity stocks. Current values have also tended to become more common in the USA, which has traditionally adopted a stricter view that historical cost should be the basis of generally accepted accounting principles. In the UK, the ASB adopted in 1994 the value to the business criterion, which was used as the valuation basis of CCA, as a basis in FRS 7 for measuring fair values in acquisition accounting. However, the partial use of value to the business or other forms of current value in accounts is far removed from the reintroduction of CCA. The latter seems extremely unlikely, despite the apparent belief of some that the reintroduction of CCA is on the ASB's agenda (Paterson 1996). In reality, the ASB has committed itself to evolutionary reform of the status quo, by putting the present system of mixed valuation (historical cost and current value) on to a more consistent basis, and, in its analysis of capital maintenance systems (in its draft *Statement of Principles* of 1995), has not even discussed the gearing adjustment and monetary working capital adjustment, which were integral components of SSAP 16. Thus, 1985 really did see the end of SSAP 16 as an accounting standard for the foreseeable future, and probably for ever, although the pressures to report more up-to-date costs and values remain and will no doubt influence the future development of accounting practice and standards.

We turn now to the experience of the USA, which resembles that of the UK in many respects.

THE US EXPERIENCE

The USA's inflation accounting standard, SFAS 33 'Financial Reporting and Changing Prices' (published in September 1979), preceded the UK's SSAP 16 by six months. Unlike SSAP 16, which required only one form of price-level-adjusted information, SFAS 33 required both current cost and CPP data. As a result of the deliberation of the special industry task groups, companies engaged primarily in the exploitation of natural resources or the ownership of income-producing real estate property were exempt from the current cost requirements of SFAS 33 but were subject to special requirements published in 1980.[1]

The CPP information did not require comprehensive restatement and, in particular, did not require a stabilised balance sheet: a restated income statement was required, with the gain or loss on net monetary assets shown separately. The current cost adjustments were confined to inventory, property, plant and equipment used in the operations of the business. Income from continuing operations on a current cost basis was required together with the current cost amounts of inventory, property, plant and equipment at the end of the fiscal year, and changes during the year and the current cost amount of these items net of inflation.

The current cost concept was, as in the exposure draft, based upon the replacement cost of the actual assets held and used, modified to the value of the firm by applying what was now called 'recoverable amount' when this was less than replacement cost. This definition of current cost caused problems and may have been one of the reasons for the lack of support of the standard by users.[2] A five-year summary of selected financial data was also required.

The standard came into effect for the fiscal years ending on or after 25 December 1979, although the publication of the current cost data could be delayed for one year. It was promised at the time the standard was issued that it would be reviewed within five years of its publication. In preparation for the review, the FASB encouraged a wide range of research studies to learn about the experiences of preparers, users and auditors with both historical cost/CPP information and current cost/CPP information.

The early results were discouraging: for example, studies by Berliner (1983) and Norby (1983) revealed evidence of limited use of SFAS 33 data by analysts. Berliner's survey of 190 analysts revealed that half of the respondents ignored the supplementary price-level information. Only 10 per cent used it frequently. The main concerns of the analysts were the 'non-comparability' of SFAS 33 information and doubts about the data's relevance and reliability, while a significant number believed the information to be redundant as appropriate data could be obtained elsewhere.

Berliner found that the analysts expressed no great enthusiasm for CPP data, a finding that was also supported by Norby who discovered that current cost data were being employed (if sparingly) in company analysis. Norby gave an indication that approximations of SFAS 33 data could be derived from publicly available sources in that the factors affecting the magnitude of the adjustments were well known, i.e. inventory turnover, inventory method, capital intensity and the age of assets. Once the initial adjustments were reported, the subsequent adjustments were predictable and information about changing prices was readily available throughout the year. Consequently the availability of other information could have limited the direct demand for SFAS 33 data.

In a major report, published by the FASB, Beaver and Landsman (1983) examined the impact of SFAS 33 data on changes in share price. Their findings were dramatic:

1 Once historical cost earnings were known, SFAS 33 earnings variables provided no additional explanatory power with respect to differences across firms in yearly stock price changes.
2 Even after any one of the SFAS 33 earnings variables was known, knowledge of historical cost earnings still provided additional explanatory power. In this sense, historical cost earnings dominated the SFAS 33 earnings variables.

In July 1983, a task force was appointed by the FASB to assist the Board in evaluating whether to continue the SFAS 33 requirements after the initial five-year period and, if so, what changes should be considered. An FASB Invitation to Comment 'Supplementary disclosures about the effects of changing prices' was published with the assistance of the task force and was designed to supplement the research studies by soliciting the advice of users, preparers and auditors. Four-hundred responses were received and they confirmed that SFAS 33 information was not widely used. A large number of the responses suggested that the costs of preparing the disclosures had outweighed the benefits, some stating that, although inflation was considered in assessing results of operations, mandatory disclosure requirements were unnecessary because users had developed their own methods for those assessments. Others supported supplementary CPP or current cost information but suggested that the presentation of two methods of accounting for inflation had led to confusion.

The results of the various surveys and the lack of use of constant dollar information led the Board to remove the CPP requirements of SFAS 33, and by SFAS 82 (1984) the requirements for all companies were eliminated.[3]

In December 1984 an exposure draft, 'Financial Reporting and Changing Prices: Current Cost Information', was issued, proposing the combination without significant change of all existing FASB pronouncements relating to reporting supplementary information on the effects of changing prices. A standard based on the exposure draft would have differed from existing requirements in two respects. The five-year summary of selected financial data would have been stated in average-for-the-current-year units of purchasing power, i.e. the SFAS 33 options to use base year dollars or the end-of-the-current-year consumer price index would have been eliminated. In addition, a gain or loss on disposal or write-down of inventory, property, plant and equipment included in income from continuing operations in the primary statements would have been adjusted to reflect the current cost basis of the item prior to its disposal or write-down when included in income from continuing operations on a current cost basis.

More than a hundred respondents commented on the exposure draft, a large majority recommending that the Board discontinue the existing requirements, arguing that the data did not appear to have been used by the institutional investment community, bankers or investors in general. Several reasons were cited for the lack of interest in the price-level-adjusted data: the lack of relevance or reliability of the data; the difficulty of comparisons caused by the flexibility of the methods of application; doubts about the quality of the information used to prepare the changing prices information; the failure to disclose assumptions; and the cost of preparing the data compared with its benefits.

Many respondents argued that even an improved set of disclosures would not be useful because investors had developed other sources of data on the effect of changing prices. Many also commented on the fall in the inflation rate which led to interest in more important factors than changing prices for investment decisions, namely the ability to raise capital from outside sources to finance replacements of productive capacity and the effects of interest rates on monetary assets and liabilities.

Despite the fact that only a minority of respondents argued that the supplementary disclosures required by SFAS 33 should be continued, the Board considered alternatives suggested by respondents. The Board recognised that reducing the data required could result in substantial cost savings but doubted whether users would gain much from such limited data.

Eventually the FASB decided to continue the requirements of SFAS 33 for a further year throughout 1985, while the Board continued a project to develop more effective and useful disclosures. In particular, the Board developed a comprehensive changing prices model that reflected both current cost and general price-level adjustments of financial statement items and considered which aspects of such a model were sufficiently relevant and reliable to be included as supplementary disclosures and financial reports.

To tackle this project the Board considered the four factors which determine whether to undertake a major project:

1 *The pervasiveness of the problem.* It was clear that the problems of changing prices were pervasive yet there was little interest shown in SFAS 33 information and enterprises generally provided only the minimum disclosures required.
2 *The potential for developing an alternative solution.* The Board was concerned that many of those who did not accept SFAS 33 disclosures believed that they were not sufficiently relevant or reliable for some or all enterprises and these opponents may not have accepted any eventual technical solution.

3 *The technical feasibility of the problem.* SFAS 33 did not require presentation of a 'bottom line' alternative to net income. If a project on this issue were to be undertaken, the Board would have had to readdress many complex issues of recognition and measurement which had been considered as part of the conceptual framework but which remained contentious and unresolved.

4 *Practical consequences.* Without a clear indication of alternative accounting solutions, it was difficult for the Board to assess whether others (such as the SEC or Congress) would be inclined to act if the Board did not. Government interest in any requirement to continue the disclosures of SFAS 33 appeared to have diminished.

As a result of these considerations the Board decided not to proceed with the project to develop a comprehensive changing prices model and concluded that supplementary disclosures required by SFAS 33 should not be required. Instead an exposure draft 'Financial Reporting in Changing Prices' was issued in September 1986, proposing voluntary disclosure of supplementary information on the effects of inflation and changes in specific prices.

The exposure draft received 215 responses, 93 per cent supporting the withdrawal of the mandatory nature of SFAS 33. The main arguments in favour of voluntary disclosures were that: supplementary price-level information was not used (mentioned by 47 per cent of respondents); the costs outweighed the benefits (30 per cent); and the information was misleading (12 per cent) or irrelevant (10 per cent). The few opposing the exposure draft and arguing for the retention of SFAS 33 feared that inflation would return and the progress made would be lost. (Inflation had fallen from 13.5 per cent in 1980 to 1.9 per cent in 1986.)

While the Board agreed with many of the concerns expressed by those few respondents supporting continuance of a changing prices requirement, the lack of use of the data and the effort involved in rectifying the deficiencies of the existing disclosure requirements would have been so expensive and time consuming that it was believed that no reasonable cost–benefit relationship could have been attained.

Consequently, in December 1986, the Board withdrew SFAS 33 by issuing SFAS 89 'Financial Reporting and Changing Prices' which encouraged but did not require companies to disclose supplementary information on the effects of changing prices with effect for financial reports issued after 2 December 1986.[4] The decision was not, however, unanimous. Three of the seven members of the Board dissented, believing in the words of one dissenter that:

accounting for the inter-related effects of general and specific price changes is the most critical set of issues that the Board will face this century. It is too important either to be dealt with inconclusively as in

Table 8.3 Number of companies producing supplementary information required by SFAS 33

Fiscal year	1979	1980	1981	1982	1983	1984	1985	1986
CPP information	326	450	459	352[a]	291	91[b]	5	0
CCA information	119	406	450	462	462	455	475	98[c]

Source: *Accounting Trends and Techniques*, AICPA, various years
Note: Number of companies surveyed = 600 (industrial and merchandising companies registered with the SEC, a majority of which are traded on the New York Stock Exchange)
[a] Affected by SFAS 70.
[b] Affected by SFAS 82.
[c] Affected by SFAS 89.

the original Statement 33 or to be written off as a lost cause as in this Statement.

The dissenters argued for continuing the experiment to avoid losing systems and data continuity. One of those arguing against the issue of the standard even suggested that an articulating set of adjusted statements should be produced. It was not to be. In effect, the issue of SFAS 89 ended the inflation accounting experiment in the USA. Table 8.3 shows the dramatic change in the use of supplementary price-level-adjusted information between accounting years 1979 and 1986. By 1987 companies were simply including a discussion of inflation in the Management's Discussion and Analysis of Financial Condition and were not displaying supplementary price-level-adjusted information in the financial statements. In the words of one prominent FASB member the issue was 'dead in the water'.

DEVELOPMENTS IN AUSTRALASIA

Australia

At the time of our earlier study (1984), the Australian professional accounting bodies had just issued a non-mandatory recommendation, Statement of Accounting Practice No. 1 (SAP 1), 'Current Cost Accounting', 1983. This recommended a supplementary profit and loss account and balance sheet on a current cost basis, using value to the business as the valuation method and with operating capability, rather than financial capital, as the capital maintenance concept. We observed at that time that the status of SAP 1 as a recommendation rather than a mandatory standard reflected the widespread opposition to price change accounting in Australia, particularly amongst the business community, following the failure of the government to base corporate taxation on a CCA method, as recommended in the Mathews Report (1975).

Subsequent events were no more favourable to the voluntary adoption of CCA, and Jim Paul of the Australian Accounting Research Foundation[5] summarises the response to SAP 1 as follows: 'Not surprisingly, given its non-mandatory status and the "worldwide" decline in interest in accounting for changing prices the application of SAP 1, particularly by companies, has been underwhelming'. Table 8.1 shows lower inflation rates in Australia from 1984 onwards, which must have been relevant. However, as a result of its non-mandatory status and widespread neglect, SAP 1 has not been withdrawn, and thus has survived longer than any other CCA recommendation or standard in the countries which we have studied.

Thus, CCA never took root in Australian private sector financial reporting practice, despite a lively debate on the subject in the 1970s. However, in Australia as in the UK there was subsequent interest in applying CCA to government-owned enterprises. This occurred at the same time as the Byatt Report was under discussion in the UK and it had a similar motivation. The Australian development of CCA in the public sector was led by the state of Victoria, which issued Accounting Policy Statement (APS) 1 'Rate of Return Reporting', in July 1986. This required five major commercial public authorities to produce supplementary balance sheets and profit and loss accounts on a current cost basis, including real holding gains and losses (i.e. gains and losses relative to movements in a general price index) in the measure of profit. The latter distinguished APS 1 from SAP 1 and was necessary because APS 1 was concerned with measuring a real rate of return on assets from the perspective of the provider of finance (the government in this case) rather than the enterprise itself. Thus a financial measure of capital maintenance was preferred to an operating capability measure. A similar approach was adopted, for the same reason, by the UK's Byatt Committee (1986) and it was followed later by the South Australian Treasury in a paper issued in 1989.

In 1990, the Council of Australian Governments set up a Steering Committee for National Performance Monitoring of Government Trading Enterprises, and in 1994 this issued *Guidelines on Accounting Policy for Valuation of Assets of Government Trading Enterprises using Current Valuation Methods*. These guidelines propose the measurement of non-current physical assets on the value to the business basis. They are not binding on state governments, but have in practice been influential in determining the accounting requirements placed by governments on statutory authorities and government departments.

Thus, an element of CCA has developed in practice in the public sector in Australia. In the private sector, on the other hand, the only small residue of CCA practice is in the option to re-value non-current assets and the requirement for downward revaluation to recoverable amount, which is regulated by the accounting standard AASB 1010 (revised, June 1993).

This results in a system which is best described as modified historical cost and resembles current practice in the UK.

New Zealand

The New Zealand current cost accounting standard, CCA-1, was issued in 1982. Its salient characteristics, as described in Tweedie and Whittington (1984: Table 10.2) were supplementary disclosure of current cost information (including a balance sheet), with a choice of capital maintenance adjustments (either specific index-based gearing and monetary working capital adjustments or general index-based adjustments). Failure to comply with the standard would not lead to a formal qualification in the audit report but was required to be reported by the auditor. Thus, the content and status of the standard were broadly consistent with the UK's SSAP 16.

Whereas SSAP 16 in the UK initially achieved a high compliance rate, CCA-1 in New Zealand was an instant failure, in so far as only a small minority of companies complied with it. A survey of compliance in its first year of application, 1983, by Peterson *et al.* (1984) found that, of 147 companies surveyed, only twelve (just over 8 per cent) complied with CCA-1. This poor compliance rate did not improve in subsequent years, and CCA-1 was finally withdrawn in 1985. This effectively marked the end of the CCA experiment in New Zealand, a country which had contributed substantially to the international development of CCA through the work of the Richardson Committee, although voluntary supplementary CCA disclosures were still permitted, and, as in the UK, the current cost valuation basis achieved an after-life in the utility industry (particularly in the 1994 New Zealand electricity legislation). There are thus strong similarities with the experience of CCA in Australia, where CCA was never widely practised in the private sector but did find a role in the public sector.

The reasons for the failure of the New Zealand CCA experiment appear to have been compatible with the factors which led to similar failures in the UK and the USA, although one factor which was present in the UK and the USA, rapidly declining inflation rates, was less important in New Zealand. Table 8.1 shows that inflation rates were substantially lower in 1983 and 1984, the first two years of CCA-1's application, but this was under the influence of a wage and price freeze, which ended in 1984 and was followed by a return of much higher inflation. However, the wage and price freeze itself probably had an important effect on attitudes to CCA-1. The nature of the freeze meant that there was no scope for negotiating higher prices on the basis of CCA costs, and the government was unwilling to give corporation tax concessions on the basis of CCA, because this would upset the delicate balance between the incomes of labour and capital. Baskerville (1994), in a report of interviews with leading participants in the New Zealand standard-setting process, notes the apparent importance of the attitude of the Prime Minister (The Rt Hon. Robert Muldoon, a chartered accountant) in opposing CCA-1 at the time it was issued. Previously, governments had encouraged the development of CCA and the Richardson Report was the result of a government-sponsored inquiry. Thus, there are strong parallels between the roles of governments in the UK and in New Zealand, early support for CCA being followed by a distinct lack of support from the government.

The importance of price controls and of taxation are also common to the UK and the New Zealand experiences. The survey by Peterson *et al.* summarised the reasons for non-compliance given by fifty-three companies which amounted to ninety-four expressed reasons in all (some companies giving multiple reasons). Of these, only twelve explicitly mentioned the lack of use of CCA for tax purposes and only three mentioned lack of use for pricing purposes. However, most of the other reasons given were somewhat bland, which suggests that the reasons stated were intended to show the respondents in a favourable light (and CCA in a bad one): overt public statements of self-interest on issues such as taxation or price policy might be expected to have been avoided by the majority. A study by Wong (1988), of the characteristics of New Zealand companies which presented supplementary CCA statements on a voluntary basis, prior to 1982, suggested that such companies tended to have high effective tax rates and to have characteristics which would otherwise make them vulnerable to government intervention (e.g. high levels of industry concentration and high rates of return, which might invite attention from the competition authorities) against which CCA might provide some defence (e.g. by lowering apparent rates of return). Thus, Wong concludes that the wish to influence tax policy and avoid other government interventions provided a motive for adopting CCA disclosures. This is also consistent with the opinions expressed in Baskerville's (1994) interview study.

In New Zealand, as in the UK, the failure of the CCA experiment demonstrated the potential weakness of a system of voluntary accounting standards, sponsored by a professional body with only persuasive powers. In 1994 the system was replaced in New Zealand by a new body appointed by the government and having legal backing for its standards.

OTHER COUNTRIES

Canada

As reported in our earlier study, the Canadians also experimented with inflation accounting. A non-mandatory guideline on CPP was published by the Canadian Institute of Chartered Accountants (CICA) in 1974 followed, a year later, by a CPP Exposure Draft. The current cost revolution, however, changed the climate of opinion and, in 1976, a current value discussion paper was issued, to be replaced in 1979 by a CCA Exposure Draft. This publication bore a close resemblance to the UK's ED 24 published earlier the same year, but given the close economic ties with the USA it was not surprising that the CICA reconsidered its position and moved towards the SFAS 33 position, publishing in 1981 a revised exposure draft, followed in October 1982 by an inflation accounting standard (Handbook section 4510 'Reporting the Effects of Changing Prices') in which all the supplementary information required by SFAS 33 was recommended (but not required) to be shown, with the exception of CPP income from continuing operations.

In addition, however, two financing or gearing adjustments were to be shown. The first was calculated by reference to the two current cost adjustments, i.e. depreciation and cost of sales, in a manner similar to that of SSAP 16, and the other, like the New Zealand standard published earlier that year, being based on realisable holding gains of the period, i.e. the changes in the current cost amounts of stock and fixed assets. The Canadian position, therefore, lay between those of the UK and the USA and close to that of New Zealand. As in New Zealand and Australia, Canada's standard was not obligatory, and it was not widely followed in practice.

At the time that Handbook section 4510 was issued, the Accounting Standards Committee indicated that it would undertake a comprehensive review of the recommendations after five years had elapsed. The review would examine the implementation of the standard and the way in which the supplementary information required was being used. A research report was duly published in May 1990 (Hanna *et al.*), and it did not encourage further experimentation. Only a minority of analysts surveyed stated that the required disclosures had been very useful, mainly because of: a low participation rate by companies preventing analysts from making comparisons; lower inflation rates; and concerns about both data reliability and the complexity of the requirements. Nevertheless, only a small minority of users believed that the section should be withdrawn, although most felt it should be improved. On the other hand, a majority of preparers opposed the section and believed the experiment was a failure, arguing that the disclosures were too subjective and misleading. Not surprisingly, given that preparers bear the costs of preparation of the accounts, only 31 per cent rated the issue of accounting for changing prices as important compared with 70 per cent of analysts.

The report's authors stated that in their opinion the current version of section 4510 should be removed and resources should not be invested to improve it. They believed the experiment failed, partly because of measurement errors, caused largely by inadequate adjustments for technological change, and because disclosure was not mandatory, thereby making comparisons across companies difficult.

The Accounting Standards Board withdrew section 4510 from the CICA Handbook in March 1992 and has not undertaken further work on the topic. This action was not surprising given the fall in the inflation rate from 10.2 per cent in 1982 to 1.5 per cent ten years later, the withdrawal of SFAS 33 over five years earlier by the FASB and in particular the lack of observance of the Canadian standard's requirements. A survey of 300 companies, 'Financial Reporting in Canada',[6] revealed that the proportion of companies giving supplementary information on the effects of changing prices following section 4510 changed from 14.3 per cent in 1983 to 4.7 per cent in 1986. By 1991 only two companies in the survey gave numerical financial data on the effects of changing prices – by 1994 that number had fallen to one. In 1994, sixteen companies stated that the effect of inflation was not significant during the period (eighteen in 1991) and five made other comments (eighteen in 1991).

South Africa

In South Africa, the National Council of Chartered Accountants (from 1980 the South African Institute of Chartered Accountants) produced a discussion paper in 1975 which concentrated upon a CPP approach but which also addressed the problem of relative price changes and proposed the incorporation of current values into the CPP system. The paper was produced very late in the CPP stage of evolution of price-level accounting, which probably explains the introduction of relative price changes. Given the international move towards current cost accounting commencing in 1975, CPP was not developed further in South Africa. Instead, in August 1978, a guideline proposing CCA adjustments very similar to those of the Hyde Guidelines in the UK was suggested. The non-mandatory guideline was not widely followed – a study by Davison and Westwick (1981) revealed that, in a survey of reports of 528 listed companies, only eleven included supplementary current cost income statements.

Nevertheless, in September 1986, at a time when the American and British standard setters were withdrawing their CCA pronouncements, the Accounting Practices Committee of the South African Institute of Chartered Accountants published Exposure Draft 66 'Disclosure of Current Value Information in Financial Statements' suggesting that financial statements should give information on the impact of changing prices on the results of operations and the financial position of the enterprise, either in the primary statements or in supplementary financial statements. It was further recommended that the current value of assets and the bases upon which the current values had been estimated should be disclosed.

The exposure draft was not well received being deemed too vague and extremely onerous to small companies. Commentators suggested that the proposed statement should be mandatory for listed companies only.

In the light of this reaction, the Accounting Practices Committee (APC) published a second exposure draft in 1989 – ED 77 'Disclosure of Current Value Information in Financial Statements'. Like ED 66, the exposure draft did not supersede the 1978 Accounting Guideline which remained recommended accounting practice. The APC continued to pursue the route taken by ED 66, proposing that information on the impact of changing price levels should be given either as supplementary disclosure or in the primary accounts. The new publication, however, fleshed out the basic requirements of its predecessor by giving more guidance about the appropriate methods of asset and liability valuation and new adjustments to the income statement. The APC's aim appeared to be to produce a comprehensive, effective and low-cost method of accounting for the impact of inflation (which at the time was still in double digits; see Table 8.4).

The major changes from the sparse requirements of ED 66 were new proposals to show the current value of liabilities and fuller details of the effect of price changes on income. In particular, as far as the latter was concerned, it was proposed that the current value income statement should disclose 'income or loss from operations, preferably measured after allowing for current cost of sales and depreciation, the recognised holding gains on non-monetary assets and the recognised changes in the value of monetary assets and liabilities'. The total, termed 'comprehensive income', was to be disclosed before a transfer to capital maintenance reserves was determined, based either on the financial capital or on the operating capital maintenance concept, to arrive at current value income.

In general, commentators disagreed with the principles of ED 77. Of fifty-six respondents, only eleven accepted its recommendations outright and, although a further fifteen gave qualified support, thirty rejected the proposals. The main objection related to the subjectivity and impracticability of the proposals, enabling companies to manipulate the results. Others felt the costs of preparing the information were not equalled by the benefits obtained, while some argued that if information were to be presented it should be given in the supplementary financial statements. Given the opposition to ED 77, the APC began to re-examine the subject. Senior members of the Investment Analysts Society were surveyed, the majority of whom stated that if annual financial statements were produced

Table 8.4 South African annual inflation rates

	Average 1977–86	1987	1988	1989	1990	1991	1992	1993	1994
% change in consumer prices	13.9	16.2	12.7	14.7	14.4	15.3	13.9	9.7	9.0

Source: International Monetary Fund (1995) World Economic Outlook, October, Table A12

on the basis of ED 77 the information presented would be used, particularly if it could be standardised. Encouraged by this reaction the APC submitted a revised proposal to the top thirty companies listed on the Johannesburg Stock Exchange and eight other companies who had submitted meaningful comments on ED 77, suggesting that any inflation-adjusted information could be presented in supplementary financial statements or by way of notes. It was proposed that the income statement adjustments would be in line with the original guideline, similar to the Hyde Guidelines, and that consideration should be given to reflecting the net balance of the current cost adjustments (cost of sales, depreciation and financial gearing) in the primary income statement as a transfer, below the line, to a capital maintenance reserve. Furthermore the current value of non-monetary assets should be shown either by way of a note or in a supplementary balance sheet.

Of thirty companies replying, only 25 per cent stated that they would be willing to comply with the proposals if they became compulsory, those opposing the suggested pronouncement arguing that a standard set of rules would not work in practice given that the performance of companies was now measured by a widespread number of methods in the inflationary environment.[7] The APC ultimately concluded that amending ED 77 or the guideline would be pointless as it was clear that any price-level accounting proposals would not gain general acceptance. Overseas experience reinforced this view.

In the 1992 *Survey of Financial Reporting* (SAICA 1992, the latest survey available at the time of writing) it was revealed that, out of a hundred companies surveyed, only nine provided current cost income statement information and only six a current cost balance sheet, a position that has been virtually unchanged from 1982. While the non-mandatory guidance issued in 1978 has not been officially withdrawn, CCA in South Africa, as in other countries, is very much a minority practice, despite the fact that, as Table 8.4 shows, inflation has continued at a significant rate.

The Netherlands

Tweedie and Whittington (1984) described the important contribution made by the Netherlands to the evolution of a form of CCA, known there as replacement value accounting. Whereas historical cost was majority practice, a significant minority of companies (including the very largest, such as Philips and Shell) produced either partial or complete current cost information either as a substitute for or as a supplement to historical cost. This practice has continued, albeit with changes of fashion. Dutch practice in 1985 was surveyed by Van Offeren (1990) and a survey of practice in 1989 appears in Van Offeren *et al.* (1991). A recent survey by Brink and Langendijk (1995) suggests that the application of current cost increased in the period 1975–86, possibly as a lagged response to the high inflation rates of the period 1971–82. This was followed by a slow decline until 1990 and a more rapid decline after that. However, even in 1994, there was still a substantial amount of current cost disclosure: of 145 listed companies surveyed by Brink and Langendijk, only 37 per cent failed to provide any current cost information.

On the legislative front, the Netherlands incorporated the provisions of the EC Fourth Directive, in a 1983 revision to the Accounting Act, in such a way that Dutch companies were permitted to present accounts either on a historical cost basis or, under the alternative accounting rules, on a current cost basis. This ensured that existing Dutch practice could continue, in conformity with EC requirements.

The theoretical debate in the Netherlands had also continued to be lively during the inflation of the 1970s. Van Offeren (1988) gives an account of this and, in particular, of the discussion of the introduction of inflation adjustments for capital maintenance purposes, including gearing adjustments. In the early 1980s, several Dutch companies experimented with gearing adjustments. Brink and Langendijk (1995) report that, in 1985, six of the listed companies that they surveyed were using gearing adjustments; all were large international companies and they included Shell, Philips and Unilever. By 1994, their survey showed that the application of the gearing adjustment had disappeared completely, and the need for international comparability of accounts of internationally listed companies was a probable factor in this. Similarly, these international companies reduced or abandoned their current cost disclosures: in 1992 even Philips, the flagship of Dutch replacement value accounting, ceased its practice of basing its main accounts on a comprehensive replacement value system.

Apart from the pressures of the international decline of CCA (particularly in the USA and the UK), which were bound to be important to an economy like that of the Netherlands, with a high level of international trade and some very large international companies, the relative decline of CCA in the Netherlands is attributed by Brink and Langendijk to the lower inflation rates after 1983, which can be seen in Table 8.1. The Dutch experience of inflation in this period was, however, more moderate than that of the USA and the UK, and its replacement value accounting methods had evolved over a longer period. Thus, the Netherlands did not experience a 'current cost revolution' in the 1970s, and it did not subsequently experience a dramatic collapse, or 'counter-revolution' in the 1980s. The pattern was more one of increasing interest in replacement values, followed by decreasing interest but not abandonment. The degree of individual discretion allowed to Dutch companies and their auditors has enabled a wide variety of practice in which partial disclosure of current cost information, particularly in relation to fixed assets, is still the predominant practice.

An interesting postscript to the Dutch experience is that in the Netherlands, as elsewhere, there has been some interest in CCA reporting by public utilities. A survey by Berghouwer *et al.* (1996) revealed that, in the financial year 1994, six of forty-three public utilities investigated were still using the gearing adjustment, although five of these were combining it with historical cost. The reasons for this arose from the regulatory frameworks and financial strategies (target debt/equity ratios) of the companies concerned.

Latin America

At the time of our previous work (1984), a number of countries of Latin America had experienced hyperinflation and had adopted general index adjustments of the constant purchasing power (CPP) variety, rather than CCA. The leading exponent of this method was Brazil, which had adopted this type of system in 1964. Other examples cited were in Argentina, Chile and Uruguay. Accounting of this type has since been recommended by an IASC standard (IAS 29) for use in hyperinflationary economies.

Thus, Latin America is in a sense irrelevant to the story of the decline of CCA, since the system did not take root there, and has not done so since. However, the Latin American experience does serve to illustrate one important feature of the motivation for systems of price-adjusted accounting, whether of the CCA or CPP variety, namely the influence of inflation rates. Brazil, one of the exemplars of CPP, retained this system throughout the 1980s and it was strengthened in 1987 by a stock exchange requirement for listed companies to produce fuller CPP information, consistent with the requirements of IAS 29. However, from 1 January 1996, the allowance of CPP adjustments for tax purposes (the original motivation) has been withdrawn, as has the requirement for adjustment in the statutory accounts, and the stock exchange requirement has been reduced to the status of an option. This dramatic weakening of the CPP system in Brazil follows a considerable reduction in the rate of inflation associated with currency reforms designed to terminate the process of hyperinflation.[8]

The only Latin American country to experiment with CCA valuation methods has been Mexico where, in 1984, Bulletin B10 of the Mexican Accounting Principles Board required that the effects of inflation be reported in financial statements. General index adjustments were to be applied to equity, but non-monetary items could be adjusted either by reference to a general index or on a current cost basis. Essentially, this gives a choice between a CPP system (general indexation of historical cost for equity and non-monetary assets) and a real terms system (specific price adjustment of non-monetary assets and general price-level adjustment of equity), and is consistent with the international standard (IAS 15). B10 has been widely followed, especially by listed companies, because failure to comply leads to a qualified audit report. However, there has recently been pressure to withdraw the current cost option, led by the Mexican Securities Commission, which believes that some asset values are being overstated, and it is proposed to remove the option in 1997.

The other three Latin American countries which we cited in 1984 as having forms of CPP accounting were Argentina, Chile and Uruguay.

In Argentina, requirements for CPP adjustments have been withdrawn, following a government decree of August 1995. This followed four years of very low inflation (the wholesale price index increased by 3 per cent in 1992, 0.1 per cent in 1993 and 1.6 per cent in both 1994 and 1995). The Argentine professional standard setting body (FACPCE), which devised the CPP system used in Argentina, has responded to the government decree by stating that, when inflation is less than 8 per cent per annum, the absence of inflation adjustment does not constitute a deviation from generally accepted accounting principles.

In Chile, the CPP system that was introduced in 1974 has remained in place, possibly because inflation has remained at double-digit annual levels. In 1994 consumer prices rose by 11.4 per cent, which was the lowest annual rate in the period 1987–94. The average annual rate for 1977–86 was 31.3 per cent. The Chilean method of CPP adjustment does allow for replacement cost restatement of inventory, and thus contains one element of current cost adjustment.

In Uruguay, inflation rates have remained high. Consumer prices rose by 44.7 per cent in 1994, which was the lowest in the period 1987–94. Against this inflationary background, companies have continued to make partial adjustments for inflation, although not legally obliged to do so. Inflation adjustments continue to be made for tax purposes, but these adjustments are not required to appear in the accounts. Recently the Central Bank of Uruguay has required inflation adjustment of the accounts of financial intermediaries (from December 1994), insurance companies and pension funds (from 1995), and large debtors to the banking system (from 1993). The methodology used is of a CPP variety.

CONCLUSIONS

It is apparent from our survey that the use of CCA, and its support by standard setters, has declined drastically since the early 1980s. In the light of history, the early 1980s can now be seen as the high point of the 'CCA revolution'.

The decline was led by the USA and the UK, the countries which had pioneered the introduction of CCA standards. Important factors in both countries were a decline in the rate of inflation and a related change in government policies towards inflation. The other English-speaking countries lagged in their introduction of CCA standards, so that, unlike the cases of the USA and the UK, CCA never took root in majority practice and ultimately disappeared. This was the case in Canada, Australia, New Zealand and South Africa. The Netherlands has a much longer tradition of replacement value accounting, on a voluntary and often partial basis, and experienced neither a Current Cost Revolution nor its subsequent collapse. Nevertheless, the Netherlands did see an increase in the popularity of replacement values in the early 1980s and a subsequent decline.

Latin America has experienced more severe inflation rates in the past and has therefore tended to prefer general index adjustments of a CPP type. In Argentina and Brazil, these have recently been withdrawn as a result of lower inflation rates and new economic policies. In Chile, CPP is still practised, as it is, on a mainly voluntary basis, in Uruguay, against a background of high inflation. Mexico has experimented with both CPP and CCA, but CCA has recently fallen out of favour, owing to its alleged subjectivity.

At the beginning of our survey, we proposed five factors which appeared from our earlier work to have influenced the adoption of CCA. We can now comment on how each of these seems to have operated since 1983:

1 *Economic events* (notably inflation rates). These have clearly been important in all of the countries which we have surveyed. Lower inflation rates in the 1980s or later have tended to lead to lower support for CCA in the English-speaking countries and the Netherlands. Equally, the conquest of hyperinflation in Argentina and Brazil has been associated with the abandonment of CPP. The Argentine statement that inflation at a rate above 8 per cent per annum would lead to a need for price-level adjustments in accounts is a specific acknowledgement of the role of inflation in creating a demand for some form of inflation accounting (whether CCA or CPP).

2 *Self-interest.* The influence of taxation was perhaps most obvious in the UK, where the decision not to adopt CCA for tax purposes clearly helped to reduce support for it. There is evidence also from Australia and New Zealand that the adoption of CCA for tax purposes would have increased support for it. Another self-interest motive comes from the regulated sector, and it is notable that CCA has been supported by regulated companies in the UK, the Netherlands, Australia and New Zealand, even after it has been abandoned in the non-regulated sector.

3 *Ideas.* The relative popularity of CCA in the regulated sector has been supported not only by the self-interest of regulated bodies but also by new thinking on the subject, such as that in the Byatt Report (1986). Nevertheless, in a period in which interest in price change adjustments has been declining, it is perhaps not surprising that the intellectual debate on CCA has been less vigorous than in the earlier period of the CCA revolution.

4 *International influences.* Such influences have certainly been strong. The

USA and the UK tended to lead the English-speaking world in the introduction of CCA. Equally, they led the withdrawal of CCA, and the effect of this was felt in other countries, notably Canada, Australia, New Zealand and South Africa, where leading companies did not comply with CCA recommendations and professional bodies and standard setters lost heart in their support for CCA.

5 *Accidents of history.* Despite the systematic effects listed above, there are still factors which they are unable to explain, which can be attributed to the historical inheritance of particular countries, or special circumstances prevailing at particular times. The survival of the Dutch replacement value system, for example, is partly due to the unique inheritance of the Dutch accounting profession which, in turn, is partly due to the efforts of certain influential individuals as well as to the unique historical experience of the Netherlands.

Apart from these broad historical factors, it is possible to detect some technical weaknesses in the CCA proposals of the early 1980s which would probably have led to a need for reform even if the other factors had not indicated total withdrawal. In the UK these weaknesses included the conceptually suspect and intuitively unappealing monetary working capital adjustment and gearing adjustment. In both the USA and the UK, the method of valuation was perhaps left too imprecise, so that the use of broad-brush indices was permitted and the users of accounts did not regard the new information as being valuable, particularly in the presence of factors such as technical progress, which renders simple indexation inappropriate. Thus, the compromises and simplifications resulting from the debate described in our earlier book may have left the CCA standards of the 1980s fatally flawed, even if lower inflation rates and a different economic environment had not intervened to destroy the demand for CCA.

NOTES

* The authors wish to acknowledge the help of many colleagues in providing information, including Phil Bell, Steve Zeff, Todd Johnson and David Mosso for the USA; Bob Rutherford and John Carchrae for Canada; Rosanne Blumberg and Trevor Derwin for South Africa; Jim Paul for Australia; Rachel Baskerville and Alan Robb for New Zealand; Ray Hinton and his partners in Arthur Andersen for Latin America; Francisco Papellas for Brazil; Carlos Menendez for Argentina, Chile and Uruguay; and Juan M Gras for Mexico; Ron Paterson for additional information on Latin America; and Dick van Offeren and Henk Langendijk for the Netherlands. Any errors are, of course, the responsibility of the authors.

1 SFAS 39 'Financial Reporting and Changing Prices: Specialized Assets – Mining and Oil and Gas'; SFAS 40, 'Financial Reporting and Changing Prices: Specialized Assets – Timberlands and Growing Timber'; SFAS 41, 'Financial Reporting and Changing Prices: Specialized Assets – Income-Producing Real

Estate'. Later, other specialised standards, SFAS 46 and SFAS 54, dealt with motion picture films and investment companies, respectively.

2   Some would argue (see Swanson and Schriver 1987) that measurement errors in estimating the current cost of fixed assets, in particular inadequate adjustments for technological change, led to the data not being widely used by financial analysts or incorporated in stock prices. The drafting of SFAS 33, arguing that current cost measures should relate to the assets owned and used by the enterprise and not just the other assets that might be acquired to replace the assets owned, led companies not to adjust for technological change. This was particularly severe in technologically advanced companies such as those in telecommunications. While this was not the intention of SFAS 33, companies clearly interpreted the standard as not requiring changes for advancing technology and this may have led many companies to lose confidence in the numbers provided. See, for example, United Telecommunication quoted in Swanson and Schriver (1987: 75).

3   SFAS 70 (of 1982) had previously eliminated the requirements to disclose CPP data for companies that did not use the dollar as their functional currency.

4   In addition to withdrawing SFAS 33, SFAS 89 also superseded SFAS 39 (dealing with mining and oil and gas), SFAS 40 (timberlands and growing timber), SFAS 41 (income-producing real estate), SFAS 46 (motion picture films) and SFAS 54 (investment companies). In addition SFAS 70, SFAS 82 and certain paragraphs of SFAS 69 were also withdrawn.

5   Private communication, April 1996. This section draws heavily on material supplied by Mr Paul.

6   Published by the CICA.

7   For further details see Singer (1991).

8   'From December 1993 to June 1994, consumer prices in Brazil rose 763 per cent. Following the introduction of the real on 1 July 1994, monthly inflation fell to $5\frac{1}{2}$ per cent in July. From June 1994 to December 1994, consumer prices increased by 17 per cent'. International Monetary Fund (1995) *World Economic Outlook*, October, p.108.

REFERENCES

Baskerville, R. F. (1994) *Dimensions of CCA-1: An oral history of the failure of the inflation accounting standard in New Zealand*, Thesis submitted to the Victoria University of Wellington.

Beaver, W. H. and Landsman, W. R. (1983) *Incremental Information Content of Statement 33 Disclosures*, FASB.

Berghouwer, M., Brink, H. L. and Langendijk, H. P. A. J. (1996) 'Application of current cost accounting by public utilities' (Toepassing van actuele waarde bij openbare nutsbedrijven), *Tijdschrift voor Bedrijfsadministratie* January/February: 33–42.

Berliner, R. W. (1983) 'Do analysts use inflation-adjusted information? Results of a survey', *Financial Analysts Journal* March/April: 65–72.

Brink, H. L. and Langendijk, H. P. A. J. (1995) 'Current cost accounting in annual accounts' (Actuele waarde in de jaarekening), in H. L. Brink and L. G. van der Tas (eds) *Jaar in Jaar int 9*, Deventer: Kluwer, pp. 1–30.

Byatt, I. C. R. (1986) *Accounting for Economic Costs and Prices: A Report to HM Treasury by an Advisory Group* (The Byatt Report), 2 vols, London: HMSO.

Carsberg, B. and Page, M. (eds) (1984), *Current Cost Accounting: The Benefits and the Costs*, London: ICAEW/Prentic Hall International.

Davison, I. H. and Westwick, C. A. (1981) 'Inflation accounting around the world' paper presented to the *16th Conference of the International Federation of Surveyors, Montreux, 14 August 1981*, London: Arthur Andersen.

Dearing Report (1988) *The Making of Accounting Standards*, London: ICAEW.

Griffiths, I. (1986) *Creative Accounting, How To Make Your Profits What You Want Them to Be*, London: Sidgwick & Jackson.

Hanna, J. R., Kennedy, D. B. and Richardson, G. D. (1990) *Reporting the Effects of Changing Prices: A Review of the Experience with Section 4510*, CICA.

Hanson, J. D. (1989) 'Development in financial reporting over the last 20 years', in D. J. Tonkin and L. C. L. Skerratt (eds) *Financial Reporting 1988–89*, London: ICAEW.

Hoffman, L. and Arden, M. H. (1983 and 1984) 'The Accounting Standards Committee – Joint Opinion' and 'Supplementary Joint Opinion', reprinted as Appendix 3 of Deloitte Haskins & Sells, *Accounting for the Effects of Changing Prices – a Commentary on ED 35*, 1984.

Lemke, K. W. and Page, M. J. (1992) 'Economic determinants of accounting policy choice', *Journal of Accounting and Economics*, 15: 87–114.

Mathews Report (1975) Committee of Inquiry into Inflation and Taxation, *Report*, Australian Government Publishing Service.

Neville Report (1983) *SSAP 16: Current Cost Accounting – Report of the Monitoring Working Party*, Accounting Standards Committee.

Norby, W. C. (1983) 'Applications of inflation-adjusted accounting data', *Financial Analysts Journal* March/April; 33–9.

Paterson, R. (1996) *The ASB's Framework – Time to Decide*, London: Ernst & Young.

Peterson, R., Gan, H. E. and Lim, K. L. (1984) 'CCA – the day after', *Accountants' Journal* March: 88–97.

Pong, C. and Whittington, G. (1996) 'The withdrawal of current cost accounting in the United Kingdom: a study of the Accounting Standards Committee', *Abacus* March: 30–53.

SAICA (1992) *A Survey of Financial Reporting in South Africa, 1992*, South African Institute of Chartered Accountants.

Singer, M. (1991) 'Inflation accounting – the full story', *Accountancy SA* June: 164–9.

Swanson, E. P. and Schriver, K. A. (1987) 'The accounting-for-changing-prices experiment: a valid test of usefulness?', *Accounting Horizons* September: 69–77.

Tweedie, D. and Whittington, G. (1984) *The Debate on Inflation Accounting*, Cambridge University Press.

Van Offeren, D. H. (1988) 'Replacement value accounting: theory and practice', *Advances in International Accounting* 2; 23–50.

—— (1990) 'Accounting for changing prices in Dutch annual reports', *Advances in International Accounting* 3: 87–106.

Van Offeren, D. H., Sommeling, R. J. and Aardenburg, E. K. C. (1991) 'Valuation bases in annual reports' (Waarderingsgrondslagen in de jaarrekening), *Maandble. Bedrijfsadm. en Bedrijfsorg* 95: 276–82.

Whittington, G. (1994) 'Current cost accounting: its role in regulated utilities', *Fiscal Studies* 15: 88–101.

Wong, J. (1988) 'Economic incentives for the voluntary disclosure of current cost financial statements', *Journal of Accounting and Economics* 10: 151–67.

9

PLAYING THE CONGRESSIONAL CARD ON EMPLOYEE STOCK OPTIONS

A fearful escalation in the impact of economic consequences lobbying on standard setting

Stephen A. Zeff

INTRODUCTION

The lobbying in support of 'economic consequences' in the setting of accounting standards may be traced as far back as the latter part of the nineteenth century.[1] A falling price level during the last third of the century prompted railway rate regulators in the USA to favour replacement cost over historical cost: by promising shareholders a stipulated return on assets based on replacement cost, the regulators could ensure lower prices for consumers. Railway managements, of course, preferred the use of the higher historical cost in the price base in order to increase their revenues. The regulators and the railway companies swapped positions once the price level began moving upward.[2]

Economic consequences lobbying of the standard setter was evident during the sharp upturn in the price level immediately following the Second World War, when US companies wanted to record price-level depreciation so as not to exagerate their reported net incomes and also to persuade Congress that corporate income tax relief by the same use of price-level depreciation was an economic necessity.[3]

Beginning in the 1960s in the USA, economic consequences lobbying began in earnest in such areas as accounting for the investment tax credit, business combinations and goodwill, restructuring of troubled debt, oil and gas exploration, marketable securities, and employee stock options.[4]

Such lobbying has not been confined to the USA. Since the 1970s in the UK, it has been seen in connection with the standards on accounting for research and development, deferred taxes and goodwill, among others.[5] It has also been found in Sweden[6] and Australia.[7]

The recent US experience with accounting for employee stock options was marked by economic consequences lobbying at the highest levels of

177

government, which came close to imperilling the standard-setting body itself. The purpose of this paper is to give a historical account of the involvement of the US Congress, and especially the Senate, in the lobbying process.

RUN-UP TO THE CONTROVERSY

How 'hot' was the political storm over employee stock options that was kicked off by the Financial Accounting Standards Board (FASB) in the early 1990s? Hot enough to provoke the US Senate to pass a non-binding resolution in opposition to the Board's position. It was perhaps the first time in Congressional history that either the Senate or the House of Representatives had spoken out on an issue that was confined solely to accounting standards.[8]

The public controversy over the non-recognition of the expense attributable to employee stock options was part of the larger public debate, which had been launched in May 1991 at a one-day hearing of a Senate subcommittee, entitled 'The SEC and the Issue of Runaway Executive Pay'.[9] The subcommittee was chaired by Senator Carl Levin (Democrat of Michigan), who was critical of the inadequacy of the Securities and Exchange Commission's rules to enable shareholders to find out how much their companies' top executives were being paid and to have a voice in such determinations.

In early 1992, the press began to draw attention to the fact that the chief executives of large US companies were much more highly paid than their counterparts in other countries and that the greater part of their remuneration, in many instances, was in the form of stock options and other long-term incentive schemes. Questions were raised whether executive pay was aligned with performance and whether US corporate boards of directors were exercising sufficient vigilance over executive pay packages.[10]

The stage was set for the public controversy by the active discussion in the press and in Congress over the long-standing practice of companies that had been granting stock options to their executives and other employees to show zero compensation expense for the options in their income statement, a practice that was allowed by Accounting Principles Board (APB) Opinion No. 25, 'Accounting for Stock Issued to Employees', issued in 1972. Since 1984, the FASB had been working on a project to reconsider Opinion No. 25 and was giving thought to various valuation approaches to estimating the compensation expense associated with employee stock option plans.

In January 1992, Senator Levin held a half-day hearing entitled 'Stealth Compensation of Corporate Executives: Federal Treatment of Stock Options', which he used as a platform to threaten federal legislation to require 'that the accounting rules here accurately reflect the value of [stock] options to the people receiving them and the cost of these options to the companies that issue them' if either the SEC or the FASB does not act soon.[11] Senator Levin was thus pressing the SEC and the FASB to accelerate their efforts to require expense recognition for employee stock options.

During the latter part of 1992 and early 1993, the FASB gradually made known its tentative conclusions favouring a move towards income statement recognition of the expense attributable to employee stock option plans,[12] and it was reported that 'During 1992 and the first part of 1993, more than 450 comment letters were received, mostly objecting to the tentative conclusions. Many of the letters proposed disclosure in lieu of cost recognition for stock compensation.'[13]

The public controversy relating to the accounting treatment of employee stock options intensified during 1993, as company executives and other employees, directly or through trade associations, began lobbying their members of Congress to oppose the FASB's emerging proposal. While the Business Roundtable, representing the chief executive officers of more than 200 of the largest US companies, strongly opposed expense recognition for employee stock options (owing to its probable impact on their compensation packages), they wisely remained largely on the sidelines, while encouraging the representatives of emerging and high-technology enterprises to argue on the higher ground of the threat to entrepreneurial initiative and to employment in Silicon Valley.

In an editorial, *Business Week* urged the FASB to 'be strong and resist ... [the] heavy pressure to ignore the fact that stock options have real value'. It added, 'Truth is, boards would hand out options more wisely and fairly if accounting rules assigned a value to them that was charged to a company's earnings'.[14]

INITIAL EXPRESSIONS OF NEGATIVE REACTION IN CONGRESS

One of the first signs of antipathy among Senators toward the FASB's proposed accounting standard for stock options occurred on 29 June 1993 when Senator Joseph Lieberman (Democrat of Connecticut) introduced a bill known as the Equity Expansion Act. The legislation was intended to create income tax incentives for small, high-tech companies to award stock options to a larger fraction of their workforce. Such companies often have too little cash with which to pay normal salaries, and stock options were widely used as a substitute for cash.

Included in the proposed tax legislation (which was never put to a vote[15]) was a provision stipulating that the Securities and Exchange Commission (SEC) 'shall not require or permit [a company] to recognize any expense or other charge in financial statements furnished to its security holders resulting from' stock options. This provision was a direct response to the

FASB's unanimously approved Exposure Draft, which had just been issued, calling for the recognition of the compensation implicit in employee stock options as an expense in the income statement. The Bill was intended to block or overturn this proposal.[16]

In October 1993, Senator Levin and John Bryant (Democrat of Texas), a member of the House of Representatives, wrote to President Bill Clinton, saying

> We've been told that you are being lobbied by opponents of a proposed rule of the Financial Accounting Standards Board (FASB) that would require corporations to include executive stock option compensation on their books as an expense.... This accounting loophole has helped fuel the explosion in executive pay and the disconnect between pay and performance.... But stock option beneficiaries want the Administration to stop FASB and support legislation overturning its decision. This legislation would not only rob FASB of its independence, it would politicize accounting rules, damage the credibility of corporate financial statements, and perpetuate the market distortions associated with stock options' off-the-books compensation.[17]

Clinton's reply was non-committal, although he said that

> the FASB proposal has raised a great deal of concern among companies, particularly in the high tech sector of the economy, which use broad-based stock options to attract and retain employees at all levels.... I am pleased that FASB is meeting with representatives of these companies and doing field testing to attempt to assess the impact of its proposal on actual companies.... It would be unfortunate if FASB's proposal inadvertently undermined the competitiveness of some of America's most promising high-tech companies.
>
> I agree that it would be better to avoid legislation on this issue – whether to enact legislatively FASB's current proposal or to overturn it. I hope that in the course of receiving and analyzing comments and the results of the FASB field test, all issues raised by the proposal will be dealt with effectively.[18]

Also in October 1993, Senator Barbara Boxer (Democrat of California) and Senator Christopher J. Dodd (Democrat of Connecticut) took turns chairing a one-day hearing of the Subcommittee on Securities of the Senate Committee on Banking, Housing, and Urban Affairs, intended to demonstrate opposition to the FASB's proposal on accounting for stock options. Most of the witnesses invited to testify, representing companies and trade associations – as well as six Senators and the House member who represents Silicon Valley – spoke in opposition to the FASB proposal. Few FASB supporters were included in the invitation list. FASB Vice-Chairman James J. Leisenring, who defended the Board and explained its reasoning, said:

> We believe that economic goals are best achieved directly, by subsidies, tax policy, and the like. Capital markets, on the other hand, are best served by unbiased financial statements designed to inform policy makers rather than to promote policies. Decisionmakers need financial statements that tell it like it is, in short.'[19]

In a letter to Senator Dodd, Walter P. Schuetze, the SEC chief accountant, counselled that 'it is best to use the technical expertise available in the [FASB] process that currently is in place and has worked for decades, rather than intervening in that process through Congressional action.'[20]

The Washington Post, reflecting on the one-day hearing, wrote:

> There's no national interest in promoting the growth of companies, high tech or otherwise, through obscure or misleading accounting. The real interest is in the integrity of markets and efficient allocation of capital. The FASB's proposed rule deserves support. The goal in financial reporting is not only truth but the whole truth.[21]

In November 1993, Representative John D. Dingell (Democrat of Michigan), who, as the powerful chairman of the Subcommittee on Oversight and Investigations of the House Committee on Energy and Commerce, had held a number of hearings since the mid-1980s on questionable financial reporting practices, said that 'I *strongly oppose* any legislation that would undercut the ability of FASB to continue in its role as an independent standards setter and instead substitute Congressional whim as the setter of accounting principles.[22]

In December 1993, the Secretaries of the Treasury and Commerce jointly wrote to the FASB about their concerns that the implementation of its proposal 'might result in more volatile and less accurate and consistent financial statements because of the extreme difficulty of valuing long-term, non-marketable, forfeitable stock options'. Further, they argued, 'the difficulties of making meaningful estimates of value may have a disproportionately adverse impact on growing (often high-tech) industries and thus may inadvertently have a chilling effect upon the competitiveness of some of America's most promising companies'.[23]

At the end of November 1993, five Senators wrote to SEC Chairman Arthur Levitt over their concern

> that the credibility of the financial reporting process may be harmed significantly if Congress, in order to further economic or political goals, either discourages the FASB from revising what the FASB

believes to be a deficient standard or overrules the FASB by writing an accounting standard directly in the Federal securities laws.[24]

Levitt replied:

I believe that it is inappropriate for Congress to prescribe accounting standards through legislation. And, while I believe that the FASB should not view its proposals in a vacuum and should keep national priorities in mind, I also believe that it would not be appropriate to require the FASB to halt the development of an individual project because it may conflict with the economic, political, or social goals of a specific industry or group. I am concerned that if the FASB's agenda is limited to those projects that meet Congressionally favored goals, then the process no longer may be perceived as standards setting by an independent body within the accounting profession. The notion that reported information may be biased toward fulfillment of political or social goals may have serious repercussions on the credibility of the financial information that fuels our securities markets.[25]

All the while, the FASB was digesting comments on its Exposure Draft. It was reported that

The Board received 1,786 comment letters, including approximately 1,000 form letters, on the Exposure Draft. The vast majority of respondents objected to the recognition of compensation cost for fixed employee stock options – sometimes for reasons that had nothing to do with accounting. In March 1994, the Board held six days of public hearings in Connecticut and California. Representatives from 73 organizations presented testimony at those hearings.[26]

The New York Times reported that 'the emotional pitch [at the hearings] is high enough that Autozone, one Memphis company that will miss the meetings, coaxed 620 employees to sign identical protest letters'.[27]

The setting in San Jose, California, where the West Coast public hearing was held, was raucous. On 1 March 1994, the trade associations that opposed the Board's proposal sent a notice to high-tech companies throughout Silicon Valley, soliciting their support for a Silicon Valley Employee Stock Option Rally, to be held in the San Jose Convention Center from 11:00 a.m. to 1:00 p.m. on 25 March, the first day of the FASB's two-day public hearing. The notice began as follows:

The American Electronics Association, the American Entrepreneurs for Economic Growth and Bay Area Venture Capital firms are organizing a *massive* employee rally to protest the disastrous proposal by the Financial Accounting Standards Board (FASB) that will threaten our jobs. This protest rally is our last and best chance to convince the Clinton Administration that the FASB proposal is bad for Silicon Valley. It will be covered by national and local TV and print press.

An accompanying flyer contained the following, which etched the theme for the Rally:

> What sets Silicon Valley apart?
>
> ## Stock Options
>
> Why do we get the best people?
>
> ## Stock Options
>
> What's the one incentive left?
>
> ## Stock Options

'STOP FASB' posters, T-shirts, buttons, etc., and other propaganda were distributed. Emotional speeches were delivered against the FASB's position, with inspiring background music provided by a high school marching band hired for the occasion. Silicon Valley companies gave their employees time off, and they descended in large numbers on the Convention Center. An anti-FASB petition was signed for transmission to President Clinton, and a full report of the noisy proceedings was carried on the evening news by all of the local television stations and on the front page of the *San Jose Mercury News*. In a nearby hotel, the FASB was quietly holding its hearing.[28] As *The Wall Street Journal* observed, the private sector opponents of the FASB's proposal 'are treating this as a life-or-death struggle'.[29]

In April 1994, Representative Edward J. Markey (Democrat of Massachusetts), chairman of the Subcommittee on Telecommunications and Finance of the House Committee on Energy and Commerce (which had oversight authority over the SEC), wrote to SEC Chairman Levitt to clarify 'the respective roles of the FASB and the SEC', especially in the context of the stock option controversy. Referring to a recent article by SEC Commissioner J. Carter Beece, Jr,[30] criticising the FASB for not taking economic consequences into consideration in its decisions, Markey asked Levitt whether, in his view, 'there are any circumstances which should cause the FASB to take economic and social factors into account'. Pointedly, he queried: 'If the Commission does not take into account possible social and economic consequences when it reviews new accounting standards [approved by the FASB], would you explain the Commission's reasoning for declining to consider this type of information?'[31] While Markey believed that the FASB's policy of limiting its purview to improving the usefulness of financial statements 'is generally the correct one', he wanted to know when, if ever, the FASB or the SEC might justifiably take into account broader economic and political considerations when acting on accounting standards.

Markey made evident in his letter that there were views expressed in Congress on both sides of the FASB's proposal. A vivid indication of the strength with which these competing views were held was Markey's recital of the half-dozen bills that had been introduced in the House and Senate on the matter between January and August of 1993:

> Presently pending before both the House and Senate are resolutions expressing opposition to the stock option proposal, and urging the FASB to reconsider it...; legislative proposals to amend the securities laws to require accounting for stock options [i.e. endorsing the FASB's proposal] ...; and legislative proposals directing the SEC to overturn the stock options rule if it is enacted by the FASB.[32]

In his reply to Markey, Levitt acknowledged that the SEC has broader mandates than the FASB but said that 'The Commission's overriding concern of providing 'relevant, reliable, comparable, and unbiased' information to the securities markets, is consistent with these broader mandates'.[33]

THE SENATE ACTS

On 3 May 1994, shortly after the FASB had held its public hearings on its Exposure Draft, the Senate took up the subject with gusto. The matter was brought to the Senate floor with scant warning: Senator Levin's office was given twenty-four hours' notice that the issue would be raised as an amendment (No. 1668) to an unrelated Bill.[34] It was believed that certain Senators were feeling stepped-up pressure from trade associations representing high-tech and start-up companies.

Senator Lieberman, with fifteen co-sponsors on both sides of the aisle (nine Democrats and six Republicans), offered as an amendment to the Fair Credit Reporting Act a sense-of-the-Senate resolution in opposition to the position espoused in the FASB's Exposure Draft. Among the several Senators who rose to speak in favour of the resolution, Senator Boxer, one of its co-sponsors (and, together with Lieberman, one of the hardliners), said:

> I would venture to say that there are not many times in the Senate when I can read to you a list of Senators of such diverse philosophies that have come together to say that the FASB stock option proposal would be damaging to many companies in our Nation. I can certainly say, as one of the Senators from California, it would be very damaging to California's nascent economic recovery. ...

This [FASB] proposal ought to be dropped and it ought to be dropped now. It has taken them years and years to get to this point, and now they are saying they are not going to have a decision for another year. Maybe the reason it has taken so long is that in their hearts they know it is wrong. What we are saying today in the Senate – I hope what we are going to say today – is that they have to take their green eyeshades off over at FASB and pay attention to the ramifications of this proposed rule.[35]

She added, ominously, 'If we need to legislate accounting rules, I am not going to walk away from that fight...'.[36]

It was clear from the speeches on the resolution that Senators and Representatives had been holding meetings with the Chairmen of the FASB and the SEC, but to no avail. Now they were prepared to marshal the full force of the sense of the Senate.

Most Senators had little information about the issue and little time in which to educate themselves. Only Senator Levin spoke against the resolution. Levin's subcommittee had held hearings in 1991 and 1992 on executive pay, and he was astonished by the number of chief executive officers of large American corporations who had received 'more than 90 percent of their pay from stock options', and added:

What is incredible about this compensation is that it is stealth compensation. It does not show up on the books as a deduction against corporate profits. It does not show up as an expense. Unlike all other forms of compensation, no exception, stock options are not treated as an expense on the company's books. And that is what FASB is proposing to change. ...

Stock options are taken by a company as an expense on their income taxes but do not show up as an expense on their annual reports.[37]

In the course of his remarks, he submitted a letter signed by seventy accounting academics (including the author of this paper) in support of the following proposition:

Stock options have value; they impose a cost on companies that issue them; and the cost of stock option compensation ought to be charged to corporate earnings.[38]

Levin also read into the record a letter written by Warren E. Buffett, the chairman of Berkshire Hathaway Inc. and one of the nation's most respected investors, who said:

If options aren't a form of compensation, what are they? If compensation isn't an expense, what is it? And, if expenses shouldn't go into the calculation of earnings, where in the world should they go?[39]

Finally, the resolution was put to a vote, and it passed by 88 to 9. The key passages in the resolution were as follows:

It is the sense of the Senate that –

(a) the new accounting treatment of employee stock options and employee stock purchase plans, proposed by the Financial Accounting Standards Board, will have grave economic consequences particularly for business in new-growth sectors which rely heavily on employee entrepreneurship;

(b) the new accounting treatment of employee stock options and employee stock purchase plans, proposed by the Financial Accounting Standards Board, will diminish rather than expand broad-based employee stock option plans; and

(c) the Financial Accounting Standards Board should not at this time change the current generally accepted accounting treatment of stock options and stock purchase plans contained in Accounting Principles Board Decision 25.[40]

Just prior to the vote on the resolution, however, the Senate passed by a vote of 94 to 2 an amendment sponsored by Senator Levin, appealing to the conscience of the Senate that the FASB's independence in such matters should not be compromised. Its operative passage was as follows:

It is the sense of the Senate that –

(1) the status of the Financial Accounting Standards Board as a private body of independent accounting experts should be respected and safe-guarded; and

(2) the Congress should not impair the objectivity or integrity of the Financial Accounting Standards Board's decisionmaking process by legislating accounting rules.[41]

One effect of the Levin amendment was to suggest that even more Senators stood behind the independence of the FASB than would support Congressional intervention, thus weakening (it was thought) the message conveyed by the passage of the main resolution.

A columnist in *The New York Times* assailed the Senate's intrusion into accounting standard setting. The columnist named 'The nine senators with the courage to vote against what should be known as the "Shareholder Deception Act"' and characterised present-day accounting for employee stock options, by which 'a company hands out stock options to its executives [and] is usually able to act as if they are worthless', as 'one of the most egregious examples of absurd accounting now around'.[42]

THE SENATE PRESSURE CONTINUES

During the balance of 1994, several Senators continued to apply pressure on the FASB and the SEC, until, by the end of the year, it became evident to both bodies that powerful Senators were prepared to legislate accounting standards into law to prevent the FASB from acting.

On 6 October 1994, Senator Lieberman turned up the heat by introducing the Accounting Standards Reform Act of 1994, which would have prevented any new FASB standard, or modification thereof, from going into effect until it had received 'an affirmative vote of a majority of a quorum of the members of the [Securities and Exchange] Commission'.[43] With only a few exceptions, the Commission's practice had always been to require implementation of new FASB standards by assent of the Office of the Chief Accountant, but Lieberman's Bill would have required each such matter to be approved by the members of the Commission, with the prospect that they might be held directly accountable before a Congressional committee to justify their vote.

The Lieberman Bill constituted a direct assault on the independence of the FASB and would have been destructive of private sector control of the standard-setting process. It went well beyond the issue of accounting for employee stock options and brought into question the continuing viability of the FASB as an organisation. Within the FASB, this threat of legislation requiring the SEC to announce a public vote every time the FASB were to change accounting standards was a decisive factor in persuading the Board to reconsider its position on employee stock options.

The mid-term Congressional elections, in which the Republicans acquired control of both houses, led to a further threat of legislative action to block the FASB. During the second week of December, a month following the elections, Senator Phil Gramm (Republican of Texas), who was expected to become chairman of the Securities Subcommittee of the Committee on Banking, Housing, and Urban Affairs, which oversees the SEC, said that 'if the FASB insisted on forcing companies to deduct stock-option costs from profit, Congress should prohibit the SEC from enforcing the rule'.[44] On 1 December, Gramm had written to Senator Alfonse M. D'Amato (Republican of New York), who was scheduled to become the chairman of the parent committee of the Securities Subcommittee, that 'unless the FASB decides to change course at its December 14 meeting ... it would be wise and prudent that the Securities Subcommittee reconvene early in January and hold hearings on the FASB employee stock option proposal'.[45]

THE FASB SHIFTS TO DISCLOSURE

Finally, in December 1994, FASB Chairman Dennis R. Beresford announced that the Board would not proceed with a standard on the treatment of stock option compensation in the income statement even though 'The Board remains convinced that employee options have value and are compensation'.[46] Instead, the Board would develop a standard to require that the same information be included in the footnotes to the financial statements of companies that continue to show zero compensation expense for stock options in their income statements.

When Beresford met with the FASB's advisory council in January 1995, he said that the Board had come 'this close to losing its franchise', bringing his forefinger so close to his thumb that they almost touched.

But the Board was not yet 'home free'. Affected companies pressed the Board to drop even its proposed disclosure requirement. In March 1995, '380 companies, mostly in high-technology industries, said [in a communication to the Board] they "strongly disagree" with the board's requirement that the footnote disclosure select a specific value for the cost of employee stock options'.[47]

While the debate from 1991 to 1995 centred mostly on the aptness of the valuation models being considered by the Board, it seems evident that the objection was, from 1991 to 1994, to reporting an expense in the income statement and, during 1995, even to disclosing the amount of the expense in the footnotes, regardless of the acceptability of a valuation model. On the subject of footnote disclosure, however, the Congress did not intervene.

In October 1995, the FASB issued *Statement of Financial Accounting Standards No. 123*, 'Accounting for Stock-Based Compensation,' in which it expressed a preference for giving income statement recognition to the compensation expense implicit in stock-based compensation plans as determined by a fair value analysis. For companies continuing to apply APB *Opinion No. 25* and thus showing zero compensation expense for stock-based compensation in their income statement, the Board required that they disclose 'the pro forma net income and, if earnings per share is presented, pro forma earnings per share, as if the fair value based accounting method in this Statement had been used to account for stock-based compensation cost'.[48] The *Statement* was approved by a vote of 5 to 2. The two dissenters stated their belief that 'the compensation associated with employee stock options should be recognized as a cost in the financial statements and disagree with the decision to permit that cost to be reflected only in pro forma disclosures'.[49]

Clearly, the full Board still would have supported income statement recognition of the 'compensation associated with employee stock options', but the majority felt that footnote disclosure was better than nothing. In

Statement No. 123, the Basis for Conclusions includes the following passage:

> The Board believes that disclosure of the pro forma effects of recognizing compensation cost according to the fair value method will provide relevant new information that will be of value to the capital markets and thus will achieve some but not all of the original objectives of the project. However, the Board continues to believe that disclosure is not an adequate substitute for recognition of assets, liabilities, equity, revenues, and expenses in financial statements.... The Board chose a disclosure-based solution for stock-based employee compensation to bring closure to a divisive debate on this issue – not because it believes that solution is the best way to improve financial accounting or reporting.[50]

What remains to be seen is whether the fervent opponents of future FASB initiatives again 'play the Congressional card' in their effort to trump the Board. In 1972, when the FASB was about to replace the APB, Leonard M. Savoie, executive vice-president of the American Institute of Certified Public Accountants, was prophetic when he said, 'Congressional involvement contributed greatly to the demise of the APB and may loom as a threat to any successor body'.[51]

NOTES

1 For a discussion of the 'economic consequences' phenomenon, see Stephen A. Zeff, 'The rise of "economic consequences",' *Journal of Accountancy* December 1978: 56–63.

2 See Germain Boer, 'Replacement cost: a historical look', *Accounting Review* January 1966: 92–3.

3 See Stephen A. Zeff, 'The politics of accounting standards', *Economia Aziendale* August 1993: 130–2.

4 See, for example, *ibid.* Maurice Moonitz, 'Some reflections on the investment credit experience', *Journal of Accounting Research Spring 1966: 47–61; Robert Van Riper, Setting Standards for Financial Reporting: FASB and the Struggle for Control of a Critical Process*, Westport, CT: Quorum Books, 1994; and Donald J. Kirk, 'Competitive disadvantage and mark-to-market accounting', *Accounting Horizons* June 1991: 98–106.

5 See, for example, Tony Hope and Rob Gray, 'Power and policy making: the development of an R&D standard', *Journal of Business Finance and Accounting* Winter 1982: 531–58; Tony Hope and John Briggs, 'Accounting policy making – some lessons from the deferred taxation debate', *Accounting and Business Research* Spring 1982: 83–96; and Christopher Nobes, 'A political history of goodwill in the U.K.: an illustration of cyclical standard setting', *Abacus* September 1992: 142–59.

6 See Stephen A. Zeff and Sven-Erik Johansson, 'The curious accounting treatment of the Swedish government loan to Uddeholm', *Accounting Review* April 1984: 342–50.

7 See, for example, Malcolm C. Miller, 'Goodwill discontent: the meshing of

Australian and international accounting policy', *Australian Accounting Review*, June 1995: 3–16.

8 Earlier instances that were similar was the decision by Congress in 1971 to amend pending tax legislation to allow corporations to use any method of accounting for the investment tax credit, and the Haskell–Bartlett Amendment introduced in the Senate to preclude the elimination of full costing to block the FASB and the SEC in the heated controversy over accounting for oil and gas exploration costs. The latter was dropped by the House-Senate Conference Committee, and the former was an appendage to a related tax bill. See Stephen A. Zeff, 'The politics of accounting standards', *Economia Aziendale* August 1993: 134–5, and Donald E. Gorton, 'The SEC decision not to support SFAS 19: a case study of the effect of lobbying on standard setting', *Accounting Horizons* March 1991: 32.

9 Hearing before the Subcommittee on Oversight of Government Management of the Committee on Governmental Affairs, United States Senate, 102nd Congress, 1st Session (15 May 1991), Washington, DC: US Government Printing Office, 1991.

10 See, for example, the cover stories in three leading magazines: 'Paying the boss' and 'Worthy of his hire?', *Economist* 1 February 1992: 13–14 and 19–20, 22; 'Executive pay', *Business Week* 30 March 1992: 52–8; and Geoffrey Colvin, 'How to pay the CEO right', *Fortune* 6 April 1992: 60–5, 68–9.

11 Hearing before the Subcommittee on Oversight of Government Management of the Committee on Governmental Affairs, United States Senate, 102nd Congress, 2nd Session (31 January 1992), Washington, DC: US Government Printing Office, 1992, p. 45.

12 *Status Report No. 236* of the Financial Accounting Standards Board, 12 October 1992: 7; E. Raymond Simpson, 'Stock compensation', *Status Report No. 238*, 31 December 1992: 13–14; and *FASB Action Alert*, no. 93–11, 17 March 1993.

13 *Statement of Financial Accounting Standards No. 123*, 'Accounting for Stock-Based Compensation', Norwalk, CT: Financial Accounting Standards Board, 1995, para. 374. A chronology of the Board's initiatives on stock-based compensation is given in the Background Information (paras 365–79).

14 'Let stock options stand and be counted', *Business Week* 12 April 1993: 102.

15 Indeed, the Finance Committee, to which the Bill was referred, did not call a hearing, and the Bill never emerged from committee. Lieberman came to find that the Committee on Banking, Housing, and Urban Affairs was a more friendly forum for his thrusts against the FASB than was the Finance Committee.

16 *Congressional Record – Senate* 29 June 1993: S 8252.

17 Letter to The Honorable Bill Clinton from Senator Carl Levin and Representative John Bryant, dated 14 October 1993.

18 Letter to The Honorable Carl Levin from President Bill Clinton, dated 18 November 1993.

19 *Employee Stock Options*, Hearing before the Subcommittee on Securities of the Committee on Banking, Housing, and Urban Affairs, United States Senate, 103rd Congress, 1st Session (21 October 1993), Washington, DC: US Government Printing Office, 1994, pp. 62–3.

20 Ibid., p. 193.

21 'Taking stock of options', *Washington Post* 22 October 1993: A22.

22 Remarks of The Honorable John D. Dingell, The 39th Corporate Accounting and Financial Reporting Institute, 15 November 1993, p. 7 of typescript.

23 Letter to Dennis R. Beresford from Lloyd Bentsen and Ronald H. Brown, dated 27 December 1993, Letter of Comment No. 437, File Reference 1100-127 of the FASB.

24 Letter to The Honorable Arthur Levitt, Jr, signed by Senators Alan K. Simpson (Republican of Wyoming), David L. Boren (Democrat of Oklahoma), Thomas A. Daschle (Democrat of South Dakota), Dave Durenberger (Republican of Minnesota), and Carl Levin, dated 30 November 1993.

25 Letter to The Honorable Carl Levin from Arthur Levitt, dated 10 January 1994.

26 *Statement of Financial Accounting Standards No. 123*, op. cit., paragraph 376. It is only fair to point out that most commentators on FASB proposals write in a critical vein. Those who support an FASB initiative are seldom moved to write a letter of comment.

27 Alison Leigh Cowan, 'Mom, apple pie and stock options?', *New York Times* 6 March 1994.

28 The FASB has produced a videotape of the television coverage and of the speeches made at the anti-FASB rally.

29 Christi Harlan, 'High anxiety: accounting proposal stirs unusual uproar in executive suites', *Wall Street Journal* 7 March 1994: A8.

30 'A rule that stunts growth', *Wall Street Journal* 8 February 1994: A18.

31 Letter to The Honorable Arthur Levitt, Jr, from Representative Edward J. Markey, dated 28 April 1994. Both Markey's letter and Levitt's reply were published in *Accounting Horizons* March 1995: 71–8.

32 Ibid., fn. 2.

33 Letter to The Honorable Edward J. Markey from Arthur Levitt, dated 25 May 1994 (footnote omitted).

34 Communication to the author from Elise Bean, a member of Senator Levin's staff, dated 22 January 1996.

35 *Congressional Record – Senate*, 3 May 1994: S 5035.

36 Ibid., p. S 5036.

37 Ibid., p. S 5037.

38 Ibid., pp. S 5040–1.

39 Ibid., p. S 5040.

40 Ibid., pp. S 5032 (for the text of the resolution) and S 5046 (for the tally of the vote).

41 Ibid., pp. S 5039 (for the text of the amendment) and S 5044 (for the tally of the vote). The two Senators voting against the amendment were Kent Conrad and Byron L. Dorgan (both Democrats of North Dakota). Dorgan has written that 'Some could vote for the Levin amendment, and that would give them some cover for voting in favor of the [resolution] dealing with executive stock options. I was very opposed to the [resolution] and would not support any amendment that made it easier for people to support that position'. Letter to the author from Senator Byron L. Dorgan, dated 1 July 1994.

42 Floyd Norris, 'As accounting enters politics, watch out', *New York Times* 12 June 1994: Sec. 3, p. 1.

43 *Congressional Record – Senate*, 6 October 1994: S 14510.

44 Lee Berton, 'Accounting board to weigh softening its controversial stock-option proposal', *Wall Street Journal* 14 December 1994: A2.

45 Letter to The Honorable Alfonse M. D'Amato from Senator Phil Gramm, dated 1 December 1994.

46 *Status Report No. 259* of the Financial Accounting Standards Board, 27 December 1994: 1.
47 Lee Berton, 'Firms campaign to soften FASB rule on disclosing cost of stock options', *Wall Street Journal* 5 April 1995: B2.
48 *Statement of Financial Accounting Standards No. 123*, op.cit., paragraph 45.
49 Ibid., p. 17.
50 Ibid., paragraph 62.
51 Comments by Leonard M. Savoie on 'Financial accounting standards: regulation or self regulation?' by David Solomons, *Stanford Lectures in Accounting 1972*.

10

FOREIGN COMPANY LISTINGS ON THE LONDON STOCK EXCHANGE

Listing patterns and influential factors

Sidney J. Gray and Clare B. Roberts

INTRODUCTION

An important part of the growing internationalisation of financial markets has been the increasing number of companies which have listed their shares on foreign stock exchanges. The London Stock Exchange (LSE) has by far the largest number of foreign listings (see Table 10.1) of any of the world's major stock exchanges, but while the fact of this pre-eminence is well known, what is not understood is how this has happened and why it is so.

Accordingly, the purpose of this paper is to provide some insight into the historical evolution of foreign company listing behaviour on the LSE and the likely influential factors involved. First, we will review previous research on the factors influencing foreign listing decisions. Second, we will examine the listing behaviour of foreign companies from 1937 to 1994, with a view to identifying any significant time, geographical and industry patterns of foreign company listings. Finally, we will assess the influence on listing behaviour of a number of important country factors which may help to explain the geographical pattern of foreign listings. These factors include disclosure and regulatory differences, size of the economy, significance of the stock market, international trade relationships, the level of domestic investment, cultural affinity, and the membership of country groupings such as the Commonwealth and the European Union.

FACTORS INFLUENCING FOREIGN LISTING DECISIONS

While foreign company listings have been growing apace in recent years, research in this area is relatively limited. Saudagaran (1988), in a study of 481 multinational corporations (MNCs), found that the major benefits that motivated foreign listings were access to larger capital markets and

Table 10.1 Foreign company listings as at end of 1994

	Companies		
Exchange	Domestic	Foreign	Total
Europe			
Amsterdam	317	215	532
Athens	165	—	165
Barcelona	347	4	351
Belgrade	2	—	2
Bilbao	466	3	469
Bratislava	13	—	13
Brussels	155	141	296
Budapest	40	—	40
Bulgarian	13	—	13
Copenhagen	242	10	252
German	423	227	650
Helsinki	65	—	65
Iceland	24	—	24
Italian	219	4	223
Lisbon	83	—	83
Lithuania	13	—	13
Ljubljana	17	—	17
London	2,070	464	2,534
Luxembourg	55	217	272
Madrid	375	4	379
Malta	4	—	4
Moscow	58	—	58
Oporto	185	—	185
Oslo	132	14	146
Paris	459	195	654
Prague	36	—	36
Siberian	9	—	9
Stockholm	106	8	114
St Petersburg	15	—	15
Swiss Exchanges	237	242	479
Valencia	243	1	244
Vienna	94	41	135
Warsaw	36	—	36
Zagreb	36	—	36
North America			
Alberta	749	6	755
American	750	74	824
Chicago	298	1	299
Montreal	562	12	574
Nasdaq	4,577	325	4,902
New York	2,570	217	2,787
Pacific	68	2	70
Toronto	1,185	66	1,251
Vancouver	1,600	n/a	1,600

continued

Table 10.1 Continued

	Companies		
Exchange	Domestic	Foreign	Total
Far East			
Hong Kong	502	27	529
Jakarta	217	—	217
Korea	699	—	699
Kuala Lumpur	344	3	347
Osaka	1,199	10	1,209
Philippine	189	—	189
Shanghai	203	—	203
Shenzhen	120	—	120
Singapore	n/a	n/a	272
Taiwan	313	—	313
Thailand	389	—	389
Tokyo	1,689	93	1,782
Australasia			
Australian	1,144	42	1,186
New Zealand	150	57	207
South America			
Bogata	264	1	265
Buenos Aires	156	—	156
Caracas	155	—	155
Lima	222	—	222
Medellin	171	1	172
Quito	139	—	139
Rio de Janeiro	575	1	576
Santiago	293	—	293
Sao Paulo	548	1	548
Central America and Caribbean			
Barbados	19		19
Costa Rica	115	1	116
Jamaica	49	1	50
Mexican	176	—	176
Panama	77	3	80
Trinidad and Tobago	26	1	27
Africa			
Abidjan	30	—	30
Botswana	10	—	10
Casablanca	56	5	61
Ghana	17	—	17
Johannesburg	614	26	640
Nairobi	40	16	56
Namibia	8	5	13
Nigerian	177	—	177
Swaziland	4	—	4
Zimbabwe	65	—	65

continued

Table 10.1 Continued

	Companies		
Exchange	Domestic	Foreign	Total
Middle East and Asia			
Amman	95	—	95
Bombay	4,413	n/a	4,413
Cairo	700	—	700
Colombo	215	—	215
Cyprus	35	—	35
Delhi	2,889	—	2,889
Istanbul	176	—	176
Karachi	724	—	724
Kuwait	42	7	49
Mauritius	35	—	35
Muscat	100	n/a	100
Tehran	147	—	147
Tel-Aviv	350	1	351

Source: *Quality of Markets Review – Spring edition, London Stock Exchange, 1995*

increased visibility in foreign countries which may help, for example, in promoting sales in those countries. The size of the capital market would seem to be an important factor attracting foreign companies to the LSE, given its predominance in Europe. The market reason is also relevant in that a London listing provides a high level of visibility, not only in the UK but also in the rest of the European Union.

The influence of regulatory costs was examined by Biddle and Saudagaran (1989), who found that the direct and indirect costs of financial reporting and disclosure were significant in explaining foreign listing choices. In this regard, Tondkar *et al.* (1989) showed how disincentives to list in some EU countries were reduced by efforts to narrow regulatory differences. Saudagaran and Biddle (1995) further explored the issue of regulatory cost differentials across nine major stock exchanges. In their study of 459 MNCs with foreign listings they found that companies are more likely to list on foreign stock exchanges with lower financial disclosure levels relative to their own. In this regard, the level of disclosure in the UK was evaluated by experts as ranking behind the USA and Canada, but ahead of the Netherlands, France, Japan, Germany and Switzerland. So far as disclosure regulations are concerned, the LSE requirements are relatively modest for foreign companies. Mutual recognition applies to all EU member countries whereby companies complying with their local requirements are deemed to comply with the LSE requirements. Additionally, companies complying with internationally acceptable standards, such as those of the USA or the International Accounting Standards Committee, are also considered to be acceptable.

In an endeavour to explain differences in disclosure levels, Adhikari and Tondkar (1992) investigated the relationship between a number of environmental factors and the disclosure requirements of thirty-five stock exchanges around the world. A disclosure index was developed from a survey of experts to measure the overall quantity and intensity of disclosure (see Table 10.2). Factors such as the degree of economic development (measured by GNP), the type of economy (agricultural versus industrial), the size of the stock market, trading activity on the stock market, and the

Table 10.2 Disclosure scores for stock exchanges

Stock exchange (country)	Disclosure scores (unweighted)
1 Sydney (Australia)	74.64
2 Vienna (Austria)	53.52
3 Rio de Janeiro (Brazil)	68.75
4 Toronto (Canada)	78.64
5 Bogota (Colombia)	54.48
6 Copenhagen (Denmark)	66.86
7 Cairo (Egypt)	48.02
8 Helsinki (Finland)	71.05
9 Paris (France)	76.16
10 Frankfurt (Germany)	66.86
11 Athens (Greece)	59.41
12 Hong Kong (Hong Kong)	75.77
13 Bombay (India)	58.84
14 Milan (Italy)	68.39
15 Tokyo (Japan)	77.68
16 Seoul (Korea)	72.00
17 Luxembourg (Luxembourg)	66.64
18 Kuala Lumpur (Malaysia)	75.41
19 Mexico (Mexico)	70.68
20 Amsterdam (Netherlands)	72.84
21 Wellington (New Zealand)	65.91
22 Oslo (Norway)	60.59
23 Karachi (Pakistan)	55.82
24 Lisbon (Portugal)	65.50
25 Singapore (Singapore)	80.32
26 Johannesburg (South Africa)	73.48
27 Madrid (Spain)	68.36
28 Stockholm (Sweden)	60.05
29 Zurich (Switzerland)	52.39
30 Taipei (Taiwan)	71.70
31 Bangkok (Thailand)	75.41
32 Istanbul (Turkey)	50.68
33 London (United Kingdom)	84.86
34 New York (United States)	90.75
35 Caracas (Venezuela)	73.32

Source: Adhikari and Tondkar (1992: 105)

dispersion of share ownership were used to try to explain the differences identified. However, only the size of the stock market was found to be significant.

In a study of listing choice factors in the European capital market context, Gray *et al.* (1994) confirmed the importance of disclosure regulations as a factor influencing choice. It is also argued that companies based in small countries with a small stock market are likely to incur problems in raising capital locally and hence will be motivated to seek foreign listings. This view was supported by a survey of stock market participants by Arthur Andersen & Co. (1989). Cultural links were also identified as likely explanations of clusterings of foreign listings especially in respect of language, e.g. German-speaking and English-speaking clusters.

One major limitation of all of these studies is that they only looked at the position at one point in time. Thus, they try to explain the decision to list, a decision that might have occurred at any time over the last several decades, by reference to contemporary market and economic factors. If companies do not actively consider de-listing or if de-listing is driven by a different set of considerations from those driving the decision to list, there may be little or no relationship between the maintenance of a listing and the market or economic variables that have been identified as being potentially significant in explaining the initial decision to list. Therefore, before trying to develop a model that explains listing behaviour, this paper first looks at the pattern of foreign company listings on the LSE from the 1930s to the present.

FOREIGN LISTING PATTERNS, 1937–94

Data on foreign non-financial companies listed on the LSE as at the end of 1994 were gathered from stock exchange sources[1] (see the Appendix for a full list of all non-financial foreign companies with a full listing). From this it can be seen that the earliest surviving listing is that of Blyvooruitzicht Gold Mining Co. Ltd from South Africa in July 1937. Among the total of 293 companies, South Africa is indeed still well represented, with sixty-three companies listed (21.5 per cent of the total number of foreign companies listed), but the USA tops the list with 108 companies (36.9 per cent) (see Table 10.3).

We now examine the listing behaviour of foreign companies in order to identify the presence of any significant time, geographical or industrial patterns.

Time patterns

The number of companies seeking a new listing has generally increased over time, with those gaining a new listing more than doubling in the 1970s

Table 10.3 Foreign listings analysed by country
at end of 1994

Country	Number of listings
Australia	11
Belgium	1
Bermuda	10
Canada	13
Denmark	3
Finland	5
France	6
Germany	8
Ghana	1
India	6
Israel	1
Japan	14
Kenya	1
Luxembourg	1
Malaysia	8
Netherlands	6
Netherlands Antilles	1
New Zealand	2
Norway	5
South Africa	63
Spain	1
Sweden	14
Switzerland	1
USA	108
Zambia	1
Zimbabwe	2
Total	293

compared with the earlier decade (to sixty from twenty seven) and doubling again in the 1980s (121 new listings). However, peak activity was reached in the mid-1980s. Since then, the number of new listings has declined, with only thirty-four companies listing in the five years from 1990 to 1994, in comparison with sixty-three listing a decade earlier in the period from 1980 to 1984. An analysis of the foreign listings over time was carried out using the chi-square test to assess whether or not the date of listing was random. As can be seen from Table 10.4, there were consistent differences in the numbers of companies listing each year, both when the entire period 1940–94 was considered and for each ten-year subperiod. The only exception to this was in the 1960s, when the pattern of listing appears instead to be random over time.

Given the significance of the time factor, an important next step is to explore the geographical dimension over time.

Table 10.4 Time patterns of foreign listings

Period	Chi-square	Significance
1940–9	20.250	0.016
1950–9	42.455	0.000
1960–9	1.800	0.994
1970–9	23.000	0.006
1980–9	59.413	0.000
1990–4	346.069	0.000

Table 10.5 Geographical patterns of foreign listings

Listing dates	Europe	Commonwealth	South Africa	USA	Rest of world	Total
1940–4	0	0	2	0	0	2
1945–9	2	1	10	1	0	14
1950–4	2	5	15	1	0	23
1955–9	0	3	6	0	1	10
1960–4	4	3	3	0	2	12
1965–9	2	0	3	8	2	15
1970–4	6	4	3	18	2	33
1975–9	4	6	3	13	1	27
1980–4	6	9	3	38	7	63
1985–9	16	8	6	26	2	58
1990–4	9	6	5	3	11	34
Chi-square	46.71	22.71	28.81	165.78	51.85	146.78
Significance	0.000	0.012	0.001	0.000	0.000	0.000

Kruskal–Wallis test: chi-square 51.4785   significance 0.000

1	Europe	51
2	Commonwealth	45
3	South Africa	63
4	USA	108
5	Rest of world (Japan, Bermuda, Neth. Antilles, Israel)	26
	Total	293

Geographical patterns

In order to assess the nature of listing patterns across geographical areas over
time the companies were grouped into five geographical areas or countries
(see Table 10.5): Europe, the Commonwealth, South Africa, USA and the
rest of the world. Chi-square tests were conducted on the numbers of
companies listing over each five-year period for each of these five areas.
These tests show that there are significant differences in listing activity over
time within each geographical area. In addition, the Kruskal–Wallis non-

parametric test was also applied. This ranks each company in terms of its year of listing and then compares the mean rank of companies located in each geographical area. The results of this test show that the patterns of listings were also significantly different across the five areas. In particular, it is apparent that the South African companies listed significantly earlier than did companies from all other areas. This reflects the historical links between the UK and South Africa and the early reliance placed upon British finance for the exploitation of South Africa's minerals, in particular gold and diamonds. The main period for USA listings was instead the 1980s. Some of these listings were due to specific shocks in the US economy, in particular the break-up of the telecommunications industry and the formation of the 'Baby Bells', but most of the listings would seem to reflect the international expansion of US companies in general at that time. There was probably also at least a small element of fashionable or follow-my-leader behaviour by some companies.

European companies have a long history of listing in the UK, with, for example, Royal Dutch Petroleum and Unilever from the Netherlands both listing in the 1940s, SKF and Electrolux from Sweden listing in the 1950s and Thyssen, Bayer and Hoechst from Germany listing in the early 1960s. However, new listings are still fairly common in the 1990s with, for example, nine European companies listing in the period 1990 to 1994 in contrast to only three US companies. The latest entrants to the LSE include relatively more companies from the rest of the world, including most importantly Japan, with none listing before the mid-1950s but eleven of the twenty nine (38 per cent) listing in the 1990s.

Industry patterns

The assessment of industry patterns over time necessitates the analysis of companies according to their 1994 Financial Times–Stock Exchange Actuaries Industry classification (see Table 10.6). The sample was broken down into five groups: minerals, manufacturing, consumer goods, services and utilities, with the manufacturing group being further split into the two subgroups of electronics and engineering and other manufacturing. Chi-square tests show that there are significant differences within each of the five or six industries over time. The Kruskal–Wallis test was also applied to compare the behaviour of each industry group. This test shows that the patterns of listing are also significantly different across the industry groups.

In particular, minerals companies listed significantly earlier than all other sectors, which reflects both developments in exploration at the time and historical links between the UK and its colonies, especially South Africa. Most of the listed South African companies are minerals companies and, similarly, while some minerals companies from other areas are listed on the LSE, this sector is dominated by South African companies.

Table 10.6 Industry patterns of foreign listings

FT	Code	Industry	No. of companies
100s	1	Minerals	93
200s	2	Gen manufacturing	105
210–40 and 280–95	2a	Manufacturing	46
250–70	2b	Electronics and engineering	59
300s	3	Consumer goods	42
400s, 512 and 516	4	Services	36
620 and 660	5	Utilities	17
		Total	293

Date	1	2	2a	2b	3	4	5
1940–4	2	—	—	—	—	—	—
1945–9	10	1	1	—	3	—	—
1950–4	17	4	1	3	2	—	—
1955–9	9	—	—	—	1	—	—
1960–4	4	6	4	2	2	—	—
1965–9	3	6	2	4	2	—	2
1970–4	8	16	5	11	6	3	—
1975–9	7	10	3	7	4	5	1
1980–4	9	26	12	14	7	11	10
1985–9	12	23	11	12	12	8	3
1990–4	9	12	6	6	2	9	1
Chi-square	22.20	85.75	42.27	48.20	31.71	55.67	57.41
Significance	0.014	0.000	0.000	0.000	0.000	0.000	0.000

Kruskal–Wallis test: chi-square 38.8522 significance 0.000

Utilities, on the other hand, have tended to list significantly later than minerals, consumer goods or manufacturing companies, although the newest listers tend to be service companies. So far as utilities and services are concerned, these later developments can largely be explained by the impact of privatisation and economic development respectively.

EXPLANATIONS OF FOREIGN LISTINGS

Following our earlier discussion of factors influencing foreign listing decisions, we now focus on explanations of the geographical pattern of extant foreign company listings on the LSE. Our purpose is to develop an explanatory model, using regression analysis, incorporating the following six proxies for the identified country determinants of listing behaviour:

1 *Regulations and disclosure.* The disclosure requirements and levels as

reported in the research by both Saudagaran and Biddle (1995) and Adhikari and Tondkar (1992) are used as the basis for assessing disclosure requirements relative to the UK. A dummy variable was created which took the value of 1 if domestic disclosure requirements are greater than those in the UK and a value of 0 otherwise. The expectation is that more foreign listings will be forthcoming from countries with more stringent requirements and higher disclosure levels.

2 *Size of the economy.* Gross domestic product in absolute terms and per capita are used as indicators of the size and success of the economy.[2] The size of the economy is expected to be negatively related to the number of foreign listings, i.e. more listings will be forthcoming from smaller economies. GNP per capita is a measure of the economic development of a country and this should affect the demand for capital by companies. It is therefore expected that this will be positively related to the number of foreign listings, i.e. more listings will be forthcoming from relatively wealthy countries.

3 *Stock market.* The significance of the stock market is assessed on the basis of market capitalisation as a percentage of GDP. Here, a negative relationship is expected, i.e. the number of foreign listings will be higher in the case of companies based in countries with relatively less important stock markets. In addition, the model was also run using stock market turnover as a percentage of GDP. However, the model was slightly less successful when this form of the variable was used, so the results are not reported here.

4 *International trade relationships.* The nature of trade relationships is calculated by reference to exports and imports to the UK as a percentage of all exports and imports of the country. More intensive trade relationships are expected to be positively related to the number of foreign listings.

5 *Level of domestic investment.* The significance of domestic investment is assessed by reference to investment as a percentage of GDP. This provides a proxy for the availability of domestic capital for companies and the expectation here is that more foreign listings are likely when domestic investment is relatively small.

6 *Cultural affinity.* The English language, where it is a country's first language, is taken here as a proxy for cultural affinity with the UK. Hence, more foreign listings are expected from the English-speaking countries. In addition, the Commonwealth and the EU were also taken as likely significant groupings, i.e. the expectation is that more foreign listings will be forthcoming from member countries relative to others. The model was run in three forms, each looking at the importance of one of these three variables. None were found to be significant although the most successful model overall was that containing a proxy for the use of English as an official language. It is this model that is reported here.

Table 10.7 Foreign listing explanatory variables: descriptive statistics

	Mean	SD	Minimum	Maximum
GDP (£billion)	654.9	1,129.2	24.96	3,993.7
GDP per capita	11.54	6.04	0.18	19.78
Stock market capitalisation as % GDP	82.63	91.48	26.63	395.74
International trade: % imports and exports with UK	6.46	3.04	2.00	13.13
Domestic investment as % GDP	20.51	5.97	15.1	35.9

Table 10.8 Foreign listing explanatory model: regression results

	B	T	Sig. T
GDP (log)	0.5443	3.105	0.0172
GDP per capita	−0.0487	−0.705	0.5036
Stock market capitalisation % (log)	1.3946	3.046	0.0187
International trade %	0.0356	0.309	0.7665
Domestic investment %	−0.1262	−2.525	0.0395
Disclosure level	0.4387	0.491	0.6382
English	−0.4846	−0.463	0.6574
Constant	−3.3177	−1.160	0.2841

Adjusted R^2	0.6112
F	4.15
Sig. F	0.0402

Statistical results

Descriptive statistics in respect of the above variables are listed in Table 10.7. This data relates to 1992, being the latest available. The results of the regression analysis are shown in Table 10.8. The independent variable was the number of companies listed from each country. Only countries with at least two companies listed were included. Then, Zimbabwe was excluded because of the lack of available data, as was Bermuda which acts primarily as a financial centre. All the variables were tested for normality and the number of listings, total GDP and stock market capitalisation to GDP all had to be expressed as logarithms to avoid problems of non-normality.

From Table 10.8 it can be seen that the explanatory model as hypothesised has an adjusted R^2 of 0.6112 which is both relatively strong in explanatory power and statistically significant. However, in terms of the individual variables, only GDP, stock market capitalisation and domestic investment are statistically significant. Contrary to expectations, these results suggest that foreign listings tend to increase as the size of the economy and significance of the stock market increases. At the same time, foreign listings are negatively linked to the level of domestic investment. Further, contrary to the findings of Saudagaran and Biddle (1995), foreign listings do not appear to be explained by differences in disclosure levels.[3] Cultural affinity, at least as indicated by the use of English as the first language, is not significant. Finally, country groupings such as the Commonwealth and EU are also not significant.

CONCLUSIONS

The purpose of this paper was to explore the existence of patterns of foreign company listing behaviour on the London Stock Exchange during the period 1937 to 1994 and to identify some of the influential factors involved. The main findings are that, over time, the pattern of foreign listings has varied significantly. Moreover, significant geographical and industry patterns can be identified. Major explanations of the geographical pattern of current foreign listings in terms of country determinants are the size of the economy, the significance of the stock market and the level of domestic investment. However, trade patterns, differences in disclosure levels, cultural affinity and country groupings do not appear to be significant factors.

The results of this study, especially as regards differences in listing behaviour over time and country of domicile, clearly suggest that different considerations may have driven the various different types of companies to list. For example, many of the companies from the Commonwealth and in particular South Africa listed relatively early. In these cases the decision to list was probably driven by considerations of trade and cultural links. Different factors are likely to explain the behaviour of companies coming from other countries. While US companies may see a listing on the LSE as an easy and relatively cheap way of obtaining entry to European capital markets, EU companies would find a listing more expensive, given the necessity to produce English-language financial statements, and, obviously, would not need a similar point of access to the European market. Given these considerations, future research should clearly differentiate between companies from different countries. Further applications of a single model, however sophisticated, to all companies is likely to mask important differences rather than to highlight them.

NOTES

1 These data were obtained initially from the *Stock Exchange Quarterly*, Winter 1991, which contains a full listing of foreign companies as at 31 December 1991. Changes since then were obtained from individual issues of the *Quarterly*.
2 All economic data were obtained from either the IMF International Financial Yearbook or the CSO Annual Abstract of Statistics.
3 The only countries with higher disclosure levels are the USA and Canada.

Because of the sample of companies and countries used here, this variable was mainly a proxy for the USA. Consequently, the results cannot be interpreted to mean that listing requirements are definitely unimportant, rather disclosure levels cannot be easily tested when the listing behaviour inside one market only is being examined.

REFERENCES

Adhikari, Ajay and Tondkar Resoul, H. (1992) 'Environmental factors influencing accounting disclosure requirements of global stock exchanges' *Journal of International Financial Management and Accounting* 4(2): Summer.

Arthur Andersen & Co. (1989) *European Capital Markets*, London: Economist Publications.

Biddle, Gary C. and Saudagaran, Shahrokh M. (1989) 'The effects of financial disclosure levels on firms' choices among alternative foreign stock exchange listings', *Journal of International Financial Management and Accounting* 1(1): Spring.

Gray, Sidney J., Meek, Gary K. and Roberts, Clare B. (1994) 'Financial deregulation, stock exchange listing choice and the developments of a European capital market', in V. K. Zimmerman (ed.) *The New Europe: Recent Political and Economic Implications for Accountants and Accounting*, Urbana–Champaign: University of Illinois.

Saudagaran, Shahrokh M. (1988) 'An empirical study of selected factors influencing the decision to list on foreign stock exchanges', *Journal of International Business Studies* Spring.

Saudagaran, Shahrokh M. and Biddle, Gary C. (1995) 'Foreign listing locations: a study of MNCs and stock exchanges in eight countries', *Journal of International Business Studies* Second Quarter.

Tondkar, Resoul H., Adhikari, Ajay and Coffman, E. N. (1989) 'The internationalization of equity markets: motivations for foreign corporate listing and filing and listing requirements of five major stock exchanges', *International Journal of Accounting* Fall.

APPENDIX TO CHAPTER 10
Listings of foreign non-financial companies on the London Stock Exchange, 1937–94

The listing date (month/year) is given in the right-hand column.

AUSTRALIA

Australian Agricultural	Cattle, sheep and wool, grain crops	5/48
Van Diemen's Land	Farming	11/60
Foster's Brewing Group	Breweries	8/62
Western Mining	Minerals, metal, petroleum	11/79
TNT	Transportation services	10/80
News Corporation	Newspapers, TV	11/86
Pacific Dunlop	Batteries, tyres, health care equipment, etc.	1/87
Coles Myer	Food and department stores	2/87
Mayne Nickless	Freight forwarding, health care services	11/87
Goodman Fielder	Food products	12/87
CSR	Building and construction materials, timber, sugar	12/88
Cortecs International	Pharmaceuticals	12/91

BELGIUM

Petrofina	Oil exploration and refining	9/91

BERMUDA

Zambia Copper Investments	Holding company	6/71
Sea Containers	Transportation	3/84
ADT Group	Electronic security and vehicle auctions	12/84
Monarch Resources	Gold mining	7/87
Dairy Farm International	Food retail, manufacture and wholesaling	5/90

Jardine Matheson Holdings	Trading	5/90
Mandarin Oriental Int.	Hotels	10/90
Fairhaven International	Oil and gas eng. and services, project management	9/91
Vtech Holdings	Computers	10/91
Wah Shipping Holdings	Shipping and property development	6/92

CANADA

Canadian Pacific	Transportation, energy, real estate and hotels	9/52
Alcan Aluminium	Aluminium mining, refining, manuf. and recycling	8/53
Inco	Mining and precious metals	9/57
Canadian Overseas Packaging	Packaging	5/62
Ranger Oil	Oil and gas exploration and production	7/72
Seagram	Distilleries	10/73
Thomson	Info services, newspapers, leisure travel	9/78
Mitel	Electronics	9/80
BCE	Telecom. services, equip. manuf. and financial services	5/83
Northern Telecom	Telecommunications equipment	6/84
Republic Goldfields	Gold mining	7/84
Hemlo Gold Mines	Gold mining	2/87
American Barrick Resources	Gold mining	10/91

DENMARK

GN Great Nordic	Telecommunications	7/65
Novo Nordisk	Pharmaceuticals	10/78
ISS	Office cleaning	9/89

FINLAND

Amer Group	Sports equipment, motor trade, tobacco, printing	5/84
Nokia	Telecommunications	5/87
Kymmene	Paper	6/88
Enso-Gutzeit	Forestry products	6/89
Repola	Forestry products	1/91

FRANCE

Lafarge Coppèe	Cement and building materials	10/72
Total	Oil and gas	9/73
Danone	Food and drink	7/85
Compagnie de Saint-Gobain	Building materials and glass	7/87
Euro-Disney	Leisure management	11/89
Carnaudmetalbox	Packaging	4/89

GERMANY

Thyssen	Capital goods, trading, steel	7/60
Bayer	Chemicals and health care	3/61
Hoechst	Chemicals	11/61
BASF	Chemicals	5/80
Schering	Pharmaceuticals	5/86
Volkswagen	Autos	9/88
Siemens	Mechanical engineering	6/90
Daimler-Benz	Autos	12/90

GHANA

| Ashanti Goldfields | Gold mining | 4/94 |

INDIA

E.I.D. Parry (India)	General merchanting and trading	6/76
CESC	Electricity generation and distribution	4/79
East India Hotels	Hotels	10/94
JK Corporation	Diversified industrial	10/94
Shriram Industrial	Diversified industrial	10/94
Bajaj Auto	Auto engineering	11/94

ISRAEL

| Dead Sea Works | Potash, bromine manuf. and marketing | 2/57 |

JAPAN

| Toray Industries | Chemicals, plastics | 6/64 |
| Sony | Audio equipment, computers, music and film | 10/71 |

Renown	Clothing	7/76
Toshiba	Computers	10/80
Honda	Autos	6/81
NEC	Electronics	9/81
Fujitsu	Manuf. info. technology and communications products	10/81
TDK	Tapes, electronic components	5/83
Mitsubishi Electric	Electronics	9/89
Kirin Brewery	Beer	6/90
Kajima	Construction and civil engineering	9/90
All Nippon Airways	Airline	10/91
Kobe Steel	Steel	10/92
NTT	Telecommunications	10/94

KENYA

Kakuzi	Agriculture	2/53

LUXEMBOURG

Oriflame International	Cosmetics, retail	5/83

MALAYSIA

Petaling Tin Berhad	Tin mining	12/50
Riverview Rubber Estates	Rubber plantations	9/57
Kuala Lumpur Kepong	Plantations	10/73
Highlands & Lowlands	Oil palm, rubber, cocoa and coconut	1/76
Sime Darby	Industrial diversified holding company	12/79
Malaysia Mining	Mining	10/81
Golden Hope Plantation	Plantations	10/82
Gopeng Berhard	Construction, cement, property, quarrying, etc.	4/84

NETHERLANDS

Royal Dutch Petroleum	Oil and gas	10/46
Unilever	Food manufacturing	1/49
AKZO Nobel	Chemicals	10/72
Philips Electronics	Electronic and electrical products	12/73
Bols Wessanen	Food and drink marketing	11/84
Elsevier	Publishing	1/93

NETHERLANDS ANTILLES

Schlumberger	Oilfield services, meter manufacturing	4/63

NEW ZEALAND

Fletcher Challenge	Pulp and paper, forestry	3/81
Brierley Investments	Trading	12/86

NORWAY

Norsk Hydro	Natural resources processing	4/72
Bergesen D.Y.	Oil and gas tankers	6/88
Hafslund Nycomed	Medical equip., pharmaceuticals, hydroelectric	6/89
Vard	Cruise liners	6/90
Kvaerner	Shipbuilding, oil and gas, mech. eng., pulp, shipping	10/90

SOUTH AFRICA

Blyvooruitzicht Gold Mining	Gold mining	7/37
Witwatersrand Nigel	Gold mining	1/39
Anglo American Industrial	Iron, steel, eng., explosives, chemicals, etc.	5/39
Tongaat-Hulett Group	Sugar, building mats, foods, aluminium,textiles	11/39
Grootvlei Proprietary Mines	Gold mining	10/41
Gold Fields Coal	Coal mining	3/44
Gold Fields of South Africa	Mining and finance house	11/45
Middle Witwatersrand	Mining investment	5/46
St Helena Gold Mines	Gold mining	5/46
Doornfontein Gold Mining	Gold mining	4/47
Tiger Oats	Food manuf. and distribution	5/47
Free State Cons. Gold Mines	Gold mining	5/48
Vaal Reefs Exploration & Mining	Gold mining	2/49
Stilfontein Gold Mining	Gold mining	9/49

Anglo American Coal	Coal mining	10/49
Anglo-American Gold Investment	Gold mining	10/49
Hartebeestfontein Gold Mining	Gold mining	2/50
Durban Roodepoort Deep	Gold mining	7/50
East Rand Proprietary Mines	Gold mining	7/50
New Central Witwatersrand Areas	Mining finance	8/50
Bracken Mines	Gold mining and metal recovery	8/50
Simmer & Jack Mines	Gold mining	8/50
Vogelstmisbult Metal Holdings	Mining finance	8/50
West Rand Consolidated Mines	Mining title and mineral rights	8/50
Randfontein Estates Gold Mining	Gold mining	9/50
Harmony Gold Mining	Gold mining	12/50
Loraine Gold Mines	Gold mining	3/51
Consolidated Murchison	Mining antimony ore	9/51
Griqualaland West Mining	Diamond mine rights	6/54
Consolidated Company	Diamond mine	6/54
Buffelsfontein Gold Mining	Gold mining	10/54
Winkelhaak Mines	Gold mining	1/56
Rustenburg Platinum	Platinum produce and refine	2/56
New Wits	Mining finance	4/56
Western Deep Levels	Gold mining	1/59
Western Areas Gold Mining	Gold and uranium mining	10/59
Leslie Gold Mines	Gold mining	11/59
Trans-Natal Coal	Coal mining	4/63
Kloof Gold Mining	Gold mining	7/64
Kinross Mines	Gold mining	8/64
Southvaal Holdings	Gold mining finance	5/68
Barlow	Building mats, paint, autos, electricals, info. tech., etc.	3/69
Driefontein Consolidated	Gold mining	6/69
South African Breweries	Breweries	5/71
Impala Platinum Holdings	Platinum group metals supply	2/73
Unisel Gold Mines	Gold mining	10/74
Deelkraal Gold Mining	Gold mining	4/75
Elandsrand Gold Mining	Gold mining	10/75

East Rand Gold & Uranium	Gold recovery	12/77
C.N.A. Gallo	Retail, music software and publishing, film dist., etc.	8/83
Premier Group	Food and pharmaceutical products	7/84
Egoli Consolidated Mines	Gold mining and recovery	9/84
Beatrix Mines	Gold mining	3/85
H.J. Joel Gold Mining	Gold mining	6/86
United Plantations Africa	Farming	6/87
Lebowa Platinum Mines	Mining	10/87
Oryx Gold Holding	Gold mining finance	5/88
Barnato Exploration	Gold mining	8/88
Northam Platinum	Mining	2/90
De Beers Consolidated Mines	Mining and trading diamonds	6/90
Potgietersrust Platinums	Platinum mining	10/91
Sappi	Paper and pulp	6/92
Ashanti Goldfields	Goldmining	4/94

SPAIN

Telefonica De Espana	Telephone services	6/85

SWEDEN

SKF	Bearings and speciality steel	9/50
Electrolux	Household appliances etc.	9/51
Ericsson	Telecommunications equipment	8/60
ASEA	Power dist, ind and building systems, transport	4/66
Volvo	Autos	12/72
Sandvik	Tools manufacture	11/77
AGA	Industrial and medical gases	6/79
Esselte	Office products and supplies	8/79
Perstorp	Biotechnology, chemicals	3/83
Svensska Cellulosa	Forestry products	6/83
Astra	Pharmaceuticals and chemicals	5/85
Stora	Forestry products	11/89
Atlas Copco	Mechanical engineering	12/90
Arjo	Health care	11/93

SWITZERLAND

Nestlé	Food manufacturing	6/89

USA

ITT	Manuf., hotels, financial and business services	7/49
Gillette	Razors, toiletries, etc.	12/50
Chrysler	Autos	1/65
General Motors	Autos	4/65
Ford Motor	Autos	6/66
CPC International	Food manufacturing and corn refining	9/66
W.R. Grace	Chemicals and health care	6/67
GTE	Telephones	6/67
Pfizer	Health care	8/67
Texaco	Oil and gas	3/69
Monsanto	Agricultural products, chemicals	1/70
Unisys	Computers	1/70
Honeywell	Control systems	6/72
Paramount Communications	Films, publishing, TV programmes	9/72
Eaton	Auto and military components	10/72
Ingersoll-Rand	Machinery and tools	10/72
Xerox	Office equipment	10/72
Dow Chemical	Chemicals	11/72
Colgate-Palmolive	Soap etc.	11/72
Halliburton	Oil and gas ind. services, engineering, construction	3/73
Quaker Oats	Food manufacturing	5/73
TRW	Auto products	7/73
IBM	Computers	7/73
General Electric	Aircraft engines, appliances, power systems, motors, etc.	10/73
Warner-Lambert	Pharmaceuticals	11/73
Dover	Elevators, oil industry equipment	11/73
Browning-Ferris Industries	Waste recovery, recycling and disposal services	12/73
GATX	Railcars, tank storage terminals, shipping, real estate	3/74
Brunswick	Marine and recreation products, recreation facilities	7/75
United Technologies	Technological products	11/76
Mobil	Oil and gas	1/77
Time Warner	Publishing, music	2/77
Asarco	Metals, chemicals, environmental services	10/77

Dana Corporation	Components and services for auto and ind. markets	1/78
Baxter Indentational	Health care products, systems and services	4/78
Fluor	Engineering, construction and technical services	7/78
Motorola	Electronics	9/78
Sears Roebuck	Stores	10/78
Abbott Laboratories	Hospital and diagnostic products, pharmaceuticals, etc.	12/78
Rockwell International	Electronics, aerospace	6/79
Louisiana Land & Exploration	Oil and gas exploration and production	9/79
Black & Decker	Home products, info. systems and services	1/80
Boeing	Aircraft manufacture	1/80
Pennzoil	Oil	9/80
National Medical Enterprises	Health care	11/80
Amdahl	Large-scale computer systems	4/81
Sara Lee	Food manufacturing	5/81
Aluminum Company of America	Aluminium products	9/81
Lowe's Companies	D-I-Y retail	10/81
AT&T	Communication services and electronics	1/82
Aviva Petroleum	Oil and gas exploration	12/82
Campbell Soup	Food products	12/82
Rohr	Aerospace components	11/83
Nynex	Telecommunications	2/84
Pacific Telesis Group	Telephone operator	2/84
Bell Atlantic	Communication equipment and services	2/84
Bellsouth	Telephone systems	2/84
Southwestern Bell	Telephone services	2/84
US West	Communication services	2/84
Amertech	Telephone system operators	3/84
Enron	Gas production and distribution	3/84
Data General	Computer products and services	6/84
Houston Industries	Electricity	6/84
Bowater	Pulp and paper	7/84
Carter Hawley Hale Stores	Department stores	8/84
Great Western Resources	Oil and gas, coal mining	8/84
Holmes Protection Group	Fire detection systems	10/84
Chevron	Oil and gas, chemicals, coal	11/84

Limited	Clothing sale	12/84
Hasbro	Toys	12/84
Hercules	Chemicals	12/84
Centex	Construction and mortgages	12/84
American Cyanamid	Medical and agricultural products	12/84
CSX	Transportation, property, resorts	12/84
Dun and Bradstreet	Business info., software and decision-making services	12/84
Englehard	Chemicals	12/84
Enserch	Natural gas	12/84
Pall	Health care equipment	12/84
Process Systems	Microelectronics	12/84
American Brands	Consumer goods	12/85
Klearfold	Packaging	1/86
Exxon	Oil and gas	6/86
Lockheed	Aeronautical manufacturing	6/86
Caterpillar	Earthmoving, construction equip. and engines	7/86
Anheuser-Busch	Beer, baked goods and theme parks	10/86
Trinova	Engineered components and systems	11/86
Coastal	Gas, petroleum refining, oil, coal, chemicals, power	12/86
Molex	Electronic components	1/87
Allied-signal	Aerospace, auto and engineered materials	5/87
Whirlpool	White goods	5/87
WMX Technologies	Environmental engineering	6/87
Occidental Petroleum	Oil and gas	7/87
Premark International	Tupperware, food equip. and consumer products	10/87
Tenneco	Gas pipelines, constrn equip., autoparts, shipbuilding	12/87
Sotheby's Holdings	Fine art auctioneers	5/88
Texas Instruments	Electronics	5/88
SCE	Electricity supply	7/88
California Energy	Electricity generation	9/88
XCL	Oil and gas	10/88
Echlin	Auto parts	1/89
Hewlett-Packard	Electronic products and systems	4/89
Presidio Oil	Oil and gas	7/89
Philip Morris	Cigarettes and food products	8/89
Union Carbide	Chemicals	8/89
Eli Lilley	Health care products	10/89
Manpower	Employment agency	5/91

Atlantic Richfield	Oil and gas	11/92
Sunguard Data Systems	Computer software and support	6/93

ZAMBIA

Zambia Consolidated Copper Mines	Mining	6/70

ZIMBABWE

Wankie Colliery	Coalmining	4/50
Mhangura Copper Mines	Copper mining	1/58

11

THE DEVELOPMENT OF ACCOUNTING RESEARCH IN THE UK

The need to put 'accounting' back into it

R. S. Olusegun Wallace*

INTRODUCTION

The theme of this paper[1] is inspired by my growing sense of frustration at the divorce between the motivational axioms and paradigms employed in modern accounting research and the type of behaviour most practitioners believe to be real. We drill our students in analytical exercises based on these axioms and paradigms. We tell them that real-world experiences are developed on the basis of self-interested principles and argue that the principles are inadequate but offer either partly developed alternatives or none at all. By the same token accounting research is weakened.

The fact that accounting is not taken seriously by many people outside the accounting profession would have been easier to deal with if the same doubts had not infiltrated the ranks of academic accountants in the United Kingdom. Yet anyone familiar with the modern literature on accounting research cannot fail to detect the self-doubts and the not always covert dissatisfaction with the fate of being an academic accountant devoted solely to the improvement of accounting principles and practice. However, self-doubt is more crippling than the doubts of outsiders. There are three reasons for my writing on this issue. First, there is my belief that there has been a public decline in the authority, and even the credibility, of accounting and the accounting profession, and a growth in internal self-doubt of academic accountants in accounting. Second, I think that the modern academic accounting literature, in certain of its influential manifestations, has sacrificed relevance for formal linguistic and formal econometric sophistication and innovative stylistic display. And third, there is my belief that the citing of the (indisputable) complex nature of accounting (described later) as the cause of the diminishing vitality of accounting has directed attention away from the failings that are internal to the accounting craft itself.

218

Therefore, my aim is hortatory: to plead with accounting scholars to perform acts of inclusion. I argue that 'core' accounting issues are being excluded from the more recent accounting literature and suggest that this exclusion is impeding the progress of accounting research and practice. By core accounting, I refer to the theoretical and technical aspects of accounting and recommendations of different kinds of accounting. Core accounting articles deal with the measurement of income, assets, and the internal and external reporting of accounting information. To exclude core accounting issues from accounting research is to turn accounting research into a colonised or dependent discipline, an example of explicit academic subordination.

Given my Nigerian background and origin, I am in a good position to recognise colonialism. Operationally, colonialism or dependency of an academic discipline is formed through the creation of a situation where control over internal jurisdiction or external freedom of action (i.e. intellectual inspiration and methodological procedures) of that discipline is ceded to other disciplines or where the spaces of journals devoted to a discipline are taken over by cognate disciplines almost to the total neglect of that discipline. As Goldberg (1994) suggests, accounting research is in:

> a kind of treadmill, in which many, if not most, researchers appear to be driven by a need to display a mastery of a technique (often borrowed from another discipline, deemed to be more academically respectable than accounting) used to demonstrate a virtuosity concentrated on a minute aspect of little significance in the widening or deepening of our knowledge of what we call accounting, however defined.

I argue for the decolonisation of the discipline. This will occur when core accounting issues become dominant again in accounting research. My plea is in line with the call of senior academics for scholars to bridge the gap between accounting research and the needs of practitioners (Baxter 1988), not to cordon themselves off into narrow specialisms, leading to a fragmentation of the accounting literature (Zeff 1989) because those engagements are becoming more interesting (Whittington 1995), but to include core accounting issues in their research agenda because such inclusion is crucial for the health of the discipline.

I do not intend to stretch my argument to the opposite end of the spectrum – that is, to ask accounting scholars to exclude peripheral accounting issues from accounting research. The literature from this heterogeneous group of scholars has produced, in the last two decades, a variety of conceptualisations of accounting theory and practice. There is virtue in the conceptual heterogeneity of this group. Not only have they exposed aspects of accountancy practice that were once unknown to us, but they have also introduced different perspectives to the accounting literature and have, as a result, produced a respectable body of research and empirical knowledge.

What do I mean by 'accounting'? What is the scope of accounting research of which it is a part? Accounting is a process of accumulating and reporting economic information to permit informed judgements and decisions by the users of the information. Accounting is a system by which we take a picture, as of one instant, of a tremendous number of rapidly moving objects. It is concerned with the retrieval of all these rapidly moving objects so that they can be seen, by slowing them down, and making them stand still just for a particular moment – a moment accountants usually call the year-end.

In the context of research, it is advisable to adopt a broad, rather than a narrow, definition of accounting so that we can understand how the 'accounting' in accounting research has been underexplored and narrowed over time. For this purpose, I consider the 'accounting' in accounting research to include not only (a) what accountants do, or think they do, but also (b) what accountants should be doing, and (c) what non-accountants think accountants are doing and/or should be doing. Each of these components of the accounting construct is now elaborated upon.

Accounting is what accountants do

On this basis, accounting is the accountant's vocation. Accountants do a great variety of things ranging from a determination of what are described as assets, liabilities, income and costs (Sikka *et al.*, 1995: 113) to the shaping of organisational, political and social contexts (Hopwood 1994: 299). They do some of these things all the time, some at different times, and for different clients or in different circumstances/environments. The critical questions for the researcher in this context are: Why do accountants do what they do, in the way they do it, at the time or in the circumstances they do it? What explanation(s) can be provided for uniformity of and/or differences in activities? (Goldberg 1994: 12).

Accounting is what accountants think they do

One is not certain whether accountants believe that they are achieving what they think they are doing. For example, financial reports of a company are expected, by the Companies Act (since 1947), to give a true and fair view of the state of the company. Many accountants think that this is what they are doing, but the reports that are delivered often do not represent faithfully the reality because, by its nature, the underlying accounting leaves a lot of crucial (if non-financial) information out of the reckoning. In addition, auditors are neither agreed on those to whom they are addressing their opinions nor are they sure of the meaning conveyed by the wording of their opinions to the presumed, intended and/or actual recipients. If what accountants or auditors are doing varies from what they think they are doing, there is a serious expectation gap that needs resolving.

Accounting is what accountants should be doing

On several issues accountants are not agreed on what they should be doing. There are several ways in accounting and the choice of the best is often a normative quest. Early accounting scholars devoted much of their writings to this quest. However, one is not sure who should say what accountants should be doing, on what grounds, and by what criteria. This whole area raises questions of social relationships, legislation, standards and value judgements.

Accounting is what non-accountants think accountants are doing and/ or should be doing

There is hardly any agreement between the suppliers and customers of accounting as to the form which accounting product(s) should take. The specification of the product(s) would differ among heterogeneous users of information – judges in potential or actual court cases, politicians as legislators, standard setters (some of whom may be accountants) and managers of institutions needing the services of accountants.

The final authority in accounting derives from its economic consequences. The responsibility for economic consequences rests on those responsible for the actions that affect the economic outcome. As a result, changes in economic environment would invariably lead to changes in accounting. For example, the development of new financial instruments has led to a clamour for changes in accounting for those instruments.

THE PIVOTAL ROLE OF ACCOUNTING IN EARLY ACCOUNTING RESEARCH

The case for the inclusion of accounting suggests that accounting has been excluded or de-emphasised from accounting research in the UK. This will require some historical analysis of the process by which accounting research has been deprived of its very essence.

Early accounting academics tended to examine concepts and the implications of concepts – not the facts of the world. Their purpose was to find out if the arguments were cogent, felicitous, coherent and so on. But they could not find out if they were right. An explanation for such a sad state of affairs was said (Murphy 1950: 43) to have been provided by Lord

Stamp in 1924:

> English accounting practice has been developing for many years, but it
> has not made any substantial contribution to economic science over
> its own field of the analysis of the results of industry, although it has
> practically a monopoly grip of the required data. Accountants have the
> figures; other people cannot use them and if accountants will not,
> then we get nothing; economics continues its abstract declarations and
> business blunders on by individual instinct.

Early accounting research in the UK, though not without exceptions, was
carried out by individuals who were concurrently engaged in the work of
the profession of accountancy – whether in practice or in industry,
government or municipal service, or commerce. As a result, research was
mainly a part-time activity for those rare and lucid intervals of an accountant's leisure or such time that he[2] could reasonably spare from the pressure
of daily responsibilities. At the same time, in the case of co-ordinated efforts
through committees or small groups involving continuous work over a
period, such committees received with advantage the full-time assistance of
permanent research officers, if it could be made available.

A few attempts were made in the period between 1940 and 1960 to show
that, on technical grounds, the same accounting principles held for all
aggregative and non-aggregative accounting systems (Mattessich 1957:
328). As a result, the scope of the 'accounting' in accounting research
during this period extended to both national (aggregative) and individual
entities including persons, trusts, governments (local councils, the state)
and business enterprises. Since the 1960s, national (aggregative) aspects
have been excluded from what is described as accounting in accounting
research, leaving this territory to the macro economists.

Academic accounting research prior to the 1970s was, in the main,
normative deduction and description of practice (Zeff 1989: 169) each of
which was grounded in philosophy, logic, economics, law and a bit of
operations research. The efforts (many of which were critical of contemporary practice) were devoted to the improvement of accounting as an
academic discipline and as a profession. It seems relevant here to provide a
summary of early academic accounting research. This historical synthesis is
based on the works of the few persons who were appointed professors of
accounting in the UK before 1971, some details of whom are reported in
Table 11.1.

After 1970, the number of professors of accounting grew rapidly and
therefore this year can be said to mark the end of the classical age. These early
professors included: (a) those who were appointed as part-time professors of
accounting serving both as practitioners and academics (four in England and
Wales, one of whom served different tenures in two universities, and eight in
Scotland, one of whom translated from part-time to full time in 1975), and

Table 11.1(a) Professors of accounting appointed in England and Wales to 1970

Period of tenure	Name	Appointing university(ies) or body(ies)
1902–06	Lawrence Robert Dicksee	Birmingham (part time)
1907–10	Sidney Stanley Dawson	Birmingham (part time)
1914–26	Lawrence Robert Dicksee	LSE (part time)
1922–32	Charles E. Martineau	Birmingham (part time)
1926–29	Frederic Rudolph M. de Paula	LSE (part time)
1947–73	William Threipland Baxter	LSE
1947–64	Donald Cousins	Birmingham
1954–57	Frank Sewell Bray	Incorporated Accountants
1955–59	David Solomons	Bristol
1959–68	Lloyd Amey	Bristol
1962–80	Harold Edey	LSE
1968–85	John R. Perrin	Lancaster; (2) Warwick
1969–84	Gerald Hartley Lawson	Manchester Business School
1969–86	Trevor Ellison Gambling	Birmingham
1969–84	Bryan Victor Carsberg (now Sir)	Manchester; (2) LSE; (3) LBS (part time)
1969–75	John Flower	Bristol
1969–present	John Malcolm Samuels	Birmingham
1970–77	Charles Magee	Cardiff, University College
1970–84	Kenneth Hilton	Southampton
1970–84	Peter Ashby Bird	Kent
1970–present	Robert Henry Parker	Dundee; (2) Exeter
1970–present	Michael Bromwich	UWIST; (2) Reading; (3) LSE
1970–93	John Sizer	Loughborough

Table 11.1(b) Professors of accounting appointed in Scotland to 1970

Period of tenure	Name	Appointing university(ies) or body(ies)
1919–27	Thomas Patrick Laird	Edinburgh (part time)
1926–38	John Loudon	Glasgow (part time)
1927–43	William Annan	Edinburgh (part time)
1938–50	Ian Wilson Macdonald	Glasgow (part time)
1945–57	Adam George Murray	Edinburgh (part time)
1950–64	Robert Browning	Glasgow (part time)
1957–66	David Steel Anderson	Edinburgh (part time)
1964–85	David Flint	Glasgow (1964–75, part time)
1967–85	Edward Stamp	Edinburgh; (2) Lancaster
1967–94	John Rankin Small	Heriot-Watt

(b) full-time professors of accounting not undertaking any work as practitioners (fifteen in England and Wales and two in Scotland). Included in this list is Frank Sewell Bray, a professional accountant who, while combining a part-time fellowship in the Applied Economics Department of the University of Cambridge with professional practice, was appointed professor of accounting by a professional accountancy body and not by a university.[3]

Much of the writings, prior to 1971, of the professors of accounting (named in Table 11.1) can be found in professional publications such as *The Accountant*, the *Accountant's Journal* (now the *Certified Accountant*), The *Accountant's Magazine, Cost Accountant* (now *Management Accounting*), *Accountancy*, and academic publications of the period such as the nine issues of *Accounting Research* (published by the Society of Incorporated Accountants and edited from both the University of Cambridge and University College of the South West (now University of Exeter) from 1948 to 1958), the *Accounting Review* (published by the American Accounting Association), the *Journal of Accounting Research* (published and edited first by the University of Chicago and the London School of Economics, and later solely by the former) and *Abacus* (published by Sydney University Press).

Being practitioners as well as professors of accounting, early scholars were concerned with explaining practices and synthesising current practices in textbooks and professional journals. The scope of their writings covered accounting techniques such as those relating to trust accounting, insolvency, partnership accounts, auditing and taxation. The underlying discipline of their discourses was law (Whittington 1995: 6) and their writings concentrated more on the clear exposition of practice than on critical analysis (Dev 1980: 5). Early full-time accounting academics tended to argue from first principles about how to determine true accounting income – that is, to understand and explain the 'right way' to account for things and to market their normative ideas to practitioners in the hope of reforming practice.

In the first half of the twentieth century, academic economists and accountants were busy studying each other's language because they were conscious of the close relationships between their fields of operation. Teachers of accounting and economics made use of each other's terms and concepts. Economists applied accounting methods to the analysis of economic problems, the most obvious occurring in national income accounting, the analysis of balances of payments and other topics requiring the analysis of income and expenditure. Accountants needed economic concepts to explain theoretical constructs such as income and costs. Both disciplines discussed the activities of the same institutions at the micro or macro levels of the economy. Academics from the two fields often encouraged their students to look over the fence. The work of economists such as Samuelson, Boulding and Fisher are fitting illustrations.

The practice during this period (at least in England) was for the teaching of accounting to be located in university departments of economics and for accountants to be included in applied economics research teams. As a result, one finds Ronald (later Sir Ronald) Edwards, a Certified Accountant, at the London School of Economics, contributing to (and later leading) the research on the relevance of accounting procedures to business problems and, in particular, the usefulness of cost accounting for business decisions; and Frank Sewell Bray, an Incorporated Accountant and part-time Senior Nuffield Fellow in the Department of Applied Economics of the University of Cambridge, unravelling issues related to social and national income accounting.[4]

In 1945, a Joint Exploratory Committee was appointed by the Institute of Chartered Accountants in England and Wales (ICAEW) and the National Institute of Economic and Social Research to search for a territory in which accountants and economists could settle amicably together. The Committee was 'to enter into a discussion with a view to a closer understanding between accountants and economists regarding the principles applied in their respective fields of work' (Solomons 1955: 107). The Committee appointed a subcommittee of academic accountants and economists to undertake a feasibility study of the project. The subcommittee reported that the task was not feasible because their enquiry resulted in ceaseless arguments. Better, they suggested, to bring to an end the occasional traffic of the past decades between the two disciplines. This, it was thought, would ensure that they would live in mutual tolerance, but each in its own way, rather than risking, by further negotiations between them, the state of academic warfare which might grow out of the quarrels they had had during their five years of exploring a common approach to their two disciplines (Little 1952: 62). But the Committee produced a report in 1951 entitled *Some Accounting Terms and Concepts*. According to Solomons (1955: 107), 'the [subcommittee] split wide open on the rock of changing price levels'. In paragraph 78 of that report, one finds an indication of that disagreement:

> Apart from the question of the ascertainment of operating profit, economists consider that the balance sheet should also show assets in terms of current values (as the best approach to 'real' value) and should not merely reflect the historical record adopted by account-ants. ... If the economists' principle were adopted in balance-sheet presentation, it would become necessary to increase or decrease the amount of fixed assets by the increase or decrease in current values and to make a corresponding 'capital surplus adjustment'.

Solomons (1955: 107) further emphasised that '[the subcommittee] threw away an opportunity of doing much useful work [because] the economists ... seem to have confined their attention almost exclusively to aspects of the subject bearing on national income accounting'.

R. S. OLUSEGUN WALLACE

HOW THE 'ACCOUNTING' IN ACCOUNTING RESEARCH HAS BEEN MARGINALISED

The role of academic journals

Prior to 1972, academic accounting journals were rare commodities. Today, they are as numerous as dandelions in spring (Dyckman and Zeff 1984: 249). The dates when the following academic accounting journals were founded and their editorial offices are shown in Table 11.2.

Accounting and Business Research (*ABR*) began publication in 1970, as a continuation of *Accounting Research*. It is therefore the longest surviving academic accounting journal in the UK that has not changed its name. Because of its age and eclectic nature, *ABR* is chosen as a journal through which one can discern the pattern of accounting research in the UK.[5] Many of the competing UK academic journals chose the path of addressing specialist areas of accounting or specific paradigms. For example, the *Journal of Business Finance and Accounting* (*JBFA*) hardly publishes articles devoted to accounting, less than 5 per cent of its published articles are devoted to core accounting issues. *Accounting, Organizations and Society* (*AOS*) emphasises the organisational, sociological and the critical aspects of accounting. *British Accounting Review*'s record is not impressive in this respect. Although it started as an academic journal in 1980, it became a serious academic journal in 1984 when it took its present title and changed its format. Although this journal is also eclectic in its approach, the proportion of core accounting articles it published between 1984 and 1995 is less than 20 per cent.

An analysis of the contents of the articles in *ABR* over the period 1970 to 1994 is presented in Table 11.3. The entire twenty-five-year period is divided into five intervals. During the first period (1970–5), the journal was edited by the same persons who edited the professional magazine (*Accountancy*) of the ICAEW which was also the publisher of *ABR*. The editorial control of the journal was transferred to an academic (Professor Robert Parker) in 1975. He managed the journal as the sole editor until 1986 when Professor Christopher Nobes joined him as joint editor. The editorial control was gradually transferred during 1993 to a new editor (Professor Ken Peasnell). During the twenty-five-year period, the space devoted to core accounting issues fell from about 45 per cent in the first period (1970–75) to 20 per cent in the last period (1991–4). In contrast, the space allocated to finance and sociology of accounting rose from 17 per cent and 10 per cent, respectively, in the first period to about 21 per cent and about 22 per cent in the last period. With the exception of accounting history, the fortunes of research into other areas did not improve in any significant manner. Accounting history had a generous allocation of space in the second period because of a special issue on that

Table 11.2 Growth of academic accounting journals, 1926–92

	United Kingdom [*editorial office*]	*The rest of the world* [*editorial office*]
Before 1960	*Accounting Research* (1948–58) [Oxford], Society of Incorporated Accountants	*The Accounting Review* (1926) [Northwestern], American Accounting Association, USA
1961–75	*Journal of Accounting Research* (1963) [LSE co-sponsored this journal till 1973] *Journal of Business Finance* (1969), name changed to *Journal of Business Finance Accounting* in 1974 [Warwick, Hull], Blackwell *Accounting and Business Research* (1970) [Dundee 1975–77; Exeter 1977–93 (except for four years in Reading) Lancaster 1994–], ICAEW	*Journal of Accounting Research* (1963) [Chicago, USA] *The International Journal of Accounting* (1965) [University of Illinois, Urbana–Champaign] *Abacus* (1965) [Sydney, Australia].
1976–80	*Accounting, Organizations and Society* (1976) [London, Oxford], Pergamon Press	*Journal of Accounting, Auditing & Finance* (1977) [New York, USA] *The Accounting Historians Journal* (1977) [Mississippi, USA], Academy Of Accounting Historians *Accounting and Finance* (1979) Association of Accounting Teachers in Australia & New Zealand *Journal of Accounting and Economics* (1979) [Rochester, USA], Elsevier Science
1981–90	*AUTA Review* (1974), renamed *British Accounting Review* in 1984 [Essex], BAA. *Management Accounting Research* (1989) [Manchester], CIMA	*Auditing: A Journal of Theory and Practice* (1981) [USC Los Angeles, USA], Auditing Section of the American Accounting Association *Journal of Accounting Literature* (1982) [Florida, USA] *Journal of Accounting and Public Policy* (1982) [Maryland, USA], North-Holland, Elsevier Science *Journal of Extractive Industries Accounting* (1982) [Texas, A&M, USA] *Journal of Accounting Education* (1983) [Delaware, USA], IIAER *Advances in Accounting* (1984) [Virginia Commonwealth, USA], JAI Press *Contemporary Accounting Research* (1987) [Alberta, Canada], Canadian Accounting Association

continued

227

Table 11.2 Continued

	United Kingdom [*editorial office*]	The rest of the world [*editorial office*]
		Accounting Horizons (1987), [Oregon], American Accounting Association *Accounting Auditing & Accountability* (1988) [NSW, Sydney and Flinders, Australia], MCB University Press *Critical Perspectives on Accounting* (1990) [Canada and New York], Academic Press *Research in Government and Non-Profit Accounting* (1985) [Chicago], JAI Press *Advances in Public Interest Accounting* (1986) [New York], JAI Press *Advances in International Accounting* (1987) [Florida (now South Carolina)], JAI Press *Research in Accounting Regulation* (1987) [Case Western Reserve, USA] JAI Press *Journal of International Financial Management & Accounting* (1989) [New York], Blackwell
After 1990	*Research in Third World Accounting* (1990) now *Research in Accounting in Emerging Economies* [Middlesex], JAI Press *Accounting, Business & Financial History* (1990) [Cardiff], Routledge *Accounting Education* (1991) [Loughborough], Chapman & Hall. *Journal of Applied Accounting Research* (1992) [De Montfort]	*Asia-Pacific Accounting* (1990), Hong Kong *Journal of International Accounting, Auditing and Taxation* (1991), JAI Press *European Accounting Review* (1991) [Copenhagen], European Accounting Association. *Australian Accounting Review* (1992) [Sydney], Australian Society of Accountants

subject which was to honour the centenary of the ICAEW and the international conference on accounting history held towards the end of that period. Notwithstanding the appearance of a journal devoted to accounting history in 1990, there was never a time when accounting history was not accommodated during the editorship of Professor Parker. This is understandable, given a clientele effect that resulted from the editor's special interest in that subject.

The core accounting issues of the first three periods were concentrated on normative research in which their authors argued for (or against) the

Table 11.3 Percentage analysis of the classification of articles in *Accounting and Business Research*, 1970–94

Types of articles	1970–5	1976–80	1981–5	1986–90	1991–4
Core accounting[a]	44.9	40.1	24.7	19.0	20.2
Auditing[b]	4.8	3.8	9.6	7.7	9.3
Accounting history[c]	1.8	12.7	8.4	4.8	10.1
Accounting education[d]	2.4	8.9	15.2	9.5	3.8
Taxation and business[e]	18.6	11.5	11.2	16.1	14.0
Sociology of accounting[f]					
Mainstream	9.6	11.5	18.5	25.0	21.7
Radical	—	—	0.6	—	—
Finance[g]	17.4	10.2	11.2	17.9	20.9
National/social accts[h]	0.5	1.3	0.6	—	—
	100.0	100.0	100.0	100.0	100.0

[a] Articles whose principal thrust is on theoretical and technical aspects of accounting and those which recommend a kind of accounting. Such articles deal with measurement of income and assets, and the internal and external reporting of accounting information.
[b] Articles which deal with the principles and techniques of auditing.
[c] Articles which analyse accounting and auditing of the past.
[d] Articles dealing with descriptive, normative and empirical analysis of education of accountants and accounting education in universities. This classification also includes articles which review the literature, explore ideas, synthesise and develop frameworks for the improvement of accounting research, and articles discussing international accounting practices.
[e] Articles dealing with taxation and business matters such as mergers and acquisitions but not their accounting.
[f] Articles which refer to economic, political and sociological implications of accounting and the impact of accounting on society. They include articles which introduce theories or analytical techniques from other disciplines, whose main contribution seems to be this importation. They often report results of field studies or surveys, the cross-sectional or time series analyses of financial data, involving the testing of hypotheses. There are two categories here. Mainstream refers to articles that are not essentially critical of orthodox accounting and the accounting establishment, and are evolutionary in their ideas. Radical refers to critical analysis of existing practice and the establishment; the articles are revolutionary in their ideas for improvement.
[g] Articles which adopt econometric methods in their empirical analyses of earnings and the impact of accounting data on the stock market or seek to investigate the informational content of accounting numbers. This classification also includes articles dealing with the stock market and the sources and uses of finance.
[h] Articles which deal with macro-accounting issues in a society, such as accounting for the gross national product.

acceptance of a preferred kind of accounting treatment, the definition of the objectives of financial reporting or the development of a form of conceptual framework. During these periods, scholars were interested in defining income and distinguishing between accounting and economic concepts of income, grappling with how to take account of changing prices in financial reporting and the measurement of profit.

Surprisingly, however, the scope of accounting was narrowed during this period by the conspicuous absence of articles on national income and social accounting which occupied over 50 per cent of articles published in the academic journal which preceded *ABR*. Since 1990, no academic accounting journal has published any article on the topic. In addition, national income and social accounting, which was a subject of study at the LSE and Birmingham between 1949 and 1965 and on which there was a popular 1954 textbook by Professors Harold Edey and Alan Peacock, is no longer taught in any department of accounting in the UK. Accounting academics have implicitly withdrawn from this aspect of accounting, probably because they think that this is best covered in an economics course as part of public finance.

During the entire period, articles devoted to the sociology of accounting were concerned with mainstream accounting issues, seeking to provide evidence in support of the orthodoxy. They seemed to concentrate on implementation issues, users' reactions and needs, and the implications of various normative proposals to traditional financial reporting. Few tested descriptive hypotheses and only one article (Arrington *et al.*, 1983) was radically critical of extant practice in the way that is now common. This is probably inevitable given *ABR*'s orientation and the development of new journals with special interest in these topics.

The role of recruitment into the accounting faculty

The data reported in Tables 11.4 and 11.5 suggest a growth in academic accounting faculty over a period of two decades. But that growth reveals a pattern. From the point of view of the relationship between the number of accounting professors and other members of the faculty, one notices an increasing ratio in older universities. By 1972, nine of the twelve universities studied and reported upon in the Solomons Report (1974) had one accounting professor in post, two had two professors and one had three professors. On average the ratio of accounting professors to accounting lecturers was one to five in each of the twelve universities. By the end of 1993, the average ratio had become one to three and a quarter. Only one of these universities had just one in post by the end of 1993. Some even had five professors in post compared with twelve other academics below the status of professor. Note, however, that in 1994, Bristol, Exeter and Liverpool, where accounting is taught in economics departments and not in a separate accounting department, are the only three (out of twelve) universities with no more than two professors of accounting. Because there is no newer university with more than two professors of accounting in post as at the end of 1995, and many do not have any professor of accounting, it can be suggested that the newer universities will be less disposed towards the development of an accounting research profile than the older universities

Table 11.4 Full-time academic staff in selected university departments of accounting and finance, 1972 and 1994

	Professors		Other academic staff	
	1972	1994	1972	1994
Birmingham	2	4	6	12
Bristol	1	2	4	6
Exeter	—	2	1	6
Lancaster	2	5	7	9
Leeds	—	2	5	10
Liverpool	—	1	2	6
Manchester	3	6	12	27
Southampton	1	5	4	12
University of Wales (Cardiff)	1	4	2	13
Edinburgh	1	3	4	7
Glasgow	1	3	11	14
Strathclyde	1	3	8	14
Total	13	40*	66	136

Sources: Whittington (1995: 5) and Gray and Helliar (1994)
* Adjusted to remove part-time professors

and, to that extent, it seems more likely that the newer universities would rank less favourably relative to the older universities in any comparative research assessment.

On the basis of the entries in the *British Accounting Review Research Register 1994*, twenty-three of the forty-one professors in the twelve departments indicated in Table 11.4 were found to be members of accountancy bodies affiliated to the CCAB, as were sixty-four of the 136 non-professional staff (Whittington 1995: 4). However, membership of accountancy bodies is not a complete reflection of the possession of a professional accountancy qualification. From the responses to my recent survey of professorial accounting faculty, I discovered that a few of these professors who have passed the final examinations of one or more of the professional accountancy bodies affiliated to the CCAB are not members of those bodies.

Table 11.5 compares the growth of the accountancy profession with the growth in the number of professors of accounting and finance. The most important comparison is between 1972 and 1994. Over that period the number of professionally qualified accountants in the country rose from 99,000 to 223,000. However, over that same period, the number of university professors of accounting rose from twenty-four to eighty-three while the number of university professors of finance rose from five to fifty-five (of whom only one works for a newer university). About twenty of the fifty-five professors of finance are members of accountancy bodies. Because

231

Table 11.5 Growth of the accountancy profession, 1904–94 ('000)

	1904	1957	1972	1994
Chartered accountants				
in England and Wales (ICAEW)	3.2	20.1	54.0	106.0
of Scotland (ICAS)	1.0	6.0	9.0	14.0
in Ireland (ICAI)	0.1	1.0	2.0	9.0
Incorporated accountants	2.1	11.3	—	—
	6.4	38.4	65.0	129.0
Certified accountants (ACCA)	—	12.5	14.0	45.0
Management accountants (CIMA)	—	9.7	13.0	37.0
Municipal accountants (CIPFA)	—	4.7	7.0	12.0
Total	6.4	65.3	99.0	223.0
Professors of accounting and finance (not in '000)				
Accounting:				
Full-time (old universities)	—	3	24	64
(new universities)	—	—	—	19
Finance:				
Full-time (old universities)	—	—	5	54
(new universities)	—	—	—	1
Emeritus	—	—	—	5
Part time	1	3	1	7

Sources: 1904 Parker (1980: 7). The last three bodies were not in existence in 1904
1957 Parker (1980: 7) and Members' Handbooks for 1957 of the last three bodies
1972 Whittington (1995: 14) and Gray and Helliar (1994)
1994 Whittington (1995: 14) and Gray and Helliar (1994)

the research interests of these professors of finance are not concerned with core accounting issues, they seem to have contributed to the observable shift from core accounting issues.

From Table 11.6 one notices a drop in the percentage of academic accounting staff who are professionally qualified. There was a drop from 66 per cent to 52 per cent in the older universities and from 85 per cent to 73 per cent in the newer universities. In contrast, there was a slight increase in the percentage of accounting academics with postgraduate qualifications in the older universities from 63 per cent to 65 per cent with a Master's degree; and from 30 per cent to 32 per cent with a PhD. The situation in the newer universities remained the same over the period. Table 11.6 also reveals a significant dominance of accounting academics with a non-accounting PhD over those with an accounting PhD.

The decline in the proportion of academic staff with professional accounting qualifications and the greater number of academics with a non-accounting PhD can be attributed to changing conditions in the market for

Table 11.6 Number and qualifications of academics in UK university departments of accounting and finance

	Older universities		Newer universities	
	1986–7	*1992–3*	*1986–7*	*1992–3*
Number	420	628	600	858
Professional accounting qualification (%)	66	52	85	73
Master's degree (%)	63	65	46	45
PhD (%): accounting	6	7	1	2
non-accounting	24	25	2	2

Source: Whittington (1995: table 2) as amended by Gray (1995: footnote 6)

accountants, increasing erosion of academic freedom and increasing difficulty of getting published (Gray 1995). First, the business world can offer a more attractive remuneration package to any potential academic accountant than universities can. Second, there are the extra costs of retraining professionally qualified accountants to become good researchers and lecturers. And third, given the increasing difficulty of building up a sufficient publication record for confirmation and promotion, professional accountants are not finding the universities attractive. As a result, university departments of accounting find the pressure to seek recruits from other, cheaper and better research-trained disciplines irresistible (Gray 1995: 8). Among the new recruits we find most of those who specialise in finance. This group, which are now about 25 per cent of the accounting and finance faculty, do not, quite rightly, refer to themselves as accounting scholars. Other scholars include many who are yet undecided on how they should be labelled – they are often interested in joining the camp where there is a greater opportunity to succeed. Many of them are not quantitative and so would find qualitative research most congenial.

The contribution of universities to accounting education and the accountancy profession

The early history of accounting education in the UK is a tale of the accounting profession's lack of interest in intellectual pursuit. Before 1947, professional training for examination purposes was mainly in the hands of large correspondence institutions and the proportion of qualified accountants who had had a university education was very low indeed. Universities could not contribute because the training for the leading accountancy profession (Chartered Accountancy) was principally through apprenticeship in the office of a practising accountant. Training for the other professional accountancy bodies (Incorporated Accountancy, Certified Accountancy and Cost Accountancy) was done by part-time (evening) or full-time attendance at technical colleges (many of which later became universities or polytechnics in the 1960s; many of the polytechnics became universities in 1990). Many of the technical college students supplemented their lectures with correspondence courses.

In 1944, talks began between the Committee of Vice-Chancellors and Principals and representatives of the accountancy profession to work out a scheme which would enable prospective accountants to take university degrees based on the related disciplines of economics, accountancy and law and then proceed to take professional examinations (Solomons 1956: 84). In the 1947–8 academic year eleven universities began certain courses which exempted the graduate from intermediate professional accountancy examinations. Both Oxford and Cambridge were unable to join in the scheme because they considered such degrees as having vocational bias. Although the curriculum offered by the different universities varied somewhat in detail, it generally consisted of nine terms in accountancy, including costing, auditing and taxation; nine terms of economics; nine terms of law; and at least three terms each of modern foreign language, government or political thought.

This arrangement was a half-way house to the full university education for the profession. The university graduate was only exempt from the intermediate examination and still had to study for the final professional examinations through correspondence courses. The perceived inadequacy of educational arrangements for the accounting profession and for commerce in general generated sufficient clamour for the reform of commercial education in the UK and the then Minister of Education (the Rt Hon. Ellen Wilkinson) appointed a committee on education for commerce. Members of the committee included Sir Arnold Plant (Sir Ernest Cassel Professor of Commerce at LSE), Professor J. G. Smith OBE, from the Faculty of Commerce, University of Birmingham, and Frederic de Paula (a Member of Council of the ICAEW and a former Sir Ernest Cassel Professor of Accountancy and Business Methods at LSE). The committee, led by Sir Alexander M. Carr-Saunders, had the following terms of reference:

> To consider the provision which should be made for education for commerce and for the professions relating to it, and the respective contributions to be made thereto by universities and by colleges and departments of commerce in England and Wales.

The report of the committee sought to change the whole tenor of commercial education. It emphasised that study at home and by correspondence courses was undesirable and urged employers to do all in their power to make day-time study possible. Included in its report were two major recommendations relating to professional examination:

> At the stage of the intermediate examination only general commercial subjects should be prescribed, vocational training being introduced only

at the final stage. Entry upon vocational training at too early an age should be discouraged and recruits to the professions under the age of eighteen should be advised to take national certificate courses. Unnecessary variation in syllabuses in common subjects should be eliminated.

Part-time day courses, possibly on the 'sandwich' principle, giving preparation for the intermediate and final examination of the three main bodies of accountants, should be organised by the colleges of commerce and the major technical colleges on a regional basis and in conjunction with the accountancy bodies. The final course would, of course, be suitable also for graduates studying for the final professional examinations after leaving the universities.

As Kitchen and Parker (1994: 248) report, the Council of the ICAEW objected strongly to these recommendations and issued a report which sought to rebut the recommendations of the Carr-Saunders committee:

The Council would offer the strongest opposition to the disintegration of the Institute's examinations or the system of training under articles. Whatever merits the recommendations of the Carr-Saunders Committee may have in relation to other occupations – a matter with which the Council of the Institute is not concerned – the Council considers that they can have no place in the education and training for membership of the Institute.

Accounting academics in England and Wales played less important roles in the affairs of the profession before the 1970s. The directorate of research was often headed by a practitioner, not an academic, until Professor Bryan Carsberg was appointed as the part-time Director of Research by the ICAEW in 1981. In recent times, academic accountants have served as Presidents of the Chartered Institute of Management Accountants and the Chartered Association of Certified Accountants. The current President of the Institute of Chartered Accountants of Scotland is also an academic.

There are recent signs that the accounting profession is becoming more academic. The current Chairman of the Accounting Standards Board (Sir David Tweedie) is a practitioner who is also an accounting academic and the current Secretary-General of the International Accounting Standards Committee is also a renowned former accounting academic. The Accounting Standards Board and the Auditing Practices Board (including their predecessor organisations) both have Standing Committees of Academic Advisers to which they refer matters needing research or academic input.

The influence of external research funding

On the basis of available records on research funding, external funding of academic accounting research in the UK is meagre relative to academic research in the physical and social sciences and when compared with what happens in other countries. When P. D. Leake died in 1949, he left an estimated sum of £80,000 in trust with the Institute of Chartered Accountants in England and Wales, of which he was a member, for the improvement of education and research in accountancy. The first use of that trust fund was to endow a Chair in Finance and Accountancy by an annual grant of £3,000 at the University of Cambridge.[6] The first holder of that chair was Mr (later Sir) Richard Stone at the Department of Applied Economics. The curious thing was that the chair was not located in London or Birmingham where accounting was then being taught as a special subject in its own right. The reason may be that no university other than Cambridge and Oxford was held in high esteem by the profession. However, on the retirement of Sir Richard Stone in 1980, this chair was not renewed. In addition, income from the trust fund was used to offer annual fellowships from 1957 to 1966 when the management of the trust was transferred to the Research Board of the ICAEW.

In April 1957, when the research fellowships financed by the P. D. Leake Trust were launched, the object was stated as:

> to provide university facilities for an experienced accountant to carry out research in subjects with which the accountancy profession is directly concerned and within the charitable object of the P. D. Leake Trust, namely 'to benefit and advance the sciences of accounting and of political economy, including the subject of public finance and taxation'.

Nine such fellowships were established in total between 1957 and 1966 in Birmingham, London and Oxford. The recipients included John Malcolm Samuels (Birmingham) and Robert Henry Parker (LSE).

To encourage university education for accountants, the Society of Incorporated Accountants began in 1954 the annual award of the the Stamp–Martin Scholarship, to the value of £100 per annum for three years, to enable members and those who intended to enter the accountancy profession as members of the Society to undertake full-time courses of study in universities approved by the Society.

The Leverhulme Trust announced in 1955 the offer of a research scholarship, to any British-born person normally resident in the UK, with a recognised qualification in accounting and wide professional experience including work of an advisory nature, for the purpose of exploring what further contribution accounting can make to the improvement of industrial and commercial management. The value of the scholarship was not to be less than £2,000 plus the cost of any necessary travel.

The external funding of academic accounting research from the accountancy profession is meagre when compared with similar funding in the USA. In 1995, the total sums released by the 'Big-6' accounting firms in the USA to support academic accounting research was over $8 million. In contrast, the total funding available for research from all the major UK accounting firms and the professional accountancy bodies that are members of the CCAB in 1995 was £500,000. About 40 per cent of the total fund is often reserved for in-house research conducted by the professional accountancy bodies. The research funds are distributed in such a manner that no one person can get more than £20,000. However, casual observation suggests that the distribution of the research fund is asymmetrical. Like the allocation of central research funds to universities by the funding council, funding by professional accountancy bodies has become a prize-awarding system as opposed to a new research or proposal-rewarding system. Research grants are awarded as prizes for past achievements. In addition, older universities and those with more than three or more accounting professors in residence tend to get more funding than others. Young academics and those from newer universities are often disadvantaged as awards depend on a recipient's previous track record and research experience on projects sponsored by the awarding institution. There is an urgent need to target applications from newer universities and to let research funding reward proposals rather than the accomplishments of the investigators.

In the history of the funding released by the Social Science Research Council (SSRC) to academic researchers, accounting came up as a successful candidate in the late 1970s under its Accounting Research initiative. This initiative coincided with a mounting sense that accounting should be demystified and that its social implications needed to be made more explicit but that such endeavours lacked financial resources. The initiative led to the funding by SSRC of research into inflation accounting, and disclosure of information to employees and trade unions (Hopwood and Bromwich 1984: 135). The funding also included a two-year professorial fellowship (awarded to Professor Geoffrey Whittington) to cater for the provision of an overview of both the current state of knowledge in the area and the discussion of research in progress (Bromwich and Hopwood 1981: xi). The Economic and Social Research Council which succeeded the SSRC has continued to support some accounting research, albeit less than the level that was witnessed during the Accounting Research initiative of the SSRC.

Generous endowment of academic accounting research is rare in the UK. Recent experience includes the funding by Lord Rank's charitable foundation of an International Centre for Research in Accounting at Lancaster University. With this endowment, the accounting department in Lancaster was transformed into a major player in the accounting education scene. Less than 10 per cent of the accounting professorships in the UK are endowed. Such endowments usually provide sufficient funds to enable a university to translate a lectureship or senior lectureship position to that of a professor. Full funding of university chairs of accounting is rare. I know of only two:

one in Cambridge, the other at LSE.

The usage of external funds is not without its costs. There is often the potential for the provider of funds to seek to dictate the rules of engagement. Recent publicised incidents of professional interference with academic pursuits do not commend the accounting profession. For example, following the publication of an article on the accounting at the National Coal Board, one of the authors who held a funded chair was alleged to have received a threatening telephone call from a partner of the professional accounting firm which funded the chair suggesting that the article had embarrassed the firm which had been appointed as sequestrator to the National Union of Mineworkers. In the telephone conversation, it was alleged that the partner accused this co-author of biting the finger that fed the employing university. The partner concluded that the firm was not going to continue to fund the chair (Jack 1993).

Another unwholesome incident was the attempt of a professional body to silence an academic by threatening his employing university with withdrawal of the accreditation it had granted to the accounting courses of that university. The body complained to the university that it was surprised that a letter received from the academic expressing dissatisfaction with its procedure for electing members to its Council was on the university's letter-headed paper. The body concluded that the use of this letter-headed paper suggested that the university endorsed the academic's position (Jack 1993).

Indeed, very few external private funds actually come without strings. The existence of external motives is not an insuperable obstacle to the use of external funding to promote academic accounting research. In some areas, the motivations of external private funding and accounting academic interests overlap. If partially overlapping and partially divergent goals are faced squarely before specific funding contracts are signed, it should be possible to find a basis for agreements which will contribute to the development of academic accounting research.

In this connection, it is important to consider implicit (internal) funding of academic research. Of all sources of funding for accounting research in the older universities, internal funding is probably the largest. Almost all members of the accounting faculty from older universities receive about one-third time off to conduct research. This implicit funding is generally without strings, in that universities do not explicitly state what type of research a person must do. As a result, accounting research is, in large part, internally directed. Younger researchers often do what older researchers in their departments think they should do. This means that departments are likely to acquire specific research characteristics. For example, everybody knows, in a common-sensical way, that one cannot confuse Lancaster University during 1990s with its emphasis on core accounting and finance issues with LSE of 1990–5 with its emphasis on management accounting and accounting sociology, or confuse Manchester's specialisms in more than four areas with

Exeter's specialisms in international financial accounting and accounting history.

The influx of other disciplines into accounting research

Accounting research has always shown a tendency to borrow from neighbouring disciplines; this has allowed accounting researchers to ignore the subject matter of accounting. The result has been a borrowing of models, metaphors and methods from those disciplines that have (a) appeared to succeed and (b) gained the greatest amount of prestige, as measured by journal space allocated and research funding attracted. Hence, economics, mathematics, psychology and sociology have become the identity models of the contemporary accounting researcher. According to Dyckman and Zeff (1984: 267):

> The danger with borrowing, however, is that whether the theory and/ or models are likely to contribute to our body of knowledge will depend in part on how well they are (or can be) integrated into accounting contexts. ... Theories that are adapted from one field to another often carry with them a type of thinking and some of the concepts of their origin which are not always appropriate to their application in an accounting context.

There are many reasons for the influx of other disciplines into accounting research including the inability to formulate theories of accounting that would work. Despite the devotion of UK academic institutions to the individual's freedom of expression, admiring openly the 'wrong' person, achievement or issues can be costly if one's boss is likely to feel less respect for anyone who expresses such an admiration. In addition, several institutional factors are making it especially important to avoid confronting core accounting issues in a critical manner. The institutional factors include (a) the 'insecure professional status' of accounting in UK universities (e.g. no accounting academic has so far risen to the position of Vice-Chancellor in any older university and only two are Vice-Chancellors of the newer universities); (b) the feeling of inferiority that has afflicted accounting in the presence of disciplines such as economics and sociology; and (c) the low status of the fledgling departments of accounting in our universities and accounting academics' uncertainty about their prospects for promotion in departments of accounting under the control of other disciplines and about the prospects of publication in reputable academic accounting journals.

The role of mathematical economics in accounting research

In some leading academic accounting journals, accounting seems to be a branch of mathematics. Accounting scholars drawing their inspiration from the positivist school of thought and from neo-classical economics tend to reduce the rich complexity of the world of accounting to a narrow set of abstract principles that could be written on a few pages. Journal spaces are practically filled with equations. The brightest young accounting academics seem to be devoting their careers to proving theorem after theorem – whether or not these theorems have much connection with the real world. This extraordinary emphasis on mathematics is surprising. To me, a theorem is a statement about an everlasting mathematical truth – not the dressing up of a trivial observation in a lot of formalism.

I am not concerned with the mathematical rigour that is being introduced into the accounting literature. What bothers me is the weird unreality of all the mathematics. The mathematical accounting scholars seem, probably unintentionally, to be leaching accounting clean of all human frailty and passion. Their theories describe the economic person as a godlike being whose reasoning is always perfect, and whose goals are always pursued with serenely predictable self-interest. And just as physicists could predict how a particle will respond to any given set of forces, accounting economists could predict how the economic person will respond to any given economic (or accounting) situation: the person will just optimise his or her 'utility function'.

The study which introduced serious mathematics into accounting research used time series methodology to investigate the information content of the accounting numbers released to the New York stock market over a certain period. Although the pioneers of this genre (Ball and Brown 1968; Beaver 1968) are accountants and are aware of the technical antecedents of the accounting numbers which formed the bases of their econometric analyses, the research design and the analytical technique for arriving at inferences do not require that the researcher understands the underlying data or how they are constructed. In fact, the article by Ball and Brown (1968) was first rejected by *The Accounting Review* on 'the reviewer's contention that it was not an Accounting manuscript' (Dyckman and Zeff 1984: 242). It was considered a historical explication of the unintended relationship between the product of accounting and stock market prices.

This econometric genre operates and resides in a society where the economy is poised for ever in perfect equilibrium, where supply always exactly equals demand, where the stock market is never jolted by surges and crashes, where no company ever gets big enough to dominate the market, and where the magic of a perfectly free market makes everything turn out for the best. The only difference is that accounting economists seem to see the human society as a perfectly oiled machine governed by the Invisible Hand of Adam Smith, despite Chandler's (1977) eloquent testimony that the Hand is Visible.

Almost by definition, accounting studies that are governed by mathematical economics are characterised by conceptual elegance and analytical simplicity. In addition, neo-classical accounting theorists are embroidering their basic model with all sorts of elaborations to cover things such as uncertainty about the future, or the transfer of property from one generation to the next. They are adapting it to fit taxation, monopolies, international trade, employment, finance, stock market behaviour – everything economists have thought about. But none of these differing situations changes any of the fundamental assumptions. Their theories still do not describe the mess and the irrationality of the human world or what happens every day in the business world. Once you are in partnership with accounting, you have to give up that elegance and simplicity of mathematical abstraction. You are in a messy world. And from this world it is much easier to start diffusing into non-economic issues (such as the political motives of other countries, and mass psychology in the stock market). Accounting research, therefore, needs to consult sociologists, psychologists, anthropologists or social scientists in general. However, once partially immersed in the qualitative, accounting research started swimming.

Sociology of accounting

Accounting theories and practice are revealed by accounting sociologists as the products of organisational and social interaction and creators of social, organisational and behavioural consequences. This literature originates from the UK and is dominated by UK scholars. Sociology of accounting articles fill the pages of such academic journals as *Accounting, Organizations and Society, Critical Perspectives on Accounting, Advances in Public Interest Accounting* and *Accounting Auditing & Accountability*. The case for this focus on the sociology of accounting is made by Sikka *et al.* (1995: 114):

> Focusing narrowly on the development of techniques, the social conditions and consequences of accounting were routinely disregarded. However, with an increasing recognition that accounting is consequential for the generation and allocation of resources (Scott, 1931; Tinker, 1985), greater attention is now being given to the role of accounting in organizations and society. We now have a fuller understanding of how accounting information functions as an instrument of social control (Zeff, 1978) and accountability (Flint, 1982) as it shapes government policies (Loft, 1986), wages and taxation policies (Robson, 1993), divestment decisions (Bryer and Brignall, 1986), job losses (Berry et al., 1985[a]; Cooper and Hopper, 1986), social conflict (Arnold and Hammond, 1994), distribution of wealth and property rights (Tinker, 1985), etc.

Sociological enquiries in accounting research seek to question the prevailing *credat emptor* ('let the buyer trust') principle guiding the provision of services by the accounting profession. They question this *credat emptor* principle on three grounds. First, the modern secular meaning of the words 'to profess' is different from its pristine clerical meaning. Early professions were closely linked with the church and so the word 'professed' meant that one had taken the vows of a religious order. In modern times, 'to profess' means to be duly qualified. As a result, the word 'professional (or professor)' has come to mean the occupation (or subject) which one professes to be skilled (or knowledgeable) in and to follow. One should realise, however, that while a professional can only profess or claim *A*, he or she certainly may not necessarily know or perform *A*.

Second, accounting sociologists argue that the trust which society accords to accounting professionals has often been misplaced, though the profession continues to perpetuate this myth of altruism. The coincidence of (a) the increasing power and pecuniary reward attained by accounting practitioners and (b) the increasing number of business, ethical and financial problems that are unmet by the accounting practitioners raises serious questions about their claim to be serving the public interest. Scholars are unable to reconcile the professed altruism to the ever increasing exposés of the backstage (non-visible) activities of the accounting members of the profession regarding their fees, ritualistic procedures or billing for work that was never undertaken, revision of their ethical guidelines and disciplinary arrangements and the mobilisation of other agencies in support of their myth of altruism (see Sikka and Willmott 1995a, 1995b; Lee 1995). Generally, the more one gains access to the backstage activities of dominant professions, the more nefarious those activities appear to be and the greater the disparity between them and the public perceptions of frontstage activities (Gernon and Wallace 1995).

Third, the reliance of the accounting profession on the trust which society tends to accord it because society does not have a way of evaluating its professional activities depends not only on the reputation of the profession and on the esteem in which it is held by the public but also on the client's technical familiarity with the professional service and the client's need for professional accounting services. The less knowledgeable the client, the more absolute the client's trust would be. The more the client stands in awe of the professional accountant, the greater the client's tendency to accede to any demand made upon him or her for revelations or compliance to professional direction. The more the client needs help, the more likely he or she would willingly comply with the professional's requests or orders. And these needs are often created by government fiats through company and taxation laws.

Closely related to the dominance of accounting research by econometrics and sociology could be the incentives, in the accounting academic profession, for articles, not ideas. To have fame and kudos in academic accounting one has to get published. Academic accountants must publish their ideas in the form of articles, preferably in the best refereed academic journals. Books, for some reason, count for little in the academic accounting profession; books that are readable by the public count for less than nothing and can be the cause of an otherwise qualified person not staying in academic life or getting promoted. The general thrust of advice to young accounting academics is for them to write articles that are highly mathematical or highly discursive and embedded in critical theory.

To suggest that the incentives within the system are for articles, not ideas, is not to suggest that the academic accounting profession does not value ideas. If most leaders of accounting scholarship were asked, they would respond that it is good ideas and insights, not articles, that should get a person promotion and tenure. However, because ideas cannot be quantitatively measured and articles can, universities generally rely on articles as a proxy for good ideas. And when one is up for promotion or applying for appointment as professor, any article that can get published is a good idea. If there were a relatively close association between ideas and articles, this proxy would be acceptable, but there is not. Generally, the easiest impressive-looking articles to write do not involve exploring new ideas or ideas useful to accounting practice or policy; they involve using an old technique on new data, or formalising a simple idea that is well known. Therefore, that type of article predominates. Differentiating informal articles that say something from those that do not is exceptionally difficult. Consequently, to write a good, non-formalist article that will be perceived as good is risky, especially when the individuals deciding what is good take a formalist approach.

I am not saying that a formal model should not be preferred to an informal one. But when mind sets become so fixated on formal models that individuals cannot deal with ideas outside of these models, then it is not surprising that many believe that accounting research has lost its bearing (Baxter 1988).

In a perverse sort of way, the focus on mathematical modelling and critical theory nicely serves the interest of the academic accounting profession. Strong incentives for both modelling and critical theory exist in the market for accounting education. Consider, first, the student's incentives. The student's immediate interest is to get good grades, or at least to pass. In many ways, students prefer neat models because such models offer a closer correlation between study and grades than do less formal methods of conveying information. A hard-working student who learns models can assure himself or herself of a good grade. Similarly, it is often easier to criticise than to construct accounting ideas. Studying ideas is necessarily vague and will likely lead to a wider variation in grades. Lecturers (as suppliers of accounting education) also have an incentive towards modelling and critical theory. Teaching modelling and criticising accounting techniques are much easier than teaching ideas. They take less time to prepare and less thought. Thus, modelling and critical theory meet both students' and lecturers' needs. For both of these reasons, ideas that work their way into accounting textbooks are often slanted towards what is teachable and dramatic rather than towards what makes the most sense in some larger context.

BRINGING ACCOUNTING BACK INTO ACCOUNTING RESEARCH

The acceptance of an academic position in a university suggests an intellectual belief in a subject. Intellectual belief in accounting implies faith and commitment to the improvement of the art or science of accounting. To abandon the search for improved methods of accounting in favour of studying the behaviour of preparers and users of financial reports is to move away from accounting. Just as it is a misnomer to describe the study of biologists as biological research so it is to refer to the study of accountants and the outcomes of accounting as accounting research (Sterling 1993: 139). According to Sterling (1970: 450):

> The theory of accounting ought to be concerned with accounting phenomena, not [practising] accountants, in the same way that theories of physics are concerned with physical phenomena, not [practising] physicists.

In addition, to overwhelm accounting research with econometrics and sociology, without putting the accounting question in focus, is to enslave accounting.

I now turn to the programme of action needed to bring 'accounting' back into accounting research. The strategies are two-fold: to change our outlook to accounting research and to recruit more academic accountants interested in bringing core accounting issues to the fore. On the first, as accounting scholars, we need to realise that it may not be possible for us to do our work unless we, in some way, aid the professional establishment we seek to criticise. Ceasing to concentrate on accounting and financial reporting issues has led to the unfortunate situation where many account- ing and auditing standards have been developed with little or no contribution from the radical academic accounting community.

Accounting sociologists should not only be concerned with criticising mainstream accounting; they should also be concerned with specifying how their criticisms might be translated into practical action. These scholars tend to have too much sympathy for the people they describe as victims of mainstream accounting. Sympathy is not enough. Accounting sociologists should start thinking of developing new accounting modes of engagement by their victims so as to enable them to gain new understandings and to counter and demystify mainstream accounting (Johnson 1995: 500). They should be concerned with how their victims actually construct, use or are affected by accounting information in addition to how their victims should construct, use or be affected by such information if they were to behave in a rational manner (Maines 1994: 204). Accounting sociologists need to encourage accounting practitioners to think in terms of the social usefulness of the information which they collect, present and analyse, and to educate users, who are perceived to be presently marginalised by accounting practitioners, to understand accounting techniques and the possibilities of misuse or misinterpretation of technical accounting statements.

The contribution of academic research to the standard-setting process is small (Whittington 1995). For example, less than ten academic accountants responded to the call for comments on each of the exposure drafts issued by the Accounting Standards Board between 1990 and 1995. With the exception of the debate on inflation accounting, the contribution of academic accountants to the exposure drafts issued by the Accounting Standards Committee (predecessor of the ASB) was even lower. Instead of focusing on what is wrong with accounting standards, academic account-ants should be more concerned with playing a more active role in the development of such standards. It is better to embrace research that would contribute to the standard-setting process. The test of financial reporting standards will be the extent to which they improve present and future practices. Evidence of this will be the elimination of those practices that are not supported by logical reasoning, by the objective test of fairness and by everyday accepted conditions that conform to existing facts and laws for specific transactions. Accounting scholars can contribute to the process of providing such evidence. As Beresford (1994: 193), the Chairman of the US standard-setting body, FASB, suggests, a lot of conceptual questions are considered during the standard-setting process such as: What are the important issues in accounting for a particular event, transaction or item? When should amounts be recognised? How should those amounts be measured? How should the amounts be allocated to periods of time? What are the alternative ways to measure, recognise and allocate amounts? What are the likely consequences or effects of each alternative? Which alternative provides the 'best' solution in terms of theoretical consistency, technical feasibility and practical consequences? Do the expected benefits of improved reporting exceed the perceived costs of a new standard?

All these questions deal with *ex ante* financial reporting policy issues; that is, questions requiring answers prior to the release of a standard. This type of research calls for the use of data collected from experimental economics (laboratory markets), instead of the use of archival data from markets that exist naturally in the economy, to construct empirical tests of financial reporting theories. The use of experimental economics allows for the creation of 'what if' scenarios in which the effects of alternative accounting methods on decisions can be examined (Maines 1994: 205). Regrettably, however, I am not aware of any published research on UK financial reporting which has used the experimental method. This is one area where core accounting can be brought back into accounting research.

More important is the need to study the rationale behind the massive politicisation of the standard setting process in the UK and whether standard setting should remain in the hands of the private sector. There seems to be little or no critical and in-depth academic discourse on the recommendation of the Dearing Report which suggested the formation of the Accounting Standards Board and the Financial Reporting Council and recommended that the two institutions should be in the private sector. There is also the fundamental debate of whether the ASB should focus on the reliability and objectivity of financial reports to facilitate the making of economic decisions or on the potential economic and social consequences of financial reports. In short, should the focus of financial reporting be to satisfy the needs of users or to serve the needs of preparers? Not to engage in accounting research concerned with standard setting is to accept resulting standards as immutable and to weaken intellectual pursuit as a result. This re-echoes the warning of Baxter (1953: 410), forty-three years ago, that accounting standards (or recommendations, as they were then known)

> are likely to weaken the training of accountants; the conversion of the subject into cut-and-dried rules, approved by authority and not to be lightly questioned, threatens to reduce the value of accounting as a subject of higher education almost to *nil*.

On the second issue, we need to attract more recruits from the fold of professionally qualified accounting academics into the radical group. That is, we need to create the more conventional versions of the radical academic. Professor Edward Stamp's role in instigating the introduction of a standard-setting process in this country and in seeking to promote the development of a conceptual framework in both the UK and Canada is a fitting example. Working from within the profession is not, as Sikka *et al.* (1995: 127–8) suggest, a complex and even enigmatic role. Suppose academics interested in core accounting issues agree that they would like the accounting literature to include more accounting issues than is presently the case. Olson's (1965) logic of collective action predicts that suboptimal levels of this inclusiveness will be produced unless (a) there is at least one individual academic who values such inclusiveness sufficiently to bear the 'cost' alone, or (b) selective incentives are provided that make individual contributions worthwhile.

The first condition may produce the dilemma of the volunteer: a person who values the inclusion of core accounting issues in the accounting literature enough to benefit from doing the work alone, may still prefer to do nothing in the hope that someone else will do it first. As long as there is one person for whom the action is worthwhile, the decision framework for everyone else changes. Suppose a renowned accounting academic decides to devote time and effort to the cause. This initial effort will most probably increase the value of further efforts. Others will now be more enthusiastic about bringing accounting back in. Stated more formally, the initial effort will increase the marginal returns to core accounting academics that would accrue from further contributions. However, if everyone else were a rational egoist, these increasing returns would make no difference. The contribution already made would only further persuade shirkers that the best thing to do is wait around for someone else to do the (now more revolutionary) work.

There is another (more positive) side to this regeneration of core accounting work. Seeing others contribute should motivate latent conventional radical academics to contribute their share. Thus, in general, if contributions are visible and are rewarded, then non-contributors may be subject to normative social pressures to alter their behaviour. To ensure that this crusade operates without the fear of professional retaliation and eventual disillusionment, the British Accounting Association has to develop as a body capable of protecting its members from the vagaries of their academic occupation. It needs to generate financial resources, provide collegial support and legitimacy and offer members relative independence from hostile reactions from the accounting profession and their employers. If the BAA is unable to provide these supporting activities, academic accountants will remain caught between the fear of professional reaction and their criticism of professional accounting practices, never able to rise above their present mute profile to become a truly radical group seeking to change accounting for society at large.

The widening gap between current accounting research endeavours and the needs of accounting practice needs to be bridged. The bridging process can take several forms. The first form is to modify the evaluation of academic research output to include 'relevance to practice' as an explicit criterion. The second form is to institute an effective mechanism for timely communication between practitioners and researchers; and the third is for the accounting profession to distinguish between recurrent accounting problems for which research is needed and non-recurrent practice problems for which a one-time solution (consulting) is wanted (Abdel-Khalik 1994: 219). One can add to this list the need for a collaborative staff exchange scheme whereby practitioners and academics can take a sabbatical in each other's environment – a sort of intern or residence scheme. Another possibility could be the revival of the part-time professorial appointments for renowned practitioners noted for their interest in academic research. Most of the technical partners of leading accounting firms have the necessary credentials to be appointed to these positions.

Although a few accounting professors now serve as academic advisers to the ASB and the Auditing Practices Board, this is not sufficient to promote academic awareness of the Boards' activities. The two Boards can encourage accounting academics interested in financial reporting to become aware of their processes by sponsoring a regulator–academic interface whereby academics are invited to a two or three day session biannually to discuss current accounting and standard-setting issues. The session could be arranged to coincide with the meetings of the Boards so that participants can have the rare opportunity of observing each Board's deliberation.

In addition, the BAA could also liaise with the members of the CCAB so as to organise a practitioner/corporate reporter/academic session where only practitioners and corporate reporters present papers on their significant and current practice problems. Such case-study sessions could help accounting academics who are often detached from practice and the corporate reporting environment to become aware of real practical issues that practitioners and corporate reporters have to resolve and to understand the perspectives of practitioners and corporate reporters on financial accounting and corporate reporting issues. The session could also provide opportunities for interaction between practitioners and chief accounting officers on issues of common interest.

The contribution of accounting to other subjects

The present tendency to borrow from other disciplines has not allowed accounting to be perceived as a mature academic subject which is ready to lend ideas to other disciplines. If accounting is excluded from accounting research, it would be consoling to find that it is being included in the research of other disciplines. Regrettably, other disciplines do not find accounting attractive! A search of the literature of other disciplines from which accounting research is borrowing fails to reveal a reverse trend. Accounting, to my mind, has outgrown many of the disciplines which are being used to enslave it. Peasnell's (1980: 24) position on the prospect of a subject outgrowing a parent discipline is salutary:

> The process of a subject outgrowing a parent discipline has occurred numerous times in universities. The physical sciences split off from natural philosophy as they started to develop alien ways. So it has been with politics, economics and sociology which grew out of political economy. Statistics and operational research are in the process of breaking away from mathematics. So it is with accounting. The process is a natural one and occurs when it becomes increasingly clear that the concerns of the new subject are diverging from those of the older discipline.

Accounting has a lot to contribute to the study of other subjects. For example, it is a fertile ground for anthropologists and sociologists who are interested in the behaviour of people. Accounting is practised by accountants. So, how accountants behave and organise themselves should be interesting to sociologists. The environment of accounting and accountants should be an interesting laboratory for sociologists. Scholars interested in the sociology or anthropology of accounting should seek to publish in sociology and anthropology journals where their work would accordingly add to that literature, instead of seeking to publish in accounting journals that are obscure to other sociologists.

Many issues in accounting are of philosophical interest. The notions of *income, profit, true and fair view* and *going concern* are philosophical. Yet only three articles (two by philosophers who have little or no interest in accounting techniques (Lyas 1984; Harris 1987) and the third by an academic accountant with a doctorate in philosophy (Power 1986)) which discuss the interface between accounting and philosophy have been published in the philosophical literature.

The role of newer universities

Accounting research has not come of age in the newer universities. Less than 10 per cent of the accounting faculty in newer universities are research active (Whittington, 1995; Gray 1995). Only a few professors of accounting in these universities have a PhD as a terminal academic degree. The most crucial contributor to the development of accounting research is the implicit rule that to be appointed as a professor of accounting, a person has to publish in academic (refereed) journals or possess tremendous potential for attaining such goals. These days, the typical new accounting professorial appointee in older UK universities is a person who has published between six and ten articles in refereed accounting journals within the four years immediately preceding the appointment, has a professional accounting qualification and/or a postgraduate degree (MSc, MBA or PhD) in accounting or cognate discipline, but often has no experience in institutional administration. The trend in newer universities is different. Many of the recent appointments in the newer universities have been through the promotion of one or more of the existing staff to professorial status, often without a track record of publication in refereed accounting journals and with no experience of research, but with a considerable experience in teaching and institutional administration. This trend is a departure from the usual tradition in this country. Even in the earlier days, people appointed as professors often had a track record of publications. When universities decided to introduce accounting as an undergraduate degree specialism in the 1940s, and when newer universities were created in the 1960s, existing academic accountants were not translated into professors of accounting. New professorial positions were contested for by both internal and external candidates and, as was often the case, people were appointed from outside the universities.

Although a professor brought in from outside can bring in fresh ideas and a new outlook, that does not mean that professors appointed from within would lack foresight and ideas for changing the research culture. It is no problem to bring in a person from outside if the people inside believe that the person can do a better job and is perceived by peers both from within and outside the university as capable. Newer universities have to perform a balancing act between translating a known safe pair of hands to professorial status and bringing in an outside researcher with little or no administrative experience. Whatever the case, a lot of investment is needed for making a researcher out of the academic promoted from within and for making an institutional administrator out of the researcher brought in from outside. In addition, encouragement should be given to new and young people in the accounting departments of newer universities wishing to undertake research.

CONCLUSION

This paper has used both historical analysis and a study of the contents of *Accounting and Business Research* over the past twenty-five years to argue that accounting research has concentrated on the non-core rather than core accounting issues; i.e. on the context rather than content of accounting (Whittington 1996: 2). The paper traced the causes of this shift away from the content of accounting to (a) the difficulty of recruiting and retaining accounting academics who are professionally qualified and have doctorates in accounting; (b) the seeming reluctance to make accounting a graduate profession and to link professional education and development with university education; (c) the low level of external funding for academic accounting research; (d) the influx of disciplines such as law, economics, econometrics and sociology into accounting research; and (e) the dominance of accounting research by frameworks borrowed from mathematics, economics and sociology.

The salient message of this paper is the need for academic accounting research agendas to include the confrontation of core accounting issues. Bringing accounting back into academic accounting research in the UK seems inevitable for accounting scholars. And, as accounting academics,

> To encounter the inevitable –
> Is our destiny;
> To accept the inevitable –
> Is the way of wisdom;
> To rebel against the inevitable –
> Is the glory of scholarship;
> To bow to the inevitable –
> Is a tragedy;
> To seize upon the inevitable
> And steer it along the right path –
> Is the essence of greatness.

NOTES

* This paper is an amended version of an inaugural lecture delivered on 25 January 1996 at Middlesex University. I acknowledge helpful conversations with Terry Cooke, Dick Edwards, Rob Gray, Roger Groves, Anthony Hopwood, Mike Page, Bob Parker, Maurice Pendlebury, Ken Peasnell, Prem Sikka and Geoff Whittington and comments on an earlier version from Terry Cooke, Chris Nobes, Bob Parker and Rosemary Wallace. I am also grateful to the many professors of accounting and/or finance who promptly responded to my request for information and who completed the questionnaire I mailed them in December 1995.

1 This paper is dedicated to Bob Parker, who has contributed in no small measure to my academic career since I came to the United Kingdom. He provided me with the opportunity to undertake doctoral research at Exeter by agreeing to supervise my work. Together with the appointments committee, he took the gamble of appointing me to the accounting faculty at the university after eighteen months' stay as a doctoral student despite my meagre publication record at the time. Bob undertook a task of moulding a mature student who was set in his ways before coming to Exeter. This is because I had lectured at all levels of the academic spectrum in Nigeria for over twenty-five years before deciding to read for a PhD and I believed in my own ability as a scholar. Yet Bob, in his rather subtle and systematic manner, revealed to me many aspects of the academic world and its system of values that were unknown to me before arriving in the UK. Since leaving Exeter, Bob has continued to offer me his mentorial support and encouragement. He has kindly read preliminary drafts of my articles and has always helped with insightful and illuminating comments. Bob's long-serving experience as a professor of accounting in the UK is devoted to the improvement of accounting knowledge. His specialisms include financial accounting and reporting, management accounting, accounting history and comparative international accounting. This paper is a testimony that Bob's historical interest has rubbed off on me; he is always generous with his direction of how to reconstruct the past. For all these, and for his belief in my ability, I am grateful.

2 The accountancy profession was essentially dominated by men in the early part of the twentieth century.

3 The appointment of Frank Sewell Bray as the Stamp–Martin Professor of Accounting by the Society of Incorporated Accountants was described by Solomons (1974: 29) as 'a well-intentioned, probably ill-advised and certainly short-lived attempt to promote academic research in accounting outside an educational institution'. It was ill-advised because it tended to increase the mistrust between the profession and universities that was prevalent in those days. It was short-lived because the professorship was not continued after the integration of the Society in 1957 with the Chartered Institutes. This was clearly for the good of the British accountancy profession, removing as it did elements of unnecessary divisiveness and snobbishness (Parker 1980: 309).

4 Although early university departments of accounting showed an interest in social and national income accounting (i.e. macro-accounting), British academic accounting concentrated on business accounts and the needs of shareholders and various other users of corporate financial reports. However, departments of economics in those universities with nascent accounting departments and those without accounting departments such as Cambridge

251

and Oxford confined their teaching and research to macro-accounting and virtually ignored micro-accounting (Parker 1980: 316).

5 Although not all articles published by *ABR* are authored by UK academics, 72 per cent of these articles are written by them. However, this cannot be said of the articles published by *JBFA* and *AOS*.

6 The ICAEW approached Cambridge after Oxford had turned down the initial offer (Napier 1996: 20).

REFERENCES

Abdel-Khalik, A. R. (1994) 'Factors limiting the role of behavioral research in standard setting', *Behavioral Research in Accounting* 6(Supplement): 213–22.

Arnold, P. and Hammond, T. (1994) 'The role of accounting in ideological conflict: lessons from the South African divestment movement', *Accounting, Organizations and Society* 20(2): 111–26.

Arrington, C. E., Hillison, W. A. and Williams, P. F. (1983) 'The psychology of expectation gap: why so much dispute about auditor responsibility?', *Accounting and Business Research* 13(52): 243–50.

Ball, R. and Brown, P. (1968) 'An empirical evaluation of accounting income numbers', *Journal of Accounting Research* 6(2): 159–77.

Baxter, W. T. (1953) 'Recommendations on accounting theory', *Accountant*, 10 October: 405–10.

—— (1988) *Accounting Research – Academic Trends versus Professional Needs*, Edinburgh: Institute of Chartered Accountants of Scotland.

Beaver, W. H. (1968) 'The information content of annual earnings announcements' in *Empirical Research in Accounting: Selected Studies, Journal of Accounting Research* 6(Supplement): 27–37.

Beresford, D. R. (1994) 'Request for more research to support financial accounting standard-setting', AAA – Accounting, Behavior and Organizations Section, *Behavioral Research in Accounting*, 6(Supplement): 190–203.

Berry, A. J., Capps, T., Cooper, D., Hopper, T. and Lowe, T. (1985a) 'Management control in an area of the NCB: rationales of accounting practice in a public enterprise', *Accounting, Organizations and Society*: 10(1)3–28.

—— (1985b) 'NCB accounts – mine of misinformation', *Accountancy* January: 10–13.

Bromwich, M. and Hopwood, A. G. (1981) 'Introduction', in Michael Bromwich and Anthony G. Hopwood (eds) *Essays in British Accounting Research*, London: Pitman.

Bryer, R. and Brignall, S. (1986) 'Divestment and inflation accounting: an unemployment machine', *Capital and Class* Winter: 125–55.

Chandler, A. D. (1977) *The Visible Hand: The Managerial Revolution in American Business*, Cambridge, MA: Belknap Press of Harvard University Press.

Cooper, D. and Hopper, T. (1986) *Debating Coal Closures: Economic Calculations in the Coal Dispute 1984–5*, Cambridge: Cambridge University Press.

Dev. S. (1980) *An Inaugural Lecture: Accounting and the L.S.E. Tradition*, London School of Economics and Political Science.

Dyckman, T. R. and Zeff, S. A. (1984) 'Two decades of the *Journal of Accounting Research*', *Journal of Accounting Research* 22(1): 225–97.

Edey, H. C. and Peacock, A. T. (1954) *National Income and Social Accounting*, London: Hutchinson University Library.

Flint, D. (1982) *A True and Fair View in Company Accounts*, Edinburgh: Institute of Chartered Accountants of Scotland.

Gernon, H. and Wallace, R. S. O. (1995) 'International accounting research: a review of its ecology, contending theories and methodology', *Journal of Accounting Literature* 14: 54–106.

Goldberg, L. (1994) 'Whither accounting research? A personal view', *Asia-Pacific Journal of Accounting* 1 (1): 2–17.

Gray, R. (1995) 'The interesting relationship between accounting research and accounting practice: a personal reply to Professor Whittington', working draft of an article commissioned by *Journal of Applied Accounting Research*.

Gray, R. and Helliar, C. (eds) (1994) *British Accounting Review Research Register*, 6th edition, London: Academic Press.

Harris, N. G. E. (1987) 'Fairness in financial reporting', *Journal of Applied Philosophy* 4 (1): 77–88.

Hopwood, A. G. (1994) 'Accounting and everyday life: an introduction', *Accounting, Organizations and Society* 19 (3): 299–301.

Hopwood, A. G. and Bromwich, M. (1984) 'Accounting research in the United Kingdom', in Anthony G. Hopwood and Hein Schreuder (eds) *European Contributions to Accounting Research: The Achievements of the Last Decade*, Amsterdam: Free University Press.

Jack, A. (1993) 'Dons learn that "freedom" has a bottom line', *Financial Times* 9 December: 14.

Johnson, P. (1995) 'Towards an epistemology for radical accounting: beyond objectivism and relativism', *Critical Perspectives on Accounting* 6 (6): 485–509.

Kitchen, J. and Parker, R. H. (1994) 'Frederic Rudolph Mackley de Paula (1882–1954)', J. R. Edwards (ed.) *Twentieth-Century Accounting Thinkers*, London: Routledge in association with the Institute of Chartered Accountants in England and Wales.

Lee, T. (1995) 'The professionalization of accountancy: a history of protecting the public interest in a self-interested way', *Accounting Auditing & Accountability Journal* 8 (4): 48–69.

Little, L. T. (1952) 'Unsettled territory', *Accounting Research* 3: 62–9.

Loft, A. (1986) 'Towards a critical understanding of accounting: the case of cost accounting in UK 1914–1925', *Accounting, Organizations and Society* 11 (2): 137–71.

Lyas, C. (1984) 'Philosophers and accountants', *Philosophy* 59 (227): 99–110.

Maines, L. A. (1994) 'The role of behavioral accounting research in financial accounting standard setting', *Behavioral Research in Accounting* 6 (Supplement): 204–12.

Mattessich, R. (1957), 'Towards a general and axiomatic foundation of accountancy', *Accounting Research* 8 (4): 328–55.

Murphy, M. (1950) 'Research in public accountancy', *Business History Review* 24 (2): 43–50.

Napier, C. J. (1996) 'Accounting and the absence of a business economics tradition in the United Kingdom', Working Paper, University of Southampton.

Olson, M. (1965) *The Logic of Collective Action*, Cambridge, MA: Harvard University Press.

Parker, R. H. (1977) 'Men of account', Inaugural Lecture delivered at the University of Exeter on 22 April, 1977.

—— (1980) 'Memorial: Frank Sewell Bray, 1906–1979', *Accounting Review* 55 (2): 307–16.

Peasnell, K. V. (1980) 'Accounting as an academic discipline' Inaugural Lecture delivered at the University of Lancaster, in *AUTA Review* 12 (2): 7–30.

Powelson, J. P. (1955) *Economic Accounting*, New York: McGraw-Hill.

Power, M. (1986) 'Taking stock: philosophy and accountancy', *Philosophy* 61 (237): 387–94.

Robson, K. (1993) 'Inflation accounting and action at a distance: the Sandilands episode', *Accounting, Organizations and Society* 19 (1): 45–82.

Scott, DR (1931) *The Cultural Significance of Accounts*, New York: Lucas Brothers.

Sikka, P. and Willmott, H. (1995a) 'The power of "independence": defending and extending the jurisdiction of accounting in the United Kingdom', *Accounting, Organizations and Society* 20 (6): 547–81.

—— (1995b) 'Illuminating the state-profession relationship: accountants acting as Department of Trade and Industry investigators', *Critical Perspectives on Accounting* 6: 341–69.

Sikka, P., Willmott, H. and Puxty, T. (1995) 'The mountains are still there: accounting academics and the bearings of intellectuals', *Accounting, Auditing & Accountability* 8 (3): 113–40.

Solomons, D. (1955) 'The integration of accounting and economic studies', *Accounting Research* 6: 106–11.

—— (1956) 'Accounting education for new responsibilities', Inaugural Lecture delivered at the University of Bristol, *Accountant* 28 January: 83–86 and 4 February: 114–20.

—— (with T. M. Berridge) (1974) *Prospectus for a Profession: The Report of the Long Range Enquiry into Education and Training for the Accounting Profession*, London: Advisory Board of Accountancy Education.

Sterling, R. (1970) 'On theory construction and verification', *Accounting Review* 45 (3): 444–57.

—— (1993) 'The subject matters of accounting', in M. Mumford and K. V. Peasnell (eds) *Philosophical Perspectives on Accounting: Essays in Honour of Edward Stamp*, London: Routledge, pp. 123–55.

Tinker, T. (1985) *Paper Prophets* London: Holt, Rinehart & Winston.

Whittington, G. (1995) 'Is accounting becoming too interesting?', Sir Julian Hodge Accounting Lecture at the University of Wales, Aberystwyth.

—— (1996) 'Some interesting aspects of accounting', Plenary Address at the British Accounting Association 1995 National Conference, Cardiff, 27 March 1996.

Zeff, S. A. (1978) 'The rise of economic consequences', *Journal of Accountancy* 156 (12): 56–63.

—— (1989) 'Recent trends in accounting education and research in the USA: some implications for UK academics', *British Accounting Review*, 21 (2): 159–76.

INDEX

255